Permissible
Computing
in Education

Permissible Computing in Education

VALUES, ASSUMPTIONS, AND NEEDS

Ronald G. Ragsdale

PRAEGER

New York
Westport, Connecticut
London

Library of Congress Cataloging-in-Publication Data

Ragsdale, R. G. (Ronald G.)
    Permissible computing in education : values, assumptions, and
needs / Ronald G. Ragsdale.
        p.   cm.
    Bibliography: p.
    Includes index.
    ISBN 0-275-92894-2 (alk. paper)
    1. Education—United States—Data processing—Moral and ethical
aspects.   I. Title.
LB1028.43.R34   1988
370'.285—dc 19   87-35964

Library of Congress Catalog Card Number: 87-35964

ISBN: 0-275-92894-2

First published in 1988

Praeger Publishers, One Madison Avenue, New York, NY 10010
A division of Greenwood Press, Inc.

Printed in the United States of America

The paper used in this book complies with the
Permanent Paper Standard issued by the National
Information Standards Organization (Z39.48-1984)

10 9 8 7 6 5 4 3 2 1

Contents

Preface

The purpose of this book is to make explicit some of the value bases that support the various uses of computers in education. Our age of science and technology is often seen as an age of "value-free" pragmatism, with a focus on "getting the job done" using tools and procedures "that work," but the assumptions are only partly true. Indeed, many technological tools and scientific procedures are effective in accomplishing tasks that need to be done. But the danger is that the commitment of science is to that which is scientific, whether it works or not, while unnecessary technology has a similar attraction. For example, Polanyi's "Potential theory of adsorption" was rejected by the scientific community for almost 50 years, not because it was wrong, but because it was seen to be "unscientific."

What distinguishes between the scientific and the unscientific? Polanyi refers to the "powers of orthodoxy," the orthodox view of the nature of things, as being crucial. Thus, to say that humans learn languages because they have a "language acquisition device" is scientific, while to say that it is because they are "made in the image of God" is not.

This leads to a paradox which a recent article by Carl Bereiter seems to illustrate. He proposes that students can become better writers by using (among other things) the principle of "chance plus selection," being provided randomly with "strategic moves" for more effective writing. I do not know of anyone (nor does he mention anyone) who uses this method either for improving their own writing or for teaching others. On the other hand, I have met and/or read books by successful authors who make it their practice to pray before they write. The paradox is that science, that "no holds barred search for truth," accepts the former as scientific and rejects the latter as unscientific.

Our use of science and things scientific hinges on values, as do the important questions related to using computers in education. The questions may change as new applications are proposed, but the importance of a values base continues on. Although it cannot be guaranteed that all the important issues and values have been discussed here, it can be guaranteed that no "random strategic moves" were used in the writing of this book.

Non random moves, however, were used and included the help of many important people. Feedback to the first draft was given by graduate students in an OISE course in 1985, namely: Brader Brathwaite, John Brine, Bill Dodd, Luella Egerton, Dick Fransham, Byron Hermann, Marcia Johnson, Bill Littlefair, Louise Litwin, Betsy McKelvey, Peter Moyls, and Rosemary Sedley. Also part of this group, and providing me with material from their own research, were Roger Casey, Doug Hayhoe, and Gayle Rose.

The second draft was studied by a second group of OISE graduate students in 1987. They were David Bacon, Viviane Caplan, Sarah Cohen, Grant Dale, Darlene Decicco, Carol Dietrich, Carolyn Gazan, Marilyn George, Paula Goldman, Paul Hébert, Chai Ho, Kathy Inglis, Irene Lee, Paul Mallany, Kathy Marina, Margaret Roberts, Randy Saylor, Bobbi Smith, Judy Weinstein, and Craig White.

For the extra work which enabled me to spend the 1985-86 year on study leave, thanks to my faculty colleagues in the Department of Measurement, Evaluation, and Computer Applications, particularly Bob McLean.

How can a secretary help you to write a book when you do your own typing? Let me count the ways. The important factor is that Lee Tetsull not only responded to all my irritating requests and completed all the distasteful jobs, but she also did those tasks which I forgot about, including the "discovery" of a valuable reference.

But most of all, thanks to my wife Charlotte, who not only read the second draft *twice*, but also provided support and inspiration throughout.

These and many others who have gone unmentioned are responsible for the good ideas herein. I claim sole responsibility for problems of presentation and the "clinkers."

*Permissible
Computing
in Education*

1   *Permissible Computing*

"Everything is permissible,"—but not everything is beneficial.
"Everything is permissible,"—but not everything is constructive.
I Corinthians 10:23 (New International Version)

THE ROLE OF VALUES

This seems to be an age in which computers are seen as the answer to everything. If Elizabeth Barrett Browning had lived in the computer era she might have said, "How can I use computers? Let me count the ways." In actual fact, proponents of computers have said much more than that. For example, Stonier expresses it as "In the course of history, human ingenuity has created many a wondrous device. None so marvelous, however, as the computer" (Stonier, 1984, p. 252). The range for computer applications is enormous, from the ridiculous to the sublime, from video game to thinking machine.

In the midst of this computer cornucopia, the need for discernment grows. Not only in education, but in all of life, the danger exists that as new applications of computers are developed they will be adopted, not because they fill an important need for the user or society, but because they are new and exciting. For example, an article in a 1986 issue of *Time* described the use of computers in selling plastic surgery, cosmetics, hairpieces, and clothes. This chapter is about the foundation on which the necessary discernment might be based. The remainder of the book is an attempt to begin the application of the discernment process to some of the proposed applications of computers to education, not to exclude computers from the educational process, but to make informed decisions about their use.

The quote from the first letter to the Corinthians which precedes this chapter comes from a context which is strikingly similar to our own. Paul, the author of the letter, is seen as responding to specific words used in a message he has received from Corinth, for "everything is permissible" is put in quotation marks in the New International Version of The Bible. In response to their defense that they as humans were only doing what is permissible, he counters that just because something is permissible, or possible, does not mean that it is beneficial or constructive. Our response to computers should carry with it a similar discernment.

It is also worth noting that Paul's advice takes a very personal form. That is, he follows up by saying that it was not sufficient for the people of Corinth to base their rules for behavior on what was permissible for themselves as individuals, but they should consider the needs and strengths of their fellow Corinthians. The notion that the effects of computers can be extremely personal, just as were the effects of eating meat sacrificed to idols as discussed by Paul, is presented in more detail later in this chapter and in later chapters. However, it should be clear that this perspective gives a new form to the analysis of computer benefits, that what is beneficial to some computer users, particularly those who intensely enjoy computers, may not be beneficial for all.

The historical context for Paul's letter is also similar to that of today. It was a time when things seemed out of control, a time of luxury, and a time of immorality. Virgil wrote, "Right and wrong is confounded; so many wars the world over; so many wrongs." Juvenal wrote that "A luxury more ruthless than war broods over Rome. No guilt or deed of lust is wanting since Roman poverty disappeared." He also comments that one woman had eight husbands in five years, though the first 500 years of the Roman republic had seen no divorces, until 232 B.C. (Barclay, 1975).

In our age we may point to the increasing availability of television channels and movies on video tape as signs of our cultural progress, but the "permissible" violence in these media may have been responsible for the increasing number of uncontrollable children in the schools (Stott, 1985). It appears that putting our faith in our human abilities to choose that which is beneficial is not being confirmed.

The inability of humans to discern what behavior is constructive has long been recognized as a problem. Plato stated that without absolutes, that is fixed standards of behavior not subject to human choice, morals could not exist. He struggled to find the necessary absolutes, but was unable to generate them out of human experience. His effort is but one example of humanism, more recently put in the form of a *Humanist Manifesto* (Kurtz, 1973). This manifesto, signed in its 1933 version by John Dewey and in 1973 by B. F. Skinner and Henry Morgenthaler, states that humanism is a "philosophical, religious, and moral point of view as old as human civilization itself" (p. 3). Since the humanistic view tends to dominate our society, particularly in its use of technology, it is instructive to look at its major features.

The scientific method is an important part of humanism, being seen as a way to build moral values. Moral values are also to be based on human experience," with ethics being situational to match "human need and interest." Reason and intelligence are viewed as the most "effective instruments" of humans, and although science can explain causes of behavior, individuals somehow can retain freedom of choice in using them. Most important for this context, technology is seen as the vital key for development and human progress, and any attempts to censor basic research on moral grounds are rejected. The essence of the message is that humans, aided by the technology they have developed, can find the answers to all the problems of this world, without appeal to "revelation, God, ritual, or creed" (Kurtz, 1973, p. 15).

Humanism occupies a unique position in the U. S. legal system, one which allows its influence to be freely felt, particularly in education. That is, humanism is legally seen as a religion by the U.S. Supreme Court when it comes to seeking "conscientious objector" status for exemption from military service, but not seen as a religion when it comes to its doctrine being taught in the public schools (though major court decisions early in 1987 have partially reversed this view). Although many see the United States's separation of church and state as resulting in "value-free" (and nonreligious) education, in fact the dominant values are those of humanism, a self-declared religion.

The Myth of Value-Free

Unfortunately, we live in an age when the myth of value neutrality is widely accepted. However, as teachers and parents should know, failing to provide guidance for a child is not a neutral act. In discussing "value-neutral schooling," Arons comments that "It wasn't long before the absence of beliefs, commitments, and passionately held values became a goal in itself" (S. Arons, 1984, p. 24). Flaherty (1985) offers further insight into these effects from the results of asking 20 university students to name their role models, the people they admired most. Not only was their response one of total apathy, with no names offered, but they denied the value of role models (other classes duplicated the results).

A popular alternative to values based on absolutes is to put one's faith in science and technology, particularly in computers. Noble (1984) provides an illustration of this in explaining why computer literacy has been seen as essential by so many. He believes that a futuristic ideology, based on a faith in high technology, is responsible for the widespread, enthusiastic, and in his view unnecessary clamor for computer literacy.

The loss of absolutes can be seen in curriculum materials designed to help students "develop" their own ethics in regard to computer use (Hannah & Matus, 1984; Gilliland & Pollard, 1984; Taffee, 1984). The result of relative morals can be seen in the statement from a former computer "hacker," now a high school teacher. "It's one thing for a high school kid to show off how he can dial the phone for free. It is quite another for an adult to go around encouraging schoolkids to steal" (Elmer-DeWitt, 1984, p. 76). These two acts are truly different only if one has a "flexible absolute" such as "Thou shalt not steal except under certain conditions."

Of course, scientific facts are themselves dependent on the values of those who search for scientific facts, not only for their discovery, but also for their interpretation. Lincoln and Guba (1985) discuss this "moral inversion" in which values actually precede careful scientific discovery, contrary to the general public's impression of the reverse. This effect is particularly true for the social sciences, where Scarr asserts that "We do not discover scientific facts; we invent them" (Scarr, 1985, p. 499). Her reasoning is based on, among others, the "fact" that androgyny (having good characteristics of both sexes) was seen as a bad result of family breakup in the 1950s and 1960s, but a good result of the women's movement in the 1970s. Hirschheim (1986) also documents the role of a priori views in determining the impact of office automation. Scarr's point is the same made by Roszak (1986); the facts were determined by the theory, not the reverse, or one could say the assumptions resulting from underlying values determined the facts.

ROLE OF ASSUMPTIONS

Francis Schaeffer often emphasized the importance of assumptions when discussing the difficulties which others encountered in formulating satisfactory theological or philosophical positions, and the even greater difficulty they had in living with the results of these positions. He stressed that the difficulties which they faced were inevitable, given the assumptions with which they had begun (Schaeffer, 1968). Often, people may use assumptions as though they are compatible with their total outlook, when in fact they can be applied to only a part of their lives. For example, John Cage has proceeded from the assumption that the world has been created by chance to the conclusion that therefore the most profound music will be created by chance and uses this feature in his compositions. Yet he is (understandably) not willing to apply this same assumption to another important part of his life, his hobby of mycology, the collecting and identifying (and eating) of mushrooms (Schaeffer, 1968). Schaeffer traced what he saw as the undesirable implications of scientific thinking back to the initial assumption that there are no moral absolutes, or absolute moral values to guide scientific thinking and research.

David Noble, a historian of technology, has also challenged the assumption of ultimate universal benefit from technological advances. He asserts, using arguments similar to those of C. S. Lewis (1978) and Hans Jonas (1973), that the results of the struggle to harness nature have been a concentration of power and a greater control over humans (D. F. Noble, 1984a, 1984b). As Lewis put it, "Man's conquest of nature turns out, in the moment of its consummation, to be Nature's conquest of Man" (Lewis, 1978, p. 41).

A further complication in the process of technological change is that often an agreement on what needs to be done is not sufficient to get it accomplished. Seidman (1983) describes the "rational systems" approach as being inadequate in education primarily because the rational systems view is that every organizational unit will play its role in the expected, or rational manner. This view does not allow for the changes introduced at each stage as original intents are put into law by legislators, developed into guidelines by bureaucrats, implemented by school authorities, and evaluated by yet another group. Because of the changes introduced at each step (much like the party game in which a sentence is passed around the room by whispering it from one person to another) the final result may even contradict the original intent. For example, Canadian attempts to alleviate the problems of the single parent have resulted in a system that makes it more attractive financially for parents to live apart than together—presumably not one of the original goals.

VALUES OF TECHNOLOGY

The threat that technology poses to our value systems was seen several decades ago by Jacques Ellul, a French sociologist, who wrote about the dangers of "la technique" in 1954. In the English edition, he defined "la technique" as "the *totality of methods rationally arrived at and having absolute efficiency* (for a given stage of development) in *every* field of human activity" (Ellul, 1964, p. xxv). Thus, it is more general than technology, incorporating it and including administrative procedures as well as machine operations.

Ellul sees *technique** as autonomous and inevitable, with its most distressing result being an increased emphasis on the means of technique and a vanishing emphasis on the original goals. One example he gives has to do with the mechanization of bakeries, where the first machines not only took *more time*, but also gave work to *more people*. Making adjustments to the nature of bread (such as pumping air into it) has been part of the solution, but success was not achieved until human taste had also been transformed. That is, bakeries could be mechanized to produce "sliced bread" successfully only when the original goal, making the kind of bread that people wanted to eat, had been modified. In later writings, he describes such results as examples of "technological morality," in which "everything is subordinated to efficiency" (Ellul, 1980, p. 244).

The modern analog of the inevitability of *technique* can be seen in Clive Sinclair's prediction that "Quite soon, in only 10 or 20 years perhaps, we will be able to assemble a machine as complex as the human brain, and *if we can, we will* (emphasis added)" (Sinclair, 1984, p. 257). Although a more complete discussion of the computer as human brain will be left to Chapter 4, we can at this

---

*The word *technique* has been italicized to indicate use of the French word (usually translated as "technology").

point express a hope that the computer brain will not be "the greatest thing since sliced bread."

Not only does *technique* dominate over humans' goals, it also diminishes the role of humans in the efficient world. "The qualities which technique requires for its advance are precisely those characteristics of a technical order which do not represent individual intelligence" (Ellul, 1964, p. 93). Because he sees *technique* as not producing certain values but demanding the values which encourage its development, Ellul suggests that we must become "mutants" in order to have any guiding influence on *technique* (Vanderburg, 1981). By this he means that we must have a viewpoint from outside of technology on which to base the changes, that we can't make an unbiased evaluation of technology while we are dependent on, in love with, or otherwise "inside technology." Mutants would be people who used technology, but did not subscribe to its value system, with Ellul suggesting the Judeo-Christian value system as a basis for making decisions about *technique.*

Ellul (Vanderburg, 1981) also defines a contradiction derived from our use of technology, which he feels is highly characteristic of Western society. He points out that the use of technology requires greater discipline imposed on us, such as the rules necessary to keep the streets clear for traffic. At the same time as we are subject to strict discipline, the society has lost its values, discarding the absolutes in favor of a faith in technology. That is, the discipline is increasing but is less and less a function of a commonly accepted set of values. As a result, people are becoming more likely to reject all disciplines, while the discipline imposed by technology continues to increase, leading to the contradiction. Though Ellul was writing about society in general, his thoughts have special implications for education, particularly the use and acceptance of high technology.

Some people might consider Joseph Weizenbaum as one of the mutants of the computer age. Weizenbaum is a pioneer in the use of computers for artificial intelligence applications, having created the popular ELIZA program in the mid-1960s. ELIZA, like its namesake from *Pygmalion* (or *My Fair Lady*), was able to give the impression of "speaking" (through typed output) at a level beyond its true ability of understanding. In its most widely known form, ELIZA simulated a nondirective therapist, reflecting statements back to the user in the form of questions, such as "Tell me more about your father." Weizenbaum became alarmed when it was suggested that a more advanced version of his program might some day be used to treat people in need of therapy, a goal still being pursued by some psychologists (O'Dell & Dickson, 1984).

Weizenbaum is not so much concerned about what computers can or can't do, but rather about what they shouldn't do. He focuses on two types of computer applications that he feels should be avoided or approached with utmost caution. One type, "obscene" applications, includes the coupling of an animal's visual system and brain to a computer, as well as any proposal to replace human functions that involve interpersonal respect, understanding, and love by a computer system. The second type are those applications likely to have serious negative side effects, such as automatic recognition of human speech. He feels that this application could be used by governments in monitoring telephone conversations through the use of computer screening, and he asks why computer technologists should lend support to such a project (Weizenbaum, 1984a).

The preceding conflicts are examples of the means and ends controversy, that goals are sometimes supplanted by specific means of attaining them. Scheffler (1986) refers to both "absolutizing of means" and "expansion of means" in describing proposed educational applications of computers. A focus on means over ends can lead to idolatry, a process well documented in *The Silicon Idol* (Shallis, 1984), *Idols of our Time* (Goudzwaard, 1984), and *Idols for Destruction* (Schlossberg, 1983).

VALUES AND USE OF COMPUTERS IN SCHOOLS

Weizenbaum also expresses strong views about the use of computers in education, most of them negative. The basis for these misgivings is his belief that false assumptions underlie the introduction of computers into primary and secondary schools (Weizenbaum, 1984b). These false assumptions include the beliefs that computer literacy assures employment, learning computer languages is crucial, and technology can solve any problem.

One can also see the effect of values in the beliefs and work of those who promote the use of technology in education and in all of life. Sherry Turkle has written about the impact of computers on those who use them, including computer scientists (Turkle, 1984). One value that seems to be common in their minds is the importance of computers as models of human thinking, based on a mechanistic view of humans. For example, Marvin Minsky believes that it is more important for students to know the inside of a computer than the inside of a frog, not because he objects to dissection on compassionate grounds, but because he believes that understanding structure and subroutines is more valuable than understanding the "bloody mess of organic matter." However, far from trying to clarify the workings of computers, Minsky would actually prefer to make them more obscure, in order to make the computer model of human thinking more plausible. Thus, Minsky proposes that we not discuss computers in terms of electronic switches which are either on or off (the actual components of computers), but rather as a "society" as described in the movie *Tron* (Turkle, 1984).

The overall theme for the proponents of computer science as a technology to help education (and life in general) seems not to be a function of what computers can (or can't) do, nor does it seem to be based on what computers should (or shouldn't) do, but rather it appears to be more strongly influenced by what the proponents would like to have computers do. The danger of believing that computers can replace important human functions is twofold. If the replacement actually happens, such as in the automobile seriously reducing human exercise, there is a corresponding reduction in human capability and self-image.

However, even more certain is the negative impact of *believing* that the replacement will occur, such as computer systems substituting for human thinking skills. This belief has immediate consequences for human self-concept and the effort one puts into developing thinking skills, whether the prediction is true or not. This danger seems most apparent in the area of artificial intelligence and will be discussed more extensively in Chapter 4.

Since all proposals for the use of computers in education come from some value base, it is appropriate for the author to give some indication of his own value system. Throughout these chapters, I will attempt to be guided by Judeo-Christian values, particularly with respect to having equal love for one's neighbor and oneself. The necessity of this concern is highlighted by Lewis as he states, "For the power of Man to make himself what he pleases means, as we have seen, the power of some men to make other men what *they* please" (Lewis, 1978. p.37). If we do not heed this warning, we are likely to find that "Man's final conquest has proved to be the abolition of Man" (Lewis, 1978, p. 40).

This concern should also carry over into the analysis of proposed computer applications. That is, one can become convinced of having such a clear view of "truth" that all other views can be disregarded. It is hoped that the remainder of this book will reflect a concern for, and an understanding of, opposing views, leading to a *reformation*, rather than an *inquisition*.

COMPUTERS AS COMMUNICATIONS MEDIA

The effects of communications media are difficult to determine after they have occurred and even more difficult to predict, as the work of Marshall McLuhan has shown. Because computers are used as communications media, it is difficult to predict their ultimate uses and importance in our lives. Drawing on McLuhan's work, Lias (1982) described some of the principles of media, emphasizing the difficulty that people have had in predicting the ultimate uses of these media. To illustrate the point, he described an incident from 1876, when president of the United States, Rutherford B. Hayes, inaugurated a new long distance telephone line between Washington and Philadelphia. Hayes was unfamiliar with telephones and ill at ease as he carried on a short conversation to officially open the service. After performing his duties, he stepped aside and said to an onlooker, "That's an amazing invention, but who would ever want to use one of them?" (Lias, 1982, p. 2). At about the same time, a British newspaper carried an article which commented on the increasing use of telephones in North America, but pointed out that they would never be that important in Britain, because "we have a plentiful supply of messenger boys" (Lias, 1982, p. 2). In both cases, the emphasis was on the way things were currently being done, with no anticipation as to how the telephone might change their ways of doing things, a situation that is being repeated with computers today.

Forecasting the Telephone (de Sola Pool, 1983) provides another view of the expectations about technology through a collection of predictions that have been made over the years about how telephones were going to be used. Many of them are quite accurate, but a set of predictions involving the phonograph is off the mark for both media. The phonograph was originally being developed to allow people to make long-distance calls, since telephones in those days did not have enough power for long distances. The idea was that one would phone to a machine which would make a record to be played into another telephone, with this process being repeated until the call had reached its destination, in a slower version of what microwave repeater stations do today. This cumbersome ritual seemed plausible to people of that day since it compared favorably with alternatives such as the telegraph and the mail system (which was no better then than it is today). Again, it was the comparison with the current way of doing things which led to this conclusion.

Lias discusses the potential effects of computers as communications media, and in so doing, presents eight general principles of media, most of them arising from McLuhan's earlier work. All of these principles have implications for our lives, but some are disturbing—namely,

• Each medium biases or distorts the message it carries in significant ways.
• New media often generate their own market, their own need for existence.
• New media reshape societies, their governments, bureaucracies, and institutions.
• New media cause underlying social values to change through the metaphors which they instill. (Lias, 1982, p. 31)

Each of these principles is examined in the following sections.

The Biasing Effect

Each medium biases or distorts the message it carries in significant ways. One example of the way in which television biases a message is that it develops in the spectator the expectation that any worthwhile event (a good play in a hockey game, for example) will be shown again in "instant replay." A result of this expectation is likely to be a lack of attention to any events as they occur. The comparable bias arising from the use of computers in instruction may be the expectation that any question from the student will evoke an immediate response. That is, immediate responses from computerized systems may exacerbate the "instant-gratification" syndrome of our society and further devalue qualities such as thoughtful deliberation and patience.

Even more ominous is Lias's suggestion that the original reasons for using a medium are often lost as new reasons suggest themselves. As an example, he describes the growth of government records in the United States, concluding that "Such record-keeping could not be managed manually, but with computers, since it *can* be done, it *is* done" (Lias, 1982, p. 28). These principles of media suggest first that the warning of Francis Schaeffer, that which can be done, will be done (particularly if it is to the advantage of those already in power), is certainly appropriate for computer applications in government. Beyond this, however, they also suggest that human intentions and media outcomes interact continuously. That is, unanticipated outcomes (modified by media effects) alter human intentions, which again produce different outcomes, and so on. The original intentions of humans are probably less important in determining how computers will be used than are the unintended outcomes, the side effects of technology as media. Similarly, when computers are used to communicate in education, the original intentions for computer use are again probably less important than the side effects. It should be remembered that side effects do not have to be bad, such as those associated with drugs. For example, Catherine Marshall observes that happiness is more likely to come to us as a by-product of other activities than when we pursue it directly.

When the importance of side effects, either good or bad, is recognized, the way in which the use of computers in education is evaluated should change dramatically. One technique for detecting side effects is to adopt the methods of goal-free evaluation suggested by Scriven (1974). This is a type of evaluation in which "the evaluator is not told the purpose of the program but enters in the evaluation with the purpose of finding out what the program is *doing* without being cued as to what it is *trying* to do" (Scriven, 1981a, p. 68). In the goal-free method, the observer avoids (if possible) knowledge of the stated goals of the project and attempts to determine the actual outcomes (which might be the same as the stated goals), or process results, through observation. In a second phase, the observations can continue after the stated goals have been learned. In actual practice, it may be difficult or impossible to keep the true objectives hidden from the evaluator. However, the main advantage of goal-free evaluation is the removal of the blinders which focusing on the "intended" results can put on the observer. If the evaluator doesn't know what someone is trying to accomplish, or at least is not concentrating on these intended goals, very different things may be observed. Such an approach will be needed to discover the full effects of computers in education, looking beyond the effects intended by human users. In particular, it may save us from overenthusiastic computer users, who not only urge the use of computers in impractical ways, but also imply that the ultimate effects of these applications can be predicted on the basis of very restricted vision. On the other hand, those who argue against the use of computers in education may be proven wrong on the basis of good side effects, such as the unforeseen applications of telephones and phonograph records. (Some examples of side effects are given later in the chapter.)

The Marketplace Effect

New media often generate their own market, their own need for existence.
Lias's principle of media generating their own market requires further examina-

tion as well, since it can have serious and disturbing implications for education. As Sullivan has indicated, "We will either mould these new technologies to educational and societal ends, or will, through our own default, be moulded by them. . . . The medium of television, as an earlier test case, provides a sad commentary on the route computers could also take" (Sullivan, 1983, p. 26).

Observers have also raised a more specific question about the impact of the marketplace on the direction that computer technology will take. With regard to the competition between the school market and the parent market, the question is "What will happen when parents and schools are buying software for the same purposes?" Will schools be "second-guessed" by parents when the school purchases of computer courseware do not match what the parents have purchased?

One point which observers have not raised, and potentially a more serious concern, is the question of whether the home market for educational computer products will become so much larger than the school market that the characteristics of products available will be determined by the desires of parents (or perhaps sponsors of freely distributed materials), not schools or teachers. When this occurs (and the direction of courseware advertising has already changed), much less priority may be given to objectives, instructional design, and pedagogical value, than to slick, superficial packaging. A possible deterrent to such a marketplace effect, which is a consequence of deliberate corporate sales and production strategies, would seem to be a well informed public—which would mean including parents in education programs similar to those that school boards develop for their teachers. This is, in fact, a move that has already taken place in some school boards, though probably not for the same reason (for more details of this type of program, see Chapter 9). It should be noted that a well informed public does not guarantee that their purchases will reflect their level of knowledge. That is why a few school authorities have entered into cooperative buying arrangements with parents in order to affect more directly their behavior.

The marketplace effect can dominate our lives unless the question of "Why?" gets asked.

Without leaving their dorms, students will be able to access the library card catalog; they will be able to log on to a student bulletin board to exchange advice, gossip, make dates, find a ride, buy used books. They will be able to submit assignments electronically to their instructors.

Yes, these things and a dozen more *can* be computerized. But why *should* they be? . . . Indeed, it has always been my thought that an intellectually vital campus is one designed in its architecture, grounds, and general spirit to make such daily intercourse graceful and attractively frequent—rather than one that spends millions to spare its students the exercise of leaving their dorms. (Roszak, 1986, p. 61)

The Reshaping Effect

New media reshape societies, their governments, bureaucracies, and institutions. New media not only reshape societies and governments, but have particularly strong effects on their businesses and educational systems. The British government is having to wrestle, along with labor and business, with the conflicting demands of increasing consumer choice via high technology in the marketplace and increasing worker dissatisfaction brought on by high technology in the workplace (Worsthorne, 1985). The reshaping of society takes on a new twist if the choice between these two is not along class lines in the way that many people, particularly union leaders, would expect. Some British labor leaders, such as Arthur Scargill, believe that workers are willing to forego consumer choice in order to avoid the intrusion of high technology into their jobs, while Worsthorne, a political analyst, believes that blue-collar workers are more likely to accept job change to get better consumer choice than are the "upper classes."

Meanwhile, the educational system bears witness to the shaping effects of the paper and print media. Television and radio have had a major impact on business, through the effect of mass advertising for mass markets, while television has had a particularly strong effect on the election processes which determine governments. The dominant theme of this reshaping seems to be an emphasis on acquiring, not only material possessions but also power, love, self-esteem, etc., rather than a spirit of giving. Assertiveness is a key word for the "Me generation," with an advertising brochure aimed at executives illustrating this in its messages, *"GET YOUR WAY," "WHAT TO SAY OR DO TO GET WHAT YOU WANT,"* and *"HOW TO USE PEOPLE'S FEAR OF THE UNKNOWN TO GAIN POWER OVER THEM,"* (Koch, 1985).

Many effects from the media that have preceded computers into society can be seen, but the impact of computers is less clear. Although many of the effects of computers are still to be determined, possible problems have already been detected in the areas of increases in military power, changes in banking and credit systems, and concerns for individual privacy (Lias, 1982). The precise effects may not have been discovered, but the effects of computers, as with other media, are likely to be large and varied.

The societies that function within schools and particularly those within classrooms are also likely to be reshaped. Boyd (1983) notes that the classroom is no exception to the general effects of computers (and other technology) reducing human interaction. Time spent with computers can be a substitute for activities with other humans. Similarly, many teachers have noted changes in their behavior and classroom organization after they began using computers with their students. These and other changes in the classroom and society are further discussed in Chapters 7, 8, and 9.

The Value Changing Effect

New media cause underlying social values to change through the metaphors which they instill. Scholars say that through the metaphors which the new media bring to life, people come to value the dominant traits of the media on which they rely. McLuhan has described the cultural differences that the phonetic alphabet seems to have brought to the people who adopted it. Both the printing press and the alphabet have a metaphor of linearity, thus leading to the concept of the assembly line. Lias claims that the Japanese adoption of a phonetic alphabet for technical documentation during World War II brought them the metaphor of linearity, which enabled the emergence of the Japanese mechanical genius following the war.

Some observers attribute the rising tide of Islamic fundamentalism to the value changes brought on by the invasion of Western technology into the Muslim world. An example is Tunisia, where the traditional Muslim family and cultural values are being changed by Western values, communicated through both the employment of women in Western-owned factories and the tourist trade's features of topless swimsuits, alcohol, and prostitution (Woodward, 1985). Islamic fundamentalism is seen as offering a return to the values lost to "progress."

The changes in social values are often hidden during the time they occur and only become obvious when someone like McLuhan points them out. One may guess at the metaphors which will arise from our use of computers to change our values, but if past history is any indication, some of the value changes will come as a surprise. According to Lias, the dominant features of computers are: "instantaneity" and "multaneity," their equal respect for every letter or word presented, and their solution of problems through a rational and logical approach. Some see more negative aspects to the traits of computers, such as depersonalization of their users (Brod, 1984), while others see little merit in the possibility that computers will have a negative effect on social development (Dickson, 1985). In the end, results of the computer age will be determined by experience, not through prediction. Sherry Turkle provides some insights into the possible metaphors, particularly that described by the title of her book, *The Second Self* (Turkle, 1984). Because the computer can be such an intimate part of its users and also cause them to be much more aware of their own thought patterns and psychology, it almost seems to be a second self. Yet, even if this pattern of "remote introspection" prevails, its effect on social values is still not totally clear. For example, interesting speculation can arise from Kubey's (1986) research on solitude and television, particularly when linked with Tillich's (1963) discussion of, and distinction between, loneliness and solitude.

Within the realm of education, a two-year study of computers used in elementary classrooms done by Carmichael, Burnett, Higginson, Moore, and Pollard

(1985) offers many glimpses into the possible value shifts which computers might bring. Their report provides many illustrations used in the following chapters, but one small example will be given here. It has been found generally that computer study tends to displace the regular curriculum, particularly in elementary schools. That is, the more students study computers, the less they tend to study the regular curriculum. One of the teachers in this study felt that his (intermediate-level) students should be spending less time on the regular curriculum (taught by other teachers) and more time with computers. Specifically, he felt that learning the language of the computer was of greater value than English language skills. The researchers report that an intermediate-level student (not from this teacher's class) said, "We worked all week on it and we don't got nothing. I ain't going to do it no more" (Carmichael et al., 1985, p. 91).

THE MEDIA EFFECT AND EDUCATION

Events are interpreted in the context of experience and expectations. Thus, it might be said that the answer to questions about the effect of computers on education is unobtainable regardless of the researchers' backgrounds, or more precisely, because of their backgrounds. That is, our backgrounds cause us to expect certain results, preventing our clear perception of other results. It is amusing that people responded to telephones in what seems to be inappropriate ways, but 50 years from now, current views about computers may seem just as quaint and amusing. At the present time, it is clear that the ways in which computers are used have changed a great deal over the last two or three decades, but the experience of those decades does not guarantee that our predictions have improved. In 1928, the Benz company (forerunners to the makers of Mercedes automobiles, widely sold throughout the world) hired a consulting firm to estimate the *total* number of cars they might expect to sell in the next 40 years. The estimated total for the 40-year period, 1928–68, was given as up to 40,000 cars, *provided* that enough chauffeurs could be trained (Lias, 1982). In a similar fashion, one might expect that although we have several decades of computer use behind us, it is still likely that the applications of computers will continue to change over the coming decades. It may be that not only is the ultimate effect of computers not yet known, but major effects of their use have not even been anticipated.

Although the initial predictions about computers were off the mark, such as predicting that ten computers would serve all the computing needs of the entire United States, changes in use have occurred since that time, possibly permitting a better idea of where new applications are developing.

One major change in computer use, and a trend which continues, is the decreasing emphasis on mathematical applications of computers. The link between computers and numbers can be described as primarily historical, with the tabulating machine (for punched cards) being invented in the 1890s so that data collected in one U. S. census could be processed before the next census was upon them. The first North American computers were constructed to calculate artillery firing tables, with the first large computers used to do extensive calculations for atomic energy research. This emphasis was perpetuated by schools that assigned mathematics teachers to handle the computer courses and made mathematics a prerequisite for these courses (a situation which unfortunately continues in some schools).

The drift away from mathematical applications began when the prices of computers sharply decreased and the variety of devices that could be attached to computers increased. When high quality printers became available at lower prices, word processing became a popular and effective use of computers. The development of high quality graphics display devices has led to the increased use of computers in animation, resulting in one of the largest computers in the world being sold to a Hollywood film studio for animation work.

The applications of word processing and graphic animation, along with music creation, editing, and production are just a few consequences of the greater emphasis on nonmathematical applications, which leads to the general impact that computers are having on human communications. Some of the effects are clearly visible and some are hidden. For example, the current level of telephone service is taken for granted, but it has been estimated that in the United States, half of the population would have to work for the telephone companies in order to maintain today's level of telephone services if computers were entirely removed from the system (Lias, 1982). On a more visible level, many companies and universities are using electronic message systems to enhance the communications within their communities. The popular appeal of electronic communications is seen in the hundreds of "bulletin boards" which have sprung up all over the North American continent (many bulletin board features are also available on the French *Teletel* system, a part of the regular telephone system). The bulletin board allows any user with a telephone-connected computer or terminal to read notices, add notices for other users, or send and receive electronic mail, and share microcomputer programs with other bulletin board users. Many bulletin boards are for groups with special interests, such as users of a particular microcomputer, librarians, or (as in a French experiment) cancer patients.

That the connection between computers and communications is not trivial is illustrated by the business battle of the 1980s between IBM and AT&T. These giant corporations, one originally based in computers and the other in communications, increasingly have seen each other as being in direct competition for a major world market. What products these two companies will be selling 20 years from now is not known, but it seems certain that the products will involve computers and be used for communication.

If doubts about computers being communications media continue to linger, the director of electronic information programs at Link Resources was quoted as estimating that 90 percent of the use of consumer-oriented data bases such as The Source, Compuserve, and Delphi is for communications (with other people). He said, "It's very hard to make the consumer believe he needs [precreated data bases] enough to pay for it. User-generated databases are a different story, people have a basic desire to communicate" (Latamore, 1984, p. 18). Beneath the jargon, this says that people prefer to communicate with other people, rather than with vast collections of information.

If computers are important to communication, given that how they are going to be used is not known, how can current and future generations be prepared? How can research on the use of computers in education be done if the questions to be answered are still unknown? One reason the future of computers is unknown is that too much of the population is bound up in the noncomputer age. Context affects expectations and leads most people to see computers being used to do present day tasks, but do them more effectively. Those who are most likely to see new applications for computers are those who are not steeped in the culture of the past or present, namely young children. Children who grow up with computers are likely to create applications that have not yet been anticipated.

Thus, not only do most parents desire that their children be ready for the computer age, it appears that these children will also be the creators of the computer age. This is the cornerstone for the arguments in favor of introducing computers into the elementary grades. The younger the children are when they begin using computers (initially in very simple ways), the fewer preconceptions they will have about computers, and the longer they will have to refine their ideas and develop new concepts.

It would be grossly negligent to proceed from this point without considering some of the negative aspects of the thoughts expressed in the last two paragraphs. The very lack of preconceptions, which is an advantage in creating new computer applications, is also reflected in a lack of knowledge about and/or concern for the cultural values of their society. For example, they may be particularly susceptible to the threat which Mumford (1970) already sees operating, the trend toward quick decisions and snap judgments, rather than reflective, rational, cooperative interaction. It is normal for the youth of a society to question or reject the cultural norms, but they do not usually have the opportunity to remove these values so quickly. Through the increasing demand for new and creative computer applications, the youth of today have an unprecedented opportunity to modify or destroy their culture before they are even familiar with what it is. (This topic will be discussed further in Chapter 7.)

The question about the future effects of computers is still unanswered and the ultimate effects are probably impossible to determine. Yet, the location of the answer, and the procedures for finding it, are defined, at least for the near future of computer use. It is in the children who will use computers as part of their education, through elementary, secondary, and postsecondary levels that the answer will be found through careful observation and encouragement. It is important to note that this implies that the school is not only a place where the future might be predicted, but also a place where the future might be shaped. This has always been true to some extent, more so since nuclear families have declined, but the link to technology is a new feature (though evident in the use of television). Postman (1982) and Harlow (1984) both underscore the importance of shaping the future by pointing out that just because certain characteristics (both positive and negative) are *inherent* in computers, it does not have to follow that these characteristics are *inevitable*. In order to select from the inherent characteristics of computers, stress must be placed on the careful encouragement of students using computers, as well as careful observation of them.

Some will claim that the location of the answer is in the classroom, feeling that society is more likely to change schools than vice versa, but the definition of the means for finding the answer may be more severely questioned. The need for careful observation rather than controlled experimentation can be supported on the basis of experience in the area of computer programming development. Great concern has emerged over the most effective methods for creating computer programs, due to an increasing portion of programming budgets having to be allocated to modifying and correcting existing programs, mainly because they were poorly programmed when they were originally created. One response to this concern has been to do scientific studies in an attempt to identify effective programming techniques. The general result of these studies has been disappointing, however, primarily because they usually fail to show any differences between the techniques being compared (Chapter 2 gives more details as to why this has been so). On the other hand, some success has been achieved in developing more effective programming methods, generally by people who have been or have worked closely with computer programmers over a number of years. It is similar in some ways to a comparison between science and folklore, where experience with health care has shown that some (but not all) of the folklore regarding health care is a useful source of information.

This is not to say that folklore is better than science, but rather that they are best used in a complementary manner. The problem in studying programming, and in studying computer effects on children has been that sufficiently long periods of careful observation have not been done, the type of observation which enables the "folklore" to develop. Without informal, but intensive observations, the carefully controlled scientific studies are likely to be directed at studying the wrong events. The acquisition of folklore is more properly called "naturalistic inquiry" in academic circles and such inquiry is often seen as one of defining the questions that can be answered by carefully controlled studies. Lincoln and Guba (1985) see this relationship as too simplistic and favor the replacement of the cause and effect model with one of "mutual simultaneous shaping." This is probably a useful concept to apply to our study of computers in education, for the computer effect does seem to be the result of an interaction of many factors, some of which are probably still unknown. (These notions are discussed more fully in Chapter 2.)

Observations and naturalistic inquiry are important. But as mentioned earlier, when dealing with a new medium such as computers, the observer must be especially alert to unanticipated outcomes, or side effects. Searching for the unexpected is not an easy task, since what is being looked for is unknown. Attention to detail is essential and should be based on neutral expectations: information should not be excluded because of the observer's expectations. Techniques such as goal-free evaluation can assist in the detection of side effects.

One example of an unintended result comes from the business world, but it has significant implications for education. The story concerns a secretary who worked, using an electric typewriter, for two men. When the men bought a word processing system, she quickly learned to use the system and was pleased and comfortable with it. However, her two bosses had conflicting expectations about her use of the system. One believed the use of word processing meant that all printed text should be perfect, while the other felt that the use of word processing meant that initial drafts should have many errors, since they were so easily corrected. Faced with this no-win situation, where much of her work had to be viewed as unsatisfactory, she quit her job. The secretary had to quit, not because of the technology, but because of other people's expectations about the technology.

All of the participants in this story had a positive view of the technology, but the major outcome was unintended; the secretary's leaving was a negative side effect. From this we should probably conclude that it is still necessary to look for side effects from educational applications, even though all participants, teachers, students, and parents have positive views of computers.

Examples of side effects from the use of computers in education are also evident. In some of the instructional programs students are encouraged to give wrong answers because the programs give more interesting responses to wrong answers than they give to right answers. One observer noticed a student giving an immediate wrong answer to every question, in order to get a hint before making a real attempt at answering the question (Della-Piana, 1982). Some programs are described by their authors as developing one skill, while actual practice shows they develop entirely different skills.

As the number of computers in classrooms increases, it becomes more important that teachers observe their students' use of them in a careful manner. What are the side effects of both general use and specific applications? How can the good side effects be increased while the bad side effects are eliminated? Teachers are essential in identifying the factors that require further study, a point which is explored further in Chapter 10.

POSSIBLE BENEFITS OF COMPUTERS
IN EDUCATION—ASSUMPTIONS

All the statements about the value of computers in education are based on (usually unstated) assumptions and underlying values. In this section some of the possible benefits of computers will be considered, along with assumptions that might support or contradict the claims. Most of the benefits suggested here will be considered in more detail in later chapters.

Physical Presence

If one is allowed to begin on a somewhat cynical note, it often seems that computers are assumed to provide benefits for students on the basis of their physical presence alone. It is not unusual to hear parents, teachers, or even principals declare with some pride that their school has a substantial number of computers, though they don't know how they are being used. If physical presence were the key, one could envisage a simple solution to the problem of funding computer purchases, namely, the purchase of inexpensive cardboard replicas of computers.

This heavy-handed attempt at humor should not be allowed to conceal the problem of physical presence. The assumption being made is not that computers are beneficial when they are not being used, but rather that computers are beneficial no matter how they are being used. This assumption often arises out of ignorance, with people who know that all other tools can be misused appearing to hope that the same is not true for computers. Unfortunately, this assumption is not limited to those with no computer background, but is often found in those who use computers a great deal, primarily for the joy they get from such use. The computer enthusiast, or those with "misdirected enthusiasm" (Self, 1985), seems to be able to assume that video game players can increase hand-eye coordination without their being affected by the violence being displayed.

Frude (1983) refers to "electronic hammers" for cracking little human nuts and I have often used the "law of the hammer" to characterize extreme enthusiasm for computers. The law is: "If you give a hammer to a two-year old, suddenly a lot of things need hammering." Its corollary is: "If you give a computer to an educator . . . ," which indicates the nature of the problem, but not its solution. Presumably the solution lies in better informed parents, teachers, and students, with a more thorough examination of the alleged benefits, assumptions, and underlying values accompanying computer use.

The most frequently used term for describing the benefits of computers in education is computer literacy. If a commonly accepted definition of computer literacy existed, it would be useful to discuss the possible value of computer literacy. Although a great many people see computer literacy as having to do with computer programming (Ershov, 1981), a truly common definition does not exist and a discussion of computer literacy per se seems pointless. Instead, over the course of this entire book, many of the activities and concepts which are often used to define computer literacy will be treated individually. Thus, readers are free to adhere to the computer literacy definition of their choice.

How Computers Work

Understanding how computers work is often a goal of computer education. Since different levels of understanding are possible, so different assumptions can be made about the value of the understanding. An introduction to computer understanding can be done without the use of a computer, with teacher or students playing the part of the computer and obeying instructions from other members of the class, something like the ageless "Captain, may I?" (Burns, 1980). This is really an introduction to programming, which when thoroughly learned, gives an almost complete grasp of the capabilities and limitations of computers. Such instruction must be done carefully, for a small amount of programming knowledge can give a very misleading impression of how computers work. One teacher described a boy in her school who was "programming a video game," but under the mistaken impression that if he could create the display of the video game on the computer screen, the game would be complete, with all functions working (even though he had not programmed them).

The assumption that an understanding of how computers work can help students is plausible, but the main point of contention is probably on the amount of understanding required. Young children can understand much about the need for detailed instructions in programming, the arbitrary nature of the content of output messages, and the ease of changing program features (among other things) in a very short time, but the intricacies of programming are still not completely mastered by professionals with years of experience. The temptation is to use the skills acquired by professional programmers through years of intensive experience as the justification for a young person's spending a few weeks learning to program, a point which is elaborated on in Chapter 6.

How to Control Computers

Programming is usually the means of learning to control computers, that is, getting computers to do what you want them to do. An assumption that is growing increasingly less credible is that programming is the most effective way of controlling a computer. Certainly, a programmer has the greatest potential flexibility in exerting control over a computer, but must also pay the price in terms of the substantial amounts of time that true programming requires. If one wants to control computers, but does not wish to spend a great deal of time preparing to control computers (programming), it is more practical to use programs that other people have written.

Logical Thinking

It is often argued that programming also leads to more logical thinking and improves thinking skills in general. An unproven assumption is that those skills acquired for programming will transfer to other contexts. Moreover, logical thinking can be beneficial in some contexts, but an overemphasis on logical methods might be counterproductive. For example, the techniques which are often used to stimulate creative thinking are those which de-emphasize the analytical and emphasize forms of thinking which are nonlogical.

How Computers Affect Us

The effect of computers on society or individuals is often taught in a lecture setting, not in a laboratory, and for this reason is often derided by those who promote hands-on experiences with computers. One major drawback of this instruction is that with either the lecture or hands-on method, the effects on society which are studied are only those outside the classroom. That is, students and teachers typically study the current (and predicted) effects of electronic banking, airline reservation systems, government data bases, and the like, with little if any attention given to the way in which computers as word processors (to choose only one example) might be shaping student writing habits. (See Chapter 6 for more on this topic.)

How Humans Think

The notion that we can gain an understanding of our own thinking processes through studying the ways in which computers are used to solve problems seems to have a strong appeal. People who wouldn't consider studying a forklift to understand human lifting find this idea quite acceptable. When reading Minsky's derogatory assessment of "the handful of quasi-mechanical concepts at the root of earlier thinking about thinking" (Minsky, 1979, p. 393), one can't help but wonder what future generations will have to say about our fascination with electronic and programming concepts as a basis for thinking.

Several assumptions might form a foundation for our believing that computer processes can help to explain human thinking. One is that although we don't have a conscious knowledge of how we think, we might have a subconscious understanding that would be reflected in the way in which we construct computer programs. Those who support the link between computers and human thinking don't usually make this assumption, though it may be more plausible than the alternatives. However, experience has shown that our directions on how to solve problems, whether we give them to humans or computers, do not seem to bear a strong resemblance to our actual thinking processes.

The more common assumption is that because humans are "information processing machines" they must use some of the same processes as other information processing machines. This, of course, rests on a further assumption that humans are in some way machinelike, which fits in with the humanistic view of humans as an integral part of a closed, mechanistic (cause and effect) system. On the surface, the initial assumption might seem reasonable, but when examined more closely, it appears suspect.

An assumption which is rarely made, but one which is probably the most plausible, is that through the study and extensive use of computer programming, humans might modify their thinking processes to become more like computers.

This offers an intriguing solution to one of the problems of artificial intelligence—that computers can't duplicate all types of human thinking. That is, if humans were to limit their types of thinking by imitating computers, the problem could be solved. Although presented partly as a joke, the consequences of these kinds of assumptions can be severe. (Further discussion of them appears in Chapter 4.)

Help Students Learn Content

Probably the earliest use of computers in education, and one which continues to be useful, is computer-assisted instruction (CAI), the delivery via computer of instructional content to students. One explicit assumption usually made was that the use of computers allowed greater flexibility than any other nonhuman delivery system in adapting the instruction to the needs of the student. This assumption is theoretically true, but often turns out to be false in practice. The falsity can take many forms, but economics provides the basis for one example. CAI programs are economically efficient when the many hours of development cost can be spread over the use of a large number of students. It is economically inefficient to provide instructional features that will be used by very few students, the "exceptional students" who are gifted or learning disabled, hence the flexibility which is theoretically available is usually not found.

Many other assumptions underlie the use of CAI. Because CAI involves assumptions about students, teachers, and parents as well as those about the material being delivered (courseware), further discussion of these assumptions will be found in Chapters 5, 7, 8, and 9.

Help Students Learn Techniques

The argument that students would profit from the learning of techniques for the accessing of data bases, the constructing of graphic designs, the analysis of statistical data, or the processing of text is often convincing. One face of this argument is that students who are about to enter the job market need to have skills that enable them to use computer programs such as spreadsheets (matrix-type calculating programs which facilitate processes such as budget planning). This assumption is relatively strong in one sense (difficult to refute), but weak in another (may affect very few students). A stronger assumption is that students should learn these techniques as early as possible in order to use them to become more efficient learners. The weakness of this assumption is similar to that associated with the teaching of programming skills. That is, students who learn computer techniques before developing noncomputer techniques of their own will know *only* computer techniques and would be better off learning computer techniques at a later stage (Levin & Rumberger, 1986; Carlyle, 1987).

The use of computers as tools to assist the human mind (as machines assist the body) is an appealing alternative to the belief that computers can (and should) replace human thinking skills. We must be careful, however, that the appeal of the general premise does not lead us into unwise choices in specific applications. (These problems are discussed further in Chapter 7.)

Change the Range of Achievement

One of the enduring problems of the classroom setting has been the wide range of educational achievement usually present in one class, the difference between what the top and bottom students are able to do academically. Computers are often seen as changing this situation, but the way in which they will change it is often in dispute. The earliest assumption was that CAI would provide an environment in which the lower achieving students could learn more effectively, thereby decreasing the achievement range. More recently, fears have been expressed that the brighter students will make more effective use of computers (or be given greater access to them), hence increasing the range of achievement. Other alternatives have also appeared, such as boys spending more time with computers and benefitting through a rise in achievement. Conversely, in accord with Gochenouer's results from the business world (Strehlo, 1986; Gochenouer, 1985), one could suggest that boys will waste more time with computers and their achievement will fall. Or perhaps everyone will waste more time.

This proposed benefit, like physical presence, is too vague and needs a better definition of context before it can be properly debated. In particular, we need to know more about the effects of specific computer uses before considering this question. (Aspects of this problem as they relate to equity are discussed in Chapter 3.)

Change the Role of the Teacher

Experience has shown that the use of computers often does change the teacher's role, but it may be too soon to conclude that this is a necessary consequence of computer use. One alternative explanation is that those teachers most likely to change their style were the first to use computers. Another is that different educational applications place different forms of stress on the teacher, making a general statement inappropriate. For example, some teachers may choose to use computers in a way that does not require them to change (electronic blackboard, putting them in a corner, bookends), while others will choose more demanding uses.

An early assumption associated with CAI was that teachers would become "trouble shooters," with computers handling the bulk of the instruction. This view is perhaps less widespread today, but still held by some. It is probably more appropriate to consider some of the factors affecting the possible uses teachers might make of computers, such as workload changes, their social role with students, and effects on teacher professionalism, in attempting to predict changes in the teacher role. These factors will be examined in Chapter 8.

LOOKING AHEAD

The preceding paragraphs give a few indications of the assumptions that lie behind some of the claims about the uses of computers in education. The intent for the remaining chapters is to continue the examination of critical questions about these uses, the kind of questions which Sloan (1984) believes have received too little attention. Sloan speculates on the reasons why these issues have not been sufficiently considered and concludes that the common perception that the computer age is both inevitable and harmless is the major cause. On the other hand, Bezilla speaks of the "twin dangers of over-enthusiasm and extreme skepticism" (Hassett, 1984, p. 28) as threatening the computers in education movement. Menosky (1984) puts this in a more specific form, citing the popular media's preference for an "artificial dichotomy" in presenting important issues. That is, the focus on news reporting as entertainment often leads to the publicizing of extreme views at the expense of more rational ones. Those involved with computers in education have found that the fifth estate is most interested in hearing that either "computers will do everything right" or "computers will do everything wrong." The following chapters will be directed at the excluded middle, the proposition that computer applications in education, like snowmobiles in the arctic, are examples of value-laden technology (Pacey, 1983), having both benefits and drawbacks.

In examining the possible effects of educational applications of computers, it is intended that the associated assumptions will be made explicit, but this will not always be the case. As human beings, we are not used to declaring our assumptions and some will undoubtedly be missed. The assignment of "assumption spotting" is thus left to the reader, since the real purpose of this book is to increase the skill of identifying assumptions, not to provide a list of all those that have been found.

2   Sensing and Assessing Needs

THE PROBLEM

The focus of this chapter is on determining what is to be done and then deciding if it has, in fact, been done. The former, methods for determining the areas of education in which computers might have the most beneficial effects, will be called *needs assessment*. The latter, methods for estimating how successful the uses of computers have been in providing the predicted benefits, will be called *evaluation*. Evaluation is really a more general term, essentially the process of determining the value of something, which in education settings, particularly those dealing with curriculum, is seen as having two components, formative evaluation and summative evaluation. Stake is quoted as saying, "When the cook tastes the soup, that's formative; when the guests taste the soup, that's summative" (Scriven, 1981a, p. 63).

Formative evaluation has its foundation in Cronbach's (1963) analysis of methods for course improvement, although the formative-summative distinction was not made (by Scriven) until a few years later. Cronbach's emphasis was on determining which parts of a course were in need of revision and the main focus of formative evaluation could be said to be that of "improvement."

In contrast, summative evaluation is more of a "horse race," determining which process or product is most effective, but for the most part ignoring how they might be improved. It has been argued frequently that formative evaluation is more appropriate to most educational settings, particularly curriculum or courseware development, than is summative evaluation (Ragsdale, 1982). That is, it is less important to know whether course A or course B is more effective than it is to know how they might be improved (or combined) to make an even better course.

Needs assessment is often considered as a part of evaluation, though in this chapter they will be discussed separately. Determining the needs, and thereby the potential benefits, is a key part of formative evaluation, since it provides information on where significant improvements might be made. In this chapter, needs assessment will be discussed first, followed by evaluation both through the form of comparative experiments (usually a summative approach) and through the form of a multimethod style (a more formative approach), including the use of naturalistic methods.

The topics of needs assessment and evaluation, both book-length subjects on their own, will necessarily be limited for the purposes of this discussion. Needs assessment will not only be limited to the field of education, but also to determining those areas where the use of computers is of potential value. Similarly, the topic of evaluation will be considered only in the context of determining the effects of computers used in education. It should be noted that values play a prominent role in both activities, a factor to be brought out in the discussion. The unpredictability of results and the importance of side effects are other important concepts carried over from the previous chapter. Together they provide an important foundation for assessing the benefits, both potential and actual, of computers in education.

NEEDS ASSESSMENT

It might be well to begin with Ivan Illich (1977), for his position seems to reject the concept of needs, or at least generally disapproves of the word "need" being used as a noun. Actually his argument seems to be against the tendency to standardize needs or to engineer them, leading to his declaration that as we continually have our needs defined for us, our ability to shape our wants is diminished. Illich sees our needs as being manipulated by organizations, somewhat similar to the "created need" Suzuki (1985) has felt for his word processor. Suzuki sees more information as an example of a need in the process of being created, something which he feels Canadians don't actually need (Craig, 1984). Burke (1978), in analyzing the process of invention and its effects, also feels that we are in danger of being covered by an avalanche of data that cannot be understood.

A critical part of the problem seems to lie in the distinction between needs and wants. Our society often seems to be better able to meet our wants than our needs, particularly if one considers the impact of rapidly proliferating credit cards. These cards seem to strongly favor wants over needs, perhaps seen most clearly in the reluctance to their being used in food stores and their almost universal acceptance by sellers of expensive entertainment and gifts. Nevertheless, in spite of the confusion over needs and wants, teachers and educators do have the responsibility of determining the needs of students.

Definition

The theoretical definition of needs assessment is usually in terms of the difference between the way things are and the way they ought to be, the comparison between the actual and the ideal. Obviously, this is not a complete definition, but it does move us one step closer to the critical element, the definition of the "ideal" state. However, Scriven and Roth do not see the definition of the ideal state as a requirement. That is, one doesn't have to know the precise description of the ideal state, merely the direction to go in order to get there. They put more emphasis on the necessity to discriminate between needs and wants, commenting that "children who need dental care rarely want it, and patients who want Laetrile rarely need it" (Scriven & Roth, 1978, p. 2). With these considerations in mind, they propose the following definition:

"A needs X" means A is or would be in an unsatisfactory condition without X in a particular respect, and would or does significantly benefit from X in that respect; thereby moving towards or achieving but not surpassing a satisfactory condition in this respect. (p. 3)

Note that this definition is aimed at a "satisfactory" state, not the "ideal," and proposes that X is a need when an unsatisfactory condition exists, which the presence of X would reduce or eliminate. The definition also includes needs which are already being met (such as our need for oxygen), by including the case of X already being present and already a benefit. Finally, the definition rules out the "surpassing a satisfactory condition," which Scriven and Roth see as the critical discrimination between needs and wants.

Needs and Values

All of science is value-laden, a statement which was quite controversial about 30 years ago, but is now relatively well accepted. For example, Capra, a physicist, illustrates the importance of the scientist's consciousness and the values therein by describing their effect on the properties of the electron. "If I ask a particle question, it will give me a particle answer; If I ask a wave question, it will give me a wave answer!" (Capra, 1982, p. 87). As a result, Howard (1985), a psychologist, sees a large role for values in the science of psychology, where consciousness is not only present in the observer, but also in the observed. He urges a greater acknowledgement of the place of subjectivity and value judgment, along with a greater sensitivity to how human nature is being influenced by the way in which science views it.

Guba and Lincoln (1982) have looked specifically at the role of values in needs assessment. They see values entering into the process of needs assessment in at least six places. The first of these is in the identification of target state domains, or ideal states, or satisfactory conditions. That is, social skills, honesty, musical training, etc., are all possibilities for target domains, but the particular ones that are chosen, often given in a school board's statement of educational philosophy, are chosen on the basis of values, usually those of the community, but often required by some higher governmental agency. Guba and Lincoln use the term "stakeholding audiences" to describe the groups involved in this domain definition. These groups are the ones whose values must be determined in identifying the target domains.

Following closely on the identification of target domains is the choice of a particular target from the chosen domains, the second point at which values enter. That is, once you have chosen a domain, such as music training, you must then determine "how much" music training. Guba and Lincoln define six types of target states, made up of three possible levels of goal attainment at each of two different perspectives. The levels are the ideal (by definition, unattainable), the norm (typical or average), and the minimum (the essential). Each of these three levels can be defined from the perspective of either an institution (employer, school, or even a parent) or an individual (the student). Since the choice (and definition) of target may differ for the various stakeholder groups, based on group values, differences in perception can easily arise. If one group uses an ideal target state while another uses a minimum target state, their perceptions about school accomplishment will be completely different.

The third entry of values is in the actual "operational definitions" for the actual and target states, the way in which these two conditions are measured. In educational settings, this often involves the use of tests, but might also be based on observations or other information. For example, music training could be defined in terms of an "ear-training" test, performance of a musical composition, or attendance at musical performances. Choosing the type of measure and defining the level of performance is the third entry of values into the process.

Values also enter into the determination of the differences between the actual and target states which will be regarded as significant, or how far must the actual be from the ideal before it is regarded as a need? Part of the answer to this question is determined by the previous choice, the operationalizing of these states, since an inaccurate system of measurement means that small differences are likely to be masked by errors in the measuring process. The reverse threat is that extremely precise measures could be used to identify very small differences as important (see the later section on statistical significance). However, the stakeholders' values are the crucial determinant in identifying "important" differences, or needs.

The last two points of entry for values are a function of the definition of needs assessment used by Guba and Lincoln. Their definition is

A need is a requisite or desideratum generated as a discrepancy between a target state and an actual state, if and only if the presence of the conditions defined by the target state can be shown significantly to benefit an

S[ubject] and the absence of those conditions can be shown significantly to harm, indispose, or constrain an S. (Guba & Lincoln, 1982, p. 313)

Their fifth point, then, is the determination of what shall define a benefit and the sixth is similar, namely what shall constitute an unsatisfactory or harmful state. These two are taken together here, not only because of their bipolar nature, but also because they are often, unfortunately, interchangeable. For example, one set of stakeholders might see the fact that boys spend more time with computers than do girls as a benefit for the boys, while another set of stake-holders might consider that the quality of the boys' activities with computers (video games) is such that the time spent there is harmful rather than a benefit. Thus, the values of the stakeholder groups may cause a total reversal of the assessment.

Having identified the points of entry of values into the needs assessment pro-cess, Guba and Lincoln proceed to define a four-step needs assessment process. Underlying this process is the assumption that the appropriate stakeholder groups have been identified so that their values may be obtained. The first step is then the obtaining of information from (and providing information to) the stake-holder audiences.

Interaction with the stakeholders is in five parts beginning with the identifica-tion of the target domains, the areas to which they wish to give priority. The next step is the selection of particular target states in terms of level (ideal, typi-cal, or minimum) and perspective (institutional or individual). The third part involves operationalizing the target states, while the fourth is defining the size of a "significant" need. The final part is the designation of beneficial and harmful states. As can be seen, these five parts of the interaction with stakeholders in-clude all the defined entry points of values into the needs assessment procedure, although one might argue that values also enter the remaining three steps.

The last three steps of the needs assessment process involve the gathering of information and the classifying of information, with both of these processes based on the results of step one, the interaction with the stakeholders. The second step is directed toward the determination of the current or actual state in rela-tion to each of the targets selected by the stakeholders. Though this is an empiri-cal task, it does involve choices on the part of the needs assessor regarding not only the specific data to be collected, but also the manner in which they are to be collected. For example, in assessing the current level of musical ability, one must not only choose the particular skills to be assessed, but also the manner of assessment, such as testing or observation of music classes.

The third step of Guba and Lincoln's needs assessment procedure involves comparing the defined targets from step one with the estimated actual state from step two in order to identify differences that are large enough to be called needs. Since the standard of significance (how large a difference must be to be called a need) has been defined in step one, this step should be unambiguous. However, the clarity with which one can see the size of potential needs will be affected by the types of measurements used in step two. If relatively broad measures are used, subjectivity and its associated value base will be unavoidable.

The final step is to test the needs from the previous step to see if they qualify as beneficial or harmful according to the standards designated in the fifth part of step one. Guba and Lincoln describe this as being essentially a mechanical application of previously derived standards, but actual practice may prove to be less clear. If that is the case, the investigator's values may also be able to enter into this step.

Guba and Lincoln freely acknowledge that their description of the needs assessment process is brief and inadequate (and what is presented here is shorter still), but they stress that their description is far more complex and thorough than what is usually done in the name of needs assessment. They also stress that this procedure is highly context-specific, thus the results can only be applied to the area and groups where the needs assessment is carried out and are only appropriate for a limited period of time.

Guba and Lincoln conclude with a discussion of the interplay of facts and values, pointing out that any decision will be based on a particular combination of fact availability and value commitment. That is, the availability of relevant facts is high for some decision areas and low for others, while the degree of commitment to values is similarly variable. One of the difficulties of planning the use (and assessing the needs) of computers in education is that it is seen by most people as a "high fact–low value" area (Guba and Lincoln cite the field of nutrition as an example of this kind of area), that is, many relevant facts are known and values play a relatively minor role. In fact, values usually play a major role, so the decision areas should be seen either as "high fact–high value" (examples are abortion, the Amish rejecting the teaching of evolution), or even "low fact–high value" (nuclear safety is an example). The reader should keep this classification scheme in mind while considering the potential benefits and harmful effects of computers in education. For example, Brooks and Bowers (1970) state that damage to the surrounding environment is often ignored in technology assessment, so that the fuel for a new generating station is part of the cost, but not damage from smoke pollution or waste discharge. If value aspects of these decisions are important, but are not being made explicit, what are the potential consequences for students, teachers, and parents?

Needs Examples

In looking at a portion of the educational enterprise, Adams (1983) looks at the problems that research and development organizations have with "needs sensing," a term sometimes applied in place of needs assessment. She feels their problems are special because they are often temporary organizations with multiple target audiences (or stakeholders) operating on the cutting edge of changing problems. These problems are also often characteristic of the decision making about the use of computers in education, since temporary structures are frequently created to deal with what is seen as a temporary problem and the multiple stakeholder and cutting edge aspects are clearly evident. Adams's suggestions, based on the experience of some research and development organizations, are headed by an urging for more multimethod approaches. Multimethod techniques will be dealt with in more detail later, but the principal is that instead of relying exclusively on one form of data collection, be it standardized testing, census data, interviews, or observation, investigators should use several methods, integrating their results to clarify the overall patterns of response. Another caution from Adams that is relevant for computers in education is her statement that research and development organizations often pursue "hot topics" without adequate understanding of what the needs actually are. Her remedy for this problem is the increased use of futures studies. But, since futures studies are themselves a "hot topic" (see Chapter 10), a greater focus on underlying values might be a better suggestion.

Sigel (1985) and Dorn (1985) both provide analyses of business failures in the computer sector, some of which can be seen as examples of poor needs assessment procedures. Sigel considers the reasons why a number of prominent and promising software companies have gone out of business. For example, one of the companies went from zero sales in 1978 to $40 million in 1983, then had to merge with another company in 1984 to avoid bankruptcy, after having sold over 700,000 copies of one microcomputer program. The reason might be attributed to poor needs assessment. The founders of the company had created a product which not only met their needs (which they thoroughly understood), but also the needs of many other people, leading to their original success. However, it is a principle of business that companies must expand to be successful (probably a want, not a need). Thus, the company developed a new product, spending $10 million, or more than twice their annual profit at the time. Sigel points out that this was an extremely large sum for a company which had never done this kind of internal product development, but another aspect seems more telling. The new product was not directed at the founders' needs, but rather at the needs which they felt (apparently wrongly) existed in the buying public. Evidence for this contention is provided in another part of his article where Sigel lists six software companies that have been unable to produce a second product which comes near to the success of their first product. This should not be entirely surprising, since we frequently see inabilities to duplicate the first successful novel, the first Major League season, or the first creative educational idea.

Dorn's analysis contains more examples of computer manufacturers, with one of the consistent reasons for failure having to do with poor management doctrine. One large corporation assumed that division managers were interchangeable, changing the management of the computer division so frequently that engineers and designers were often unguided while the new manager learned binary arithmetic. A similar example is the company which bought a small computer manufacturer, but didn't have the management expertise (or will power, as Dorn suggests) to keep it alive. Another large corporation, which has tried to fit many computer acquisitions into its corporate mold, still has trouble believing that developers of computer products, where the sales environment is extremely volatile, have unique needs. That is, one can't expect them to wait six months (the normal procedure) for a basic decision or expect them to make detailed financial forecasts far in advance. The general theme is one of companies acting on the assumption that computers are no different (and the needs of their product developers are no different) than any other electrical appliance, or copier, or petroleum product. Perhaps the experience of these companies can serve as a warning for those educators who feel that computers are just another piece of audiovisual equipment.

Needless to say, the assessment of needs is often seen as the foundation of educational, and particularly curriculum, change. Pratt (1983) uses a needs assessment base to develop his "curriculum for the 21st century"; Salisbury (1984) uses a short needs assessment procedure to guide the use of computer-assisted instruction; and Bloom (1984) has used a form of needs assessment as the basis for his extensive research program aimed at making group instruction as effective as individual tutoring.

EVALUATION OF COMPUTER EFFECTS

The specific question is one of determining the effects of computers in education, primarily on students and teachers, but possibly on parents and other school personnel. The heart of the problem is contained in the question, "How can we say, with more confidence, that the use of computers in schools (or homes) has *caused* certain things to happen?"

Cause and Effect Model

Having stated the central question, we are immediately brought up short by Lincoln and Guba (1985) as they cast doubt on the adequacy of the cause and effect model to deal with such things as innovations in educational practice. After a comprehensive examination of the origins and shortcomings of the model, they conclude that the concept of causality is not really credible in its current (poorly defined) form. They see the problems of causality as important for all science, but particularly for social/behavioral inquiry. One reason for this conclusion is that humans may produce an "effect" in anticipation of a "cause," a factor which seems to be part of the computer effect, particularly in areas such as artificial intelligence (see Chapter 4). Their third conclusion is that it has been (and is) impossible to separate causality from human subjectivity, factors such as experience, judgment, and insight. On the basis of these three conclusions, they state their belief that the concept of causality should be replaced.

Lincoln and Guba suggest replacement rather than abandonment of causality because of the need for explanation and management, understanding why, and shaping our environment. The metaphors that they feel can serve to explain and to manage, while replacing the billiard table metaphor of causality, are webs, nets, or patterns. Their suggested replacement for causality is *mutual simultaneous shaping*, the notion that "everything influences everything else." Components of the definition of mutual simultaneous shaping include the continuous interaction of all elements in a situation, the unique response of each element to the configuration of all others, the possibility of more than one plausible explanation for a particular event, and the fleeting of any given pattern of circumstances.

Lincoln and Guba attempt to demonstrate the value of their new concept in the following way. Evaluation is shaped by our belief in causality, in that we attempt to evaluate teacher workshops in terms of the change in behavior of their students. This implies an implausible chain of events, while with the shaping concept, the children's behavior could be seen as shaping the workshop!

Burke (1978) provides additional instances from his analysis of the invention process, indicating that a single inventor is rarely entirely responsible for an invention and that seemingly unrelated developments are often decisive. That is, simple cause and effect is a simple, but inaccurate way of describing the development of most inventions.

The last examples are important ones, for they demonstrate that causality not only has the possible value of explanation, but also the possible negative value of leading us to search for impossible explanations. Perhaps the most obvious instance of this can be seen in the areas of programming and writing (see Chapter 6).

Comparative Experiments

Having looked at the theoretical (and practical) difficulties with the concept of causality, it is useful to look at a related problem, that of comparing two types of educational innovations, or an innovation against "normal practice." Understanding the flaws in this procedure is important, for it is often used to justify or validate educational decisions. The particular example which will be used is that of comparing curriculum materials, or evaluating courseware materials (instructional materials delivered via computer).

One curriculum area which has inspired a great deal of rhetoric, without much illumination, is the discipline (?) of computer science, particularly that portion which deals with the teaching of programming skills. Although effective teaching of programming creates great and continuing interest, most of the discussion seems to take place on the level of opinion and persuasive argument. In an earlier article (Ragsdale, 1978), many of the problems associated with the comparison of curriculum materials were discussed, most of them also applying to the comparison of courseware packages.

The problems discussed under this heading will be those found in studies which attempt an experimental comparison of curricula, sometimes called the "agricultural botany" approach. This term is used because the model for such comparisons is that used for comparing types of seeds, fertilizers, etc., where all other growing conditions are assumed to be the same for all the products tested. An examination of the literature on studies in programming instruction reveals that the following are common flaws in such studies.

The most frequent, and probably the most serious flaw, is that of nonrandom assignment. When subjects are assigned to experimental conditions on a non-random basis, it introduces another possible explanation for any differences in the ways the groups perform. Some experimenters attempt to compensate for nonrandom assignment through the use of pretests, or statistical techniques such as analysis of covariance. (Analysis of covariance is a technique for adjusting one set of scores, such as a posttest, on the basis of another set of scores, such as a pretest.) However, the pretest may not be a good indication of success on the materials of the experiment and analysis of covariance may be biased if the assignment to groups should happen to be correlated with pretest scores. For example, well organized students who register early to get the preferred class sections might also be better prepared for the pretest, making the class sections systematically different in this respect.

One problem which often occurs in curriculum comparisons is the assumption that instruction has been identical for all groups, except for the intentional variations which are studied in the experiment. This problem may not be as severe when making courseware comparisons, since if both types of material are presented via computer, it is easier to control the extraneous factors. The problem is obvious when one instructor teaches two or more sections and modifies the presentation for the later groups on the basis of feedback from the earlier groups. Using CAI for presentation of both types of material is not a sure solution, since it is still possible to introduce unintended differences, particularly if different authors create the two versions. Clark (1983) points out that the difference between CAI and other curriculum materials is substantially decreased when the same author(s) creates all the materials.

One possible cause of hidden differences between experimental conditions (or between courseware versions) is the bias of the experimenter, another common methodological problem. Pepper (1981) describes an experiment in which the results were the opposite of the experimenter's expectation, but it is interesting to note that a second experiment was done to confirm this unexpected result. One subtle effect of experimenter bias is that results that agree with the experimenter's expectation do not have to be confirmed.

Other common sources of error include the use of available resources and the short duration of most studies. Available resources refer to such things as using FORTRAN (a specific computer programming language) to compare the learning of programming via batch (using punched cards) and time-sharing systems (using computer terminals), even though FORTRAN is not particularly well suited as a language for time sharing, but was available. The second problem refers to the common practice of obtaining evidence from a one-week experiment in order to determine how a one-year (or more) curriculum should be designed.

Problems in the measurement and analysis of these experiments are often related to the use of "home-grown" tests, with no reliability or validity data, plus the use of improper statistical techniques, such as the use of individual students as the *unit of statistical analysis*, when the more appropriate approach is to use the classroom as the unit of analysis. The latter point is based on the violation of the assumption (underlying the use of statistical tests) that all experimental units are independent (in the way they respond). When a unit of instruction is presented to a group, individual students do not learn independently, but are influenced by the actions of their fellow students. If the action of one student prevents all the others from proceeding to the next topic of instruction, it is inaccurate to analyze the data as though the students were independent units. (This point is less of a problem with courseware evaluation.)

Statistical significance

Statistical significance is often a problem because of undue emphasis. The level of significance should not be used to judge the importance of results, but often, results significant at the .01 level (likely to happen by chance alone less than 1 time out of 100) are judged *better* than those significant at the .05 level (likely to happen by chance alone less than 5 times out of 100). Since the level of significance for a given experiment can be raised (say from .05 to .01) in a number of ways, such as increasing the number of subjects in the experiment, it is not a valid indicator of importance. In fact, it could be argued that in many instances obtaining statistically significant results may tell you very little, perhaps nothing at all of value (see the Appendix for an illustration of this).

Internal and external validity

The decision that often has to be made in designing a comparison of curriculum materials or strategies is based on the conflicting demands of internal versus external validity. Internal validity relates to being able to say what caused the effects of an experiment. It is based on control of experimental conditions and the elimination of alternative explanations (other than the experimental treatments) for the observed results. External validity relates to being able to say that the results of the experiment are likely to apply to other situations. It is based on the selection of the subjects and the experimental environment so that they are typical of the subjects and environments to which the results should apply. Internal validity is necessary in order for an experimenter to conclude that the experimental treatment was responsible for the change in performance (causality), while external validity is necessary for the results of an experiment to be generalizable to a large number of situations. Unfortunately, by the very nature of these two characteristics, attempts to increase the internal validity of a comparison usually lead to a corresponding decrease in the external validity of the results. That is, the control that is used to minimize extraneous variables in the experiment, such as having individual students use computers in private rooms, is what makes the experimental situation unlike the classroom. Traditional comparative experiments would be classified, in most cases, as being high in internal validity and low in external validity. At the same time, other techniques exist, sometimes called naturalistic studies, which tend to produce results of a reverse nature, low in internal validity and high in external validity, such as systematic observation of an existing classroom.

Naturalistic methods of evaluation are not discussed in detail here. The flaws in traditional comparative experiments are given a more thorough treatment based on the assumption that their results are more likely to be blindly accepted. These flaws should then suggest the alternative of naturalistic methods, the techniques of which can be found in books such as *Participant Observation* (Spradley, 1980) or *Naturalistic Inquiry* (Lincoln & Guba, 1985), or overview articles (Williams, 1986; Dorr-Bremme, 1985; Jacob, 1987). The Lincoln and Guba book contains the development of mutual simultaneous shaping, which leads to naturalistic inquiry as a method, just as the concept of causality leads to the comparative experiment.

Another drawback of the comparative experiment is the length of the typical research cycle. From the point of an experimental question being formed, a considerable time usually elapses before the process of experimental design, treatment, data collection, analysis, and dissemination finally produces information for the intended audience. In the case of short experiments, these other stages can add a substantial overhead to the time required, although some studies are lengthy on their own. Examples of lengthy studies which were required to produce the desired information are the 16-year follow-up of preschool education (Shanker, 1984) and the ten-year study of factors affecting heart disease (the MRFIT study).

Multimethod Evaluation

Although naturalistic methods have not been discussed in detail, the relative strengths of the naturalistic and experimental methods suggest a combination which merits immediate attention. The strength of experimental studies in internal validity and the greater strength of naturalistic studies in external validity (assuming, of course, that they are competently carried out), suggests the possibility that these complementary strengths might be combined. This approach to studies of computers in education has been specifically suggested by Hazen (1980) in the form of an appropriate combination of techniques.

Hazen discussed the problem of the conflicting demands from external and internal validity concerns, plus the varying shortcomings of a variety of evaluation methods. She compared five methods of data collection in terms of their respective advantages and disadvantages. The methods were final examinations, attitude questionnaires, naturalistic observation, interviews, and archival data analysis.

Final examinations or achievement tests are the most frequently used measurements in evaluations of course instruction on student learning. Their primary advantage is in allowing evaluators to define their measures in terms of very specific skills. Another advantage has to do with ease of scoring and general use. The disadvantages of this method relate to a lack of a broad range of information, as well as possible validity problems, particularly in using paper and pencil measurements of abstract qualities.

Attitude questionnaires are often used to measure more general goals, but with an impressive amount of precision. Large amounts of questionnaire data can be collected with much less effort than that required for interviews or observations. Their primary disadvantage is due to the difficulty of establishing the validity of such scales, which in extreme cases seem to prompt the formation of attitudes which did not exist prior to reading the questionnaire. This problem can be reduced through the technique (fortunately, one that is frequently used) of developing the questionnaire on the basis of relatively unstructured interviews, which provides a basis for defining the attitudes to be measured.

Naturalistic observation methods have been extensively used in such disciplines as sociology and anthropology, but are less well known in the domain of educational research and evaluation. Observation methods can include participant observation, where the observer is not seen as a stranger, but as a participating member of the group being observed. As one might expect, having considered the deficiencies inherent in other forms of data collection, naturalistic observation is increasingly being used in the evaluation of computer applications in education. The primary advantage of the observation methods is in terms of their external validity, since the actual environment being observed has little change imposed on it. This method can also be employed without the observer making initial assumptions about what is going to be discovered, hence it is more useful for building theory, or searching for unintended outcomes. The major disadvantages lie in the amount of observer time required and possible reliability problems that can occur when only a single observer is used.

The interview method is used less frequently than questionnaires, although informal interviews are often used in developing questionnaires. Interviews can be used in either unstructured forms for theory building, or as structured instruments. Interviews are also particularly useful in obtaining feedback, such as might be used in developing educational software. The major disadvantages are the time and effort involved, plus the need to have a skilled interviewer for the more unstructured interviews.

Archival methods offer what is probably the easiest method of data collection, since it involves data that were already collected for some other purposes. As one example of archival data collection, Hazen refers to the Educational Testing Service (ETS) evaluation, funded by the U.S. government, of the University of Illinois's PLATO computer-assisted instruction project. In this evaluation, student attrition rates (number of students dropping courses, or leaving the college) were used to indicate the degree of student interest in CAI (Murphy & Appel,

1977). Although Hazen does not mention the report by House (House & Gjerde, 1973) on the same project, his emphasis on a more naturalistic approach and the differences in his conclusions would seem to support her case for the use of multiple methods.

Archival data are not only easy to collect, but the process is unobtrusive, so subjects may be unaware of the study. This also allows data collection and study to cover longer periods of time than the usual experiment. The disadvantages are related to problems in interpreting the data obtained, particularly since they have not been collected for the express purposes of the study. For example, in his investigations of a college that was part of the ETS evaluation of PLATO, House found that attrition rates at the college were greatly increased after the college president resigned, indicating that they may not have been a good indication of student interest in CAI (House & Gjerde, 1973).

The major conclusion drawn by Hazen is that the drawbacks of these various methods can be best overcome by a judicious combination of methods (not necessarily limited to those described here, but possibly including audio recording, video recording of subjects or computer displays, and self-report by subjects being studied). An example of this can be seen in the results from the PLATO evaluations (Hawkins, 1979). The quantitative results from the ETS study become more valuable when they are supplemented by the naturalistic observations made by House, and vice versa. This conclusion should also be applicable to evaluating the uses of computers in education, including software development and evaluation. Quantitative, test-based measures might indicate the presence of trouble within a software package, but it would probably require other forms of investigation to shed light on the source of the problem.

A recent and large example of the multimethod approach is found in the two-year study of elementary school computer use done by Carmichael et al. (1985). Their main techniques were observation and interviews, but they also made substantial use of achievement testing, attitude questionnaires, and archival data. The interaction among the results obtained from testing of student achievement in the use of LOGO, interviews with teachers, and direct observation of the students provides rich sources of insight into the process they were attempting to study. Further examples of techniques which might be applied can be found in Schwarz's (1985) "reconnaissance" method of evaluation, a flexible, decision-oriented approach, and Ingle's (1984) video case studies.

EVALUATION AND VALUES

It is truly impossible to avoid values when discussing evaluation, since the definition of evaluation is the process of determining the value of something. However, it is not this obvious assigning of value which concerns us here, but the hidden role that values can play in determining this assessment. Although the belief that social science should be value-free still abounds, a growing number of publications have made the value link explicit. Krathwohl (1980) and Lincoln and Guba (1985) provide excellent discussions of the role of values in evaluation and these will be used in creating the structure of this section.

Krathwohl examines the values in evaluation question by looking at three forms in which values can enter into the evaluation process. The first is as means become ends. The basis of this form is the process-product continuum, or to what extent the evaluator (or the client) values the process used in evaluating (the means) over the product or result (the ends) of an investigation, or vice versa. Although few sponsors consider process as an important reason for engaging an evaluator, the process of evaluation may appear to be more beneficial in their eyes than the product.

The second form of value entry is when choices are made among means and among ends. Krathwohl considers four main points at which these occur, in selecting a problem, and at the start, middle, and final parts of the evaluation. The problem selection phase applies to the sponsor who is choosing among positive, neutral, and hostile evaluators, as well as to evaluators choosing tasks. Lincoln and Guba view problem selection and other choices affected by the personal values of the investigator as having "weak" or trivial impact, since it holds for "value-free" and "value-aware" evaluators alike. They consider that when the investigator recognizes and acknowledges the importance of these values, the whole character of the study can change.

Krathwohl sees the choices at the beginning of the evaluation as revolving around the issue of "who will control the evaluation?", leading to the decision of whose values will predominate. Choices in the middle of the evaluation are influenced by those made before and include such items as evaluation design and types of data collection. Choices at the end are primarily concerned with the relative emphasis on various results.

The third form of value entry is that of ends justifying means and is given relatively few words by Krathwohl. Yet this is an area that seems to be relevant to the shortage of critical examination and evaluation of computers used in education. That is, the decision is often made that the end of knowing the effects of computers is not worth the means required, primarily in terms of costs, but also in terms of a lack of time and resources.

Lincoln and Guba provide a number of examples of the ways in which values have influenced inquiry in science. One of these is the case of Galileo, who was censured by the Church not because of the results he had found, but because his methods of inquiry did not conform to Church doctrine. As Schaeffer (1976) recounts, Thomas Aquinas had incorporated Aristotle's view of science into his thinking, which then became a part of Church doctrine. Galileo's conflict was with Aristotle (or more accurately perhaps, with the humanism which led to the reformation) and it was for this that he was censured. This example is useful for correcting a frequent assumption that methods of inquiry are open to free choice and that results from any method are accepted as equally valid. This correction is particularly important if the method of studying computer effects is naturalistic and the bulk of the relevant population feels that controlled experiments are the only valid method for obtaining such knowledge.

Lincoln and Guba also discuss the emotional battle between the neo-Darwinians and the modern Lamarckians in regard to their versions of the theory of evolution. It is amazing that those who feel the Bible must be rejected because they mistakenly think it was contradicted by Galileo and is thus incompatible with science can so easily ignore the violence done to science by either of the main competing forms of the theory of evolution. The case of the ostrich's calluses, present at birth in just those points of the ostrich which touch the ground (when it sits), is one of the many instances of conflict between these two variants of evolution. Though Darwin had an open mind about whether acquired characteristics (such as calluses) could be inherited, Lamarckians insist they can, and that this is why the ostrich is born with calluses, while geneticists reject the notion entirely as conflicting with science. However, the neo-Darwinian position that the ostrich's calluses developed in these places and no others purely by chance, is seen by the Lamarckians as equally untenable. Lincoln and Guba quote a distinguished biologist, the late Gordon Rattray Taylor as saying,

> That takes a lot of believing even if you practice—like the White Queen—believing three impossible things before breakfast. I myself can only believe it on certain days and not a few biologists have failed to manage it altogether. (G. Taylor, 1982, p. 37)

Polanyi sees this as only one instance of science holding onto inadequate theories, such as evolution, because no "scientifically acceptable" alternative exists. He regards this as "the most dangerous application of scientific authority" (Green, 1969, p. 95). That is, for example, if one begins with the value assumption that creation cannot be true, then one form of the theory of evolution must be accepted, regardless of its absurdity.

Lincoln and Guba provide other examples, such as the influence of the political climate on a scientific debate between Pasteur and Pouchet, and then follow with an analysis of the consequences of the value-free claim and the impact of values. However, their excellent discussion will not be summarized here, but will only be recommended to the reader. Instead of continued exploration of the values issue (though the values issue should be constantly kept in mind), a small model for needs assessment in the area of computers in education will be developed.

ASSESSMENT OF COMPUTER NEEDS IN EDUCATION

Claims regarding the potential benefits of computers in education are frequently of a very broad nature, though occasional nuggets of specificity appear. In general, these proposed benefits have proven to be too vague as a basis for planning, or as a framework for evaluation. Therefore, the following is proposed as the outline of a procedure to be used in determining the needs which computers might be used to meet in education. It is not intended as a substitute for the needs assessment techniques discussed earlier, but as a more specific procedure, aimed directly at a particular set of needs, incorporating what we have learned about needs assessment from investigating other techniques.

Due to the changing nature of computer characteristics, it seems reasonable that this assessment of needs (and, indeed, most assessments of needs) will be a continuous process. Moreover, it is important that the focus of the process be on the curriculum (future, as well as current), not on the attributes of the technology. Also, it may be that an experience with computers will be more of a hindrance in determining these needs, because of the biasing effect on our expectations about computer use. In order to be as specific as possible about the computer uses, the outcome of the process should be in the form of software attributes (though possibly hardware), based on curriculum goals, independent (as much as possible) of specific hardware characteristics. (The intention of the last restriction is to prevent pure hardware requests, such as 1,000 by 1,000 full color screen resolution, without any indication of the uses, in the form of software capabilities, for the hardware). It should be noted, in practice, that this separation is very difficult to achieve. For example, a hardware development may make possible an entirely new class of software. However, hardware requirements must usually be set well in advance of the creation of software, though new software may be developed on "simulated systems" after the design, but before the creation of new hardware. This can create a difficult timing problem, since it is important for researchers and software developers to work with advanced hardware to develop new techniques, but one must not get too far ahead of the potential users. The danger is that while researchers are projecting user preferences onto new hardware, the users may be developing new styles and preferences while using the old hardware.

The curriculum orientation of this needs assessment procedure assumes that a curriculum, based on the values and requests of the various stakeholding groups, has been developed. This is not to rule out computers as an object of study in some curriculum streams, particularly computer studies, but merely to make this procedure generalizable to all discipline areas. The focus on curriculum would include what we do now, as well as what we would like to do.

It is almost impossible for most people to focus on the curriculum without using any knowledge or consideration of the potential of computers, but worth trying in an attempt to reduce the technology bias. The intention is to follow the noncomputer phase with one in which computer characteristics are explicitly considered, an approach similar in some ways to the goal-free evaluation methodology suggested by Scriven.

The requirement for a continuous needs assessment procedure means the process must be iterative (or repeating the cycle with new information on each repetition). Any needs which are identified can only be tentative, a feature consistent with Lincoln and Guba's (1985) concept of mutual simultaneous shaping.

Alterations to the needs will occur for a number of reasons, among them changing curriculum goals, technology advances, and most important, the results of previous need-assessing cycles. The most important force in changing the needs will probably be the changing applications of the new technology. Not that new applications will be discovered and "need" applying to the school, but that applications of computers will alter the school environment. For example, word processing is itself a new need on the language arts horizon, but already its use in a growing number of classrooms is helping to bring other needs into focus (see Chapter 6).

Step One—Needs Candidates

The first part of this step is to ask the relevant stakeholders to identify what they see as the greatest educational needs in a given curriculum area, without directing their attention to the use of computers. That is, students would be asked about the concepts that they were having the most difficulty in learning (or perhaps, those which were most difficult in their previous year), teachers would be asked about concepts that they had difficulty in presenting or their students had trouble grasping, and similar questions for parents, employers, etc.

The follow-up to the first part is to ask the same groups to now identify needs (in the same curriculum areas) that seem to be related to computer functions. This would probably mean that most of them would have to be supplied with some computer background between these two questions. Care would have to be taken to avoid introducing excessive bias in the computer background, limiting it to a description of the nature of computers (binary, fast, algorithmic, etc.) and a general description of certain tasks and how computers perform them, but avoiding the description of popularly proposed educational applications.

The trade-off between the relatively unbiased (a word which is too often used as a synonym for ignorant) views from nonusers and the more informed views from computer users is a troublesome factor. In either case, the danger exists that the needs will be based on intuition, which may not be supported in practice. An example of this might be found in the use of touch screens, where one may choose elements from a computer display by merely touching the screen with one's finger. This function seems intuitively very desirable, but in practice it can be a negative factor if frequent selections are required, bringing about arm fatigue.

Step Two—Critical Competitors

After the lists of general curriculum needs have been collected, it is necessary to identify the alternative means of satisfying the potential needs. Particular attention should be paid to the alternatives to computer functions if the purpose of the needs assessment is to define computer uses (even if the purpose is more general, the restriction can still be useful). The term "critical competitor," used in Scriven's treatment of product evaluation (Scriven, 1981b), gives some of the flavor one should associate with this search for alternatives to using computers. Scriven stresses that a great deal of imagination may be required in identifying critical competitors.

Scriven gives an example from an incident in Berkeley in which complaints were voiced about the time spent in waiting for elevators on the main floor of a new building. No indicators had been installed on the main floor to show what floor the elevators were on and this seemed to make the delay longer. A proposed solution of installing these floor indicators on the main floor was rejected as being too expensive and the problem was delegated to one person, who fortunately was able to come up with an ingenious answer. His solution was to propose a "critical competitor" to the expensive display, that of installing full-length mirrors next to the elevators. When this was done, the problem vanished.

It is tempting to see the full-length mirrors as only a distraction and not a real solution. If the real problem is that the elevators do not arrive quickly enough, then the expensive display is only a distractor. But, if the problem is that the delay *seems* too long, then the display is a solution. The crucial point is that in either case, the full-length mirror is a critical competitor to the display, that is, an alternative which provides comparable results. Thus, in this instance, we should be asking if alternatives exist that can provide similar results (in terms of educational outcomes or processes) as the proposed use of computers. For example, one critical competitor that Scriven suggests for computer-assisted instruction is the use of printed materials.

Step Three—Nominating Computer Functions

From the lists of potential needs and critical competitors, the next task is to identify the computer functions that seem most appropriate for the various curriculum areas. This is not necessarily a listing of the highest priority needs to which computers might be applied. For example, some high priority needs might be best satisfied by the allocation of more teacher time, which itself might be made available through the use of computers for less important, but time-consuming tasks. Therefore, appropriateness is not restricted to the highest priority needs and a certain amount of creativity may be required to nominate the computer functions.

Step Four—Selecting Computer Functions

This step can be seen as a continuation of the previous one, but it is separated in order to stress the advantages of looking at overall implications. In this step, patterns among needs, critical competitors, and computer functions are to be sought. For example, it may be that a particular computer function (or a particular competitor) is a marginal solution to one need, but could be an optimal solution to a collection of needs. This can be particularly important as a focus in getting teachers started with computers, since even mundane applications can be useful when they are available in sufficiently large numbers.

After the completion of step four and the selection and implementation of candidates nominated to satisfy these determined needs, the cycle repeats (on some convenient, but regular schedule) with new needs being detected. Often these new needs may arise as a result of steps taken to satisfy previously identified needs. The new needs may be a direct and anticipated result of the previous measures, such as the new needs created by new skills acquired through word processing practice, or they may be side effects, or unanticipated effects. For example, the increased written production that usually accompanies the introduction of word processing might lead to the teacher implementing a greater use of a peer approval process for written compositions. Out of this increased use of the peer review process might come another need for greater social skills for the students who are now interacting with each other in a new context. The impact of side effects, an impact that is likely to grow as we become more aware of their existence, should lead to a greater appreciation that not all applications of technology which can be done, ought to be done.

WHAT CAN (AND OUGHT TO) BE DONE

Most readers would probably agree that what can be done is not necessarily what ought to be done, though this is often the result of creating new media or new technology. Thus, it is not surprising that in the area of computer technology, as in the U.S. space program and mountain climbing, the desire to do something "because it is there" is extremely strong. Unfortunately, even when agreement is reached on the goals which should be sought, this does not guarantee that these goals will be reached, even if they are attainable.

In the case of individuals, many of us know that we "ought" to stop smoking, cut down on drinking, lose weight, exercise, etc., but agreement on what ought to occur is not enough. Often, the person who cannot do what they ought to do will find a convenient rationale for this lack of action, but it is usually to provide social acceptability for the behavior, not a serious argument against the proposed change. As a result, it is reasonable to suspect that obtaining agreement from the individuals involved, such as "computer hackers" who spend excessive periods of time using computers, may not be sufficient to change their behavior.

For organizations, examples of irrational behavior might include the automobile industry's use of robots (when full employment seems essential to their required level of sales), newspaper staff (both labor and management) who insist on working arrangements that meant the end of many newspapers, the actions of railway people who have worked to make the railroads a second choice to trucks and buses, or the postal workers and management who have been able to reduce greatly the amount of mail being sent, particularly during the Christmas season, by their consistent failure to provide adequate service.

CHANGES IN THE EDUCATIONAL SYSTEM

In looking at the components of the educational system, it seems clear that the choices to be made in the selection of appropriate technology should be based on the needs of students, teachers, parents, and other relevant stakeholders. Indeed, most of the discussion about needs in this chapter has been based on this premise. However, it also seems clear that many of these needs, at least as they intersect with the potential benefits of technology, have not been completely determined. And when the needs of the people, particularly the students, are not clearly identified, or are ignored, there are several other sources of needs that might be satisfied. The most dangerous of these are probably the needs of technology itself; they can be seen in a kind of technology implementation which focuses on the attributes of the technology and attempts to maximize the use of unique characteristics. It is equivalent to asking, "What can computers (or some other technology) do best?" Much of the planning and prediction in education seems to be based on this faculty assumption that what can be done should be done.

A second source of potential needs is at the management level, including not only the administration within school boards and districts, but also those at higher levels of government. The needs that they might like to see satisfied by technology, in addition to the normal goals of empire building and status/promotion, include those of replacing teachers, or making teachers conform to procedures set out by administrators. Several years ago, in what may have been an example of wishful thinking, a Provincial Minister of Education was quoted as predicting that teachers would be replaced by computers. Other predictions have said that the use of computers would allow (or require) the use of programs that would standardize the curriculum (and teachers' practice). Technology can also be seen by management as a means of monitoring the employees and evaluating their effectiveness. Although evaluation of teachers is an important function, that those needs which ease the life of management may be seen as more important than the learning needs of students is a continuing danger.

Although teachers might be targets of management needs, they can also be a source of competing needs. Just as with newspaper and postal service workers, staff in schools may have strong desires to see the status quo maintained, if not their own status enhanced. Technology used to implement old systems in new garments—such as the exclusive use of computers to assist teachers in lecturing to classes—is a threat not only to students but also to the successful implementation of the technology itself.

Finally, the students themselves may be a source of competition to their own needs, if their expressed *wants* are given greater weight than their actual *needs*. One of the assumptions made about the use of computers in schools has been that students will be able to learn more when they are given a choice of the way in which they will learn. This feature, called "learner control", has generally been unsuccessful in practice due to the fact that students seem to be unable to choose the learning style which is most effective for them (Clark, 1983). A more obvious instance of the clash between user needs and wants can be seen in the offerings of television. Basing choices of technology on student wants might lead to an instructional wasteland to rival the wasteland of television.

In summary, when considering the question of determining and satisfying needs, evidence seems to show that agreement on broad general goals does not lead to consensus on required actions. Similarly, a focus on the needs of the educational system does not lead to a consensus without a common basis for the source of these needs, the students. However, as discussed in the first chapter, the unpredictable effects of communications media mean that agreement on the actions required may still not be sufficient to bring about the desired results. Therefore, a procedure of continuous monitoring seems to be required.

3 Equity

DEFINITIONS AND AN ANALOGY

One of the first points to establish is that the issue is "equity" and not "equality." Most definitions of equality stress such forms as "evenly balanced," or "in the same measure," much as the general public's working definition, while equity is linked to concepts such as fairness, impartiality, and justice. The problem is that many people do not distinguish between these two terms, seeing equity as being synonymous with equality. This confusion tends to obscure the discussion of equity issues in the use of computers, since most of the evidence introduced indicates a lack of equality, some, or all of which may not in fact be indicative of inequity.

At a conference of the Educational Computing Organization of Ontario (ECOO), a group of distinguished computer educators, among them Alfred Bork, Dan and Molly Watt, Bobby Goodson, Henry Olds, and Fred D'Ignazio, met to consider the issue of computer equity. In the report of their deliberations, the definition of equity included some statements with which the following discussion will not agree. "It would be an equitable situation if students in adjacent classrooms had teachers of similar training," and "Nor would it be equitable if the software used within these classrooms was styled to be of interest to and be more effective with some students than others" (Wilton & Rubincam, 1985, p. 8).

These statements are not presented to disparage the definitions or content of the ECOO report, but merely to provide examples of the definitional differences that can arise. The point of disagreement hinges on the difference between equity and equality, illustrated by the following analogy.

As mentioned in other chapters, computers in education are not a unity, a single application, but rather many different applications with differing potential benefits and possible harmful effects. On this basis an analogy will be drawn with food, in that different types of computer applications will affect individuals differently, just as different types of food have different effects. First of all, it must be acknowledged that the analogy rests on the assumption that computers are important, perhaps even essential, though probably not quite as vital as food. (This assumption is questioned at other points, but is made here for the purpose of the analogy.) A second point worth emphasizing is that an analogy does not imply the two concepts are identical. That is, many possible implications of this analogy, such as those based on the claim that fasting clarifies the thought processes, will be left to the reader.

The point of the analogy between computers and food is to note those aspects of "food equity" which have implications for, or increase our understanding of "computer equity." For example, having equal amounts of food for each person is not in itself a sufficient definition of food equity, just as equal numbers of computers or equal amounts of computer time do not guarantee computer equity. That is, a person whose entire food consumption is sugar, or whose entire computer use is in the form of video games can be said to have an equity problem.

However, it is not just a matter of giving everyone the same balanced diet of food or computers, for different people can have different dietary or computing needs. Just as women often need more iron in their diet, so they may also need different types of activities in their computing.

Beyond the question of dietary balance, or perhaps even preceding that question, the matter of food quantity is known to be a need that varies greatly over individuals. That is, even if the diet is properly balanced, factors such as metabolism and physical activities result in needs for different amounts of food in different people. (The preceding should not, of course, be taken as meaning that because women generally have lower calorie requirements than men, that their computing needs are therefore also likely to be less.)

It may also be instructive to look at the factor of cultural differences as applied to equity. Even though the fast-food restaurant has penetrated to the core of an appallingly large proportion of the world's cities, public demonstrations against them in Rome during 1986 indicate that cultural differences in diet are still important. Although the tendency is to translate popular computer programs into any language in which sufficient sales appear to be possible, one would hope that considerations based on equity would take a more sensitive approach to cultural differences.

Another feature of food equity which may have importance for computer use is that of the "food allergy." That is, although little is known about the true nature of food allergies, some individuals may experience violent changes in body chemistry as a result of eating certain foods which appear to have no untoward effects on the general population. Interestingly, foods to which one is allergic are often ones that are "craved" by the body. In terms of computer applications, this is probably best expressed as the "personal side effect." Just as some people feel acute distress after eating shrimp, and others cannot disconnect themselves from a warm television set or telephone without great difficulty, so it may be that the use of word processing, for example, can have damaging effects for some writers (a topic explored in more detail in Chapter 6).

Finally, both with foods and with computers, it is often very easy to confuse needs with wants. In the report on equity from the ECOO conference, phrases such as "doesn't have to be the same if they don't want to," "tools to do the sorts of things they want to do," and "giving people things they don't want" are a part of the discussion. In spite of popular folklore, the empirical evidence indicates that babies do not select a proper diet when given free choice, nor do students necessarily profit from the opportunity to exercise control over their own learning activities. Similarly, it is unlikely that we can expect computer equity based on students' wants to be beneficial for all.

The preceding should have illustrated some points of disagreement with aspects of commonly accepted equity definitions such as those from the ECOO discussion report. Specific to the ECOO definitions, similar training for teachers is not an indicator that equity exists unless the students' needs are correspondingly equivalent. Similarly, it seems almost inevitable, and potentially beneficial, that software will "be of interest to and be more effective with some students than others." The task is to match interests and effectiveness with needs to maximize the learning potential for all students.

With the analogy between food and computers as a backdrop, and emphasizing again that the two concepts are not implied to be identical, it should now be appropriate to move on to a more explicit consideration of the components of computer equity.

ASSUMPTIONS

Available evidence clearly shows that not all students (or members of the general public) spend equal amounts of time with computers, nor do they all have the same opportunity to spend their time using computers. This is a clear case of inequality, but is it inequitable? Quite possibly it contains some elements of inequity, but further evidence or assumptions are needed to back up and clarify this claim.

The most common assumption seems to be that time spent with computers is good for students. This implies that using computers satisfies one or more student needs, but the nature of the needs is usually not made explicit. Some people, though it appears to be a definite minority, make the opposite assumption, that time spent with computers is bad for students. This latter assumption reverses the usual equity concerns, asserting that those who have access to computers are disadvantaged relative to those who do not have access. The safest assumption, given our lack of knowledge about the effects of computers, is that the beneficial and harmful effects of computers are dependent on the activity and the user, with any instance likely to be a combination of harmful and beneficial effects.

Some examples from Turkle (1984) may help to clarify this assumption. She provides detailed descriptions of three adult video game "addicts," all of them successful in business, who regularly spend large amounts of time playing video games. Although they all waxed lyrical over the benefits they derived from playing video games, it would be unconvincing to try and argue that most of the adult population was disadvantaged because they were not spending comparable amounts of time playing with video games. Given this background, and keeping in mind that in some classrooms much of the students' time with computers actually is spent in playing with video games, it is hard to accept statistics such as number of computers per school, or even per classroom as being direct indicators of the presence or absence of computer inequity.

It would be equally unjustified, however, to assume that all student use of video games must be harmful or useless. Turkle argues that Jimmy, a 14-year-old boy, derives benefits from the many hours he spends at home, alone, perfecting his video game techniques. Her arguments are persuasive, for Jimmy has slurred speech and an awkward gait due to a birth defect. Jimmy finds that the video game world allows him to achieve the perfection that eludes him in the physical world. At the same time, one must attend to the views of Brod (1984), a psychiatrist who has found many instances in which it appears that extensive use of video games or other computer applications have been damaging.

The preceding examples, admittedly extreme, are not intended to show that computer uses can be good or bad, but rather to show that a dichotomous classification is often inadequate. Each application, like the half-tone photographs in newspapers, is a combination of light and dark elements, giving an appearance of shades of gray, the lightness of which varies with the values of the observer.

Most of what we read or hear about computers in education emphasizes only one aspect, usually the good points, but occasionally the bad, to the exclusion of other points of view. This is at least partly due to the screening effect of the popular press, who favor the excitement of extremism over the calm of rationality, preferring in the name of "reader interest" to create what Menosky (1984) calls an artificial dichotomy.

Walker (1983) seems to provide an exception to this rule of extreme views, with his listing of seven limitations of microcomputers in education, to go along with the seven potentials he describes. Yet even his "limitations" are mainly short-term complaints, such as the existing shortage of good programs, the difficulties of planning in a time of rapid change, today's micros are hard to use, etc. Generally, his list of limitations does not go beyond cautions, or suggestions for new directions.

A full consideration of the possible benefits from the use of computers in education will not be given in this chaper. The areas to be included in such an investigation would have to include the use of computers to deliver instructional material (Chapter 5), programming (Chapter 6), word processing (Chapter 6), and computers as tools for students (Chapter 7), as well as some consideration of the interaction between computers and teachers who use them (Chapter 8).

However, an overview of some of the relevant factors in these areas will be provided at this time, in order to give some background for the following discussion of specific equity concerns.

AREAS OF COMPUTER "BENEFITS"

The use of computers to deliver content material to students was one of the first educational applications proposed and tested. The varied studies that have been done generally show a consistent saving of time for students using computer-assisted instruction (CAI), but other benefits, such as increased achievement, though possibly consistent, are usually quite small. The problem is that these results, which may be generally true for groups of students, do not give sufficient information to predict the likely results for individuals, particularly individuals with unusual or varied characteristics. On the other hand, anecdotal evidence derived from atypical cases may mislead us into expecting extreme results. Since equity questions relate to matching individual needs to the use of computers, we are left to speculate about the differential effects which CAI might have for individuals.

Individualized instruction has always been stated as a goal of CAI, but the realization has proved to be elusive. The general problem is indicated by the area of research known as ATI (Aptitude-Treatment Interaction) studies. The hope underlying these studies has been that student aptitudes could be found which would cause students to achieve differentially under different instructional treatments. That is, students who were high on a certain aptitude would do better with one type of materials or teaching, while students low on this same aptitude would do better with another type of materials or teaching. In spite of the strong desires of those hoping to find examples of ATIs, this type of research has been generally unfruitful, with the materials being tested producing results that are indistinguishable, or one type of materials or teaching being consistently better for all students (Ragsdale. 1980).

The one dimension on which instruction is consistently individualized is rate, both for CAI and some paper and pencil forms of individualization. The major advantage of rate individualization is that students are allowed (or forced) to "master" one unit of instruction before going on to the next. This is usually described as being advantageous for those students at the extremes of the achievement continuum. That is, slow achievers are able, perhaps for the first time in their academic careers, to succeed in mastering topics of instruction, even though it takes them much longer than most other students, while the high achievers are able to move more rapidly, covering more topics than the bulk of the class. The most consistent benefit of CAI, time saving, is largely a function of the high achievers no longer being held back by the rest of the group.

On the basis of the preceding, drastically oversimplified explanation of one effect of CAI, one could assert that those in the middle of the class, in terms of achievement, have the least to gain from CAI. This seems reasonable, since group instruction is typically directed at the estimated middle of the group. Thus one could assert, based solely on this simplified model of constant achievement and variable rate, that the middle of the class is not likely to benefit from using CAI and hence have no need for CAI. Further, one could also assert (based on the same model) that omitting the middle of the class (in terms of average achievement) from the use of CAI would not create an equity problem.

The purpose of the preceding hypothetical and artificial analysis is not to make equitable decisions about the use of CAI in all school environments and should not be taken as such. Rather, the purpose of the exercise has been to give some indication of the complexity such an equity analysis might entail if one cannot assume that all students benefit from (and consequently need) a particular computer application in the same amount. This example was based on the same application (CAI) being considered for different groups, but the reverse might also be considered, with different applications being available for one group. That is, for a particular group of students, similar in age and ability, one might assert that they had a need for some computer applications, say, word processing and other tool applications, but they had no need for some other applications, say, programming and CAI.

Very little empirical evidence exists to indicate that schools are taking a systematic approach to determining the most beneficial computer diet for each student. In fact, Becker (1986) has found that many schools provide more computer opportunities for their higher achieving students, though the trend is less pronounced than that found in his earlier study in 1983. In a few schools, perhaps 15 percent of the total, he found that lower achieving students were intentionally being given more time to use the computers. Differences in favor of the high achievers were more likely to be found in programming activities, rather than in CAI.

The primary reasons for teaching programming seem to be based on its value as vocational training. Only part of this is directed toward the new career paths of programmer, systems analyst, etc., with a large part of the expectation based on the changing skill requirements in established career patterns, such as accounting. Thus, the vocational basis for programming is not restricted to parents seeing their children becoming programmers, but also comes from a general belief that one's employment prospects are enhanced by a knowledge of computers, which might be acquired in the form of programming skills.

The emphasis on programming as a desirable skill is particularly evident in Canada, which has little hardware capability, but aspirations to be a major exporter of software. Canada can also serve as an example of most developed countries, in that the demand for programmers has grown rapidly over the past years, but the increase in training programs has generally failed to match this growth. Anecdotal information indicates that in recent years, the number of vacant faculty positions in Canadian computer science departments has been approximately three times as large as the average number of computer science Ph.D.s being produced annually in Canada. Meanwhile, most of these new graduates are taking positions in business, industry, or government. As a result, the university departments of computer science are finding it difficult to cope with student demand, a situation which seems to be common throughout North America and most of the developed world.

Whether this demand for programming skills will continue to grow is still a matter of some debate, a factor which may temper the desire to increase the existing educational facilities. This reticence on the part of public institutions has led to increasing numbers of private programming schools, some of these operated by computer manufacturers. It should also be noted that part of this problem of facilities is a function of the different perspectives of parents and students versus those of schools and educational authorities. In many cases, the educator's view of programming as a guarantor of employment is much more restrained than that of parents and students.

Regardless of the current level of demand for programmers, students and their parents are likely to rethink their views of the desirability of having programming as a job skill in light of the role programming typically plays, or will play in career mobility. Although programming may make an unemployed or handicapped person more employable, the kinds of computer skills that are required at higher levels of the job hierarchy are likely to be different. In particular, the managerial use of computers usually depends on an ability to use applications programs which, although they may require some skills related to programming, are much more dependent on knowledge of the business environment than knowledge of programming. Managerial use of spreadsheet programs (matrix calculation programs for budgeting, financial planning, and the like) are examples of applications that require minimal programming skills and greater knowledge of the information being manipulated, plus some aptitude for the hypothetical, conditional thinking processes involved. Note, however, Gochenouer's findings that increased use of computers by managers does not seem to lead to improved job performance, but rather the reverse, decreased job performance (Gochenouer, 1985; Strehlo, 1986).

We might conclude, therefore, that learning to program as a part of your education may not be a benefit, particularly if one considers the "opportunity cost" of giving up the learning of one subject in order to learn another. This conclusion would seem to shed an interesting light on the findings of Becker (1985), that current educational practice seems to be the provision of more opportunities for programming experiences for advanced students, while frequently using CAI for the lower, remedial students. At first glance, it might appear that the higher achieving students are being rewarded for their performance, but the negative aspects of programming skills for vocational advancement could show it as an activity to occupy their time while other students "catch up." It must be made clear that this conclusion is based purely on vocational implications of programming and not on the cognitive benefits that have been claimed for the programming experience. A more complete discussion of the possible benefits of learning to program, including the cognitive benefits, will be found in Chapter 6.

Computers used as word processors are also often seen as beneficial for all students, as a means of improving their writing skills. The evidence is insufficient to verify whether this assumption is true or false, but until its degree of truth is known, it is safer to consider word processing as a possible mixed blessing. The possible ways in which word processing might be harmful for some writers are spelled out in Chapter 6, with only an example presented here.

The writing styles of successful writers indicate that one can reach this level in many different ways. Most of us have been taught that the writing process includes the writing and revision of successive drafts, and many famous writers follow these procedures. Arthur Haley, however, provides one counterexample, for he has been described as writing one small section (500-1,000 words) per day, proceeding from his first draft to the final version of this section in one day, then going on to succeeding sections in the same way until the book is completed. Some other writers, on the other hand, rarely revise at all. Isaac Asimov and C. S. Lewis are given as two examples of writers who have produced their final version in their first draft, presumably by having done sufficient planning to ensure that no changes needed to be made.

Given the wide range of writing styles among the famous, or successful writers, one is led to the question of how word processing influences a young writer's acquisition of a unique style. Arthur Haley is reported to have adopted the use of word processing, keeping the same technique but doubling his daily output. But it could be argued, at one extreme, that writers like Isaac Asimov have no need for word processing, and never did have a need for it, for its use could have shaped them into a different and less successful style. A more direct way of expressing this is that Isaac Asimov might not have become a "first-draft" writer if he had become dependent on word processing techniques. The experience of an Arthur Haley should not distract us from the likelihood that young writers are going to be more powerfully shaped by their use of word processing.

The preceding does not give a formula for determining which students need word processing, merely a suggestion that it may not be equally beneficial for all students. Hence, we come to a conclusion similar to that for the previously considered applications, that equality of word processing may not be necessary or sufficient for equity in word processing.

Word processing is just one example of the use of computers as tools, and we might expect to find similar conclusions for tool applications in general. At an extreme, if we used a tool that allowed us to remain immobile throughout the day, this tool would not be beneficial for our physical fitness, unless other circumstances had already forced this immobility. One can also observe that mental abilities seem to be lost through disuse, or emotional capabilities as well, as Darwin laments in his autobiography about having lost his enjoyment of art, music, and poetry. The uses of computers as tools will be discussed further in Chapter 7, but one should be willing to entertain the possibility that their unrestricted use will not be entirely beneficial. Tool applications seem to be growing in importance, since Becker (1986) has found that the longer a school or teacher has used computers, the greater the proportion of time allocated to tool use.

In considering the possible negative consequences of tool applications, some have expressed the opinion that the use of computers as tools, particularly as analytical tools, will lead to a generation with a left-brain bias. It is not clear that this is a legitimate fear, since the evidence regarding the importance of brain sides is not as clear as the intuitive appeal of the concepts arising out of it. Alternatively, one could argue that the use of a tool which does analytical tasks will leave more time for the human to do nonanalytical tasks, leading to a right-brain (intuitive, creative) emphasis and the possibility of a different fear. That is, the increasing use of computers to do analytical work could lead to an apparent atrophy of the analytical functions of the human brain. However, the topic remains difficult to unravel. One of the factors in this lack of clarity may be the use of mathematics as the frequent topic of computerized study and analysis.

Although working in and studying mathematics can be either what is called a left-brain or right-brain activity, depending on the specific topic, the analytical component seems to lead most people to see it as primarily left-brain. Papert has based most of his descriptions and examples for LOGO in mathland (Papert, 1980b), but he has also alluded to other microworlds which might be more fruitful for the purpose of this discussion. Musicland would be one area for consideration, one in which some LOGO activity can be noted, but by far the most interesting applications in music learning have been outside of LOGO. In the many music systems that allow children (or serious composers) to experiment with different musical ideas, the role of computers seems to be that of an assistant (or possibly an accompanist) that can facilitate creative and intuitive (right-brain) activity by the user.

This small suggestion of evidence from musicland activities should not be taken to mean that fears of too much analytical activity are unfounded. Certainly, a focus on tools that provide assistance for analytical functions, including those in the musical domain, could lead to humans spending more time in analytical activities, with results that have so far only received speculative attention. Rather than dismissing these fears as being without evidence, a more constructive approach can be taken. It should be reaffirmed that an evaluation of computer use should not be confined to the effects intended by humans, but should also include both continuous monitoring of possible side effects and a continuous assessment of needs.

In summary, before moving on to a consideration of specific equity concerns, what might be some important factors of the equity discussion have appeared. In considering the importance of access to computers and their various applications, we will try to avoid the assumption that all contact with computers is beneficial to the student, for a focus on means leads to a constriction of ends (Scheffler, 1986). At the same time, although it is possible for students to use computers in such a way that the time appears to be wasted, they still may be obtaining some benefits from the time being spent. It can be misleading to continually place an emphasis on analogies, but in this instance it might be useful to compare the use of computers with the role of vitamins and minerals in the diet. Some substances, such as vitamin C, are useful in some amounts, but when the body has sufficient vitamin C, the rest is excreted. Similarly, some vitamins (such as A and D) or minerals (such as salt) are useful in small amounts, but larger amounts, rather than being excreted, can pose a danger to the body. Other analogies could be drawn, but the main task underlying the equity analysis and the use of computers in general seems to be to determine (for individual students) how the amounts of various computer activities are related to potential harmful and beneficial effects.

SPECIAL EDUCATION

Special education is an important area of concern in considering equity of computer use, with a large (and regularly increasing) number of subfields of activity. Not all of these subfields can be discussed here, but a distinction will be made for the purposes of discussion, between physical disabilities or handicaps and those which are nonphysical in nature. This distinction is being made with the realization that these categories are not truly independent, with many children being at a disadvantage both in physical and nonphysical ability. The reason for the distinction is to handle more adequately the types of computer needs they imply and the differing equity issues they raise.

In terms of computer equity issues, the use of computers for the physically disabled is probably more clear-cut than the applications for other concerns, whether inside or outside of special education. In many cases, the computer application is exactly that of a prosthesis, like that of a hearing aid or glasses, permitting their users to more nearly approximate the communications ability of their peers. To deny these basic functions to some students, when the technology exists to restore those functions which have been lost, is a definite source of inequity (though other factors, such as cost, are also relevant).

Goldenberg (1979) has made an extensive examination of the possible uses of technology in special education, starting with a foundation of identifying needs. In the area of "normal needs" he sees the computer as entertainer (perhaps more of a "want") and as assistant, with many of the assistant examples having a LOGO orientation. In special education, Goldenberg emphasizes the need for students to have access to "feedback loops," the communications facilities that will enable them to participate in their environments, not just observe them passively.

Goldenberg sees the computer being used with special education students in three ways, as tutor, as eyeglasses, and as a mirror. He sees serious potential risks with the use of tutor mode, feeling it is appropriate to only a fraction of the domain to which it is being applied. The eyeglasses mode is one form of prosthesis, with perhaps more of an emphasis on tools, permitting users to do things which would otherwise be difficult for them. The computer as mirror brings out the other aspect of the prosthesis, more accurate feedback and perceptions from the external world. Together, the eyeglasses and mirror functions serve to give students a clearer view of the world, more control over it, and more accurate feedback on the effects of their control.

The question of computer aids for the handicapped becomes less clear when the concept of prosthesis is merged with some other goal, such as teacher replacement. Many of these combinations involve the use of LOGO, such as those Goldenberg proposes, but the ambiguity of these applications is not easily clarified, since the prosthesis and LOGO elements of such a technique are not easily separable. That is, for students with mobility problems, the geometry aspects of LOGO or similar programs can be quite prosthetic in nature. However, the overall desirability of LOGO is a question which will have to wait until Chapters 6 and 7 for further discussion. The general rule that might be applied would have to consider at least three types of applications for the handicapped: prosthetic, therapeutic, and instructional. The prosthetic application is perhaps more easily judged, while the therapeutic, designed to put curriculum materials into a more "appropriate" form for a specific disability seem to require a more specialized knowledge for their evaluation. For the most part (except for factors such as a mismatch between the students' ages and the grades they are in) purely instructional applications would not be a part of equity concerns for the handicapped.

The nonphysical handicap side of special education involves a heavy emphasis on the therapeutic effects of computer use, some intentional and some side effects. Possibly because of our lack of knowledge about special education techniques with computers, the side effects seem to predominate in many applications. Results from some of the special education classrooms studied by the Queen's University researchers, though mainly anecdotal, illustrate this (Carmichael et al., 1985).

As with any evaluation of computer effects, some of the effects noted here are strongly influenced by the novelty of computers in classrooms and others may be influenced in less obvious ways. A clear result of novelty is seen in one teacher's description of how his students' pride had increased due to their unique situation of having a computer that the rest of the school wanted to see and learn about. To explain the new technology to students who were otherwise much more academically able than them was a great lift for these students, but clearly not an effect of computers that could be considered as permanent (although the effect on an individual student's self esteem might be permanent).

In a learning disability class, the teacher reported that students were able to spend longer periods of time concentrating on the computer work and that this extended concentration seemed to have carried over into their other work. The students were now working independently more than they had before. That this is due to the novelty of computers is a strong possibility, but not necessarily the total explanation. Some students will be more likely to exhibit this effect and careful study may be needed to discover which ones they are.

Another temporal benefit reported by the teacher of an emotional adjust-ment class was that he and the students had been able to learn together. This seems to be the same effect as that noted by Eaton and Olson (1985) and de-scribed more fully in Chapter 8, but even more important in the special educa-tion context. This may have important long-term implications, leading to joint learning activities in a number of different areas, but it is unlikely that teachers can continue to relearn the same computer skills indefinitely.

Some of the results in the special education classes gave indications that are the reverse of what is usually seen to be educationally valuable. For example, in the emotional adjustment class, the teacher initially felt that the students would often waste large amounts of time playing a particular game. The game involved manual dexterity, but the speed could be varied, allowing the students to earn very high scores at the slow speed if they took enough time. Later, the teacher saw this game as a boost that his students often needed and felt that his initial assessment of it as a time-waster was invalid.

This same teacher, in comments not printed in the final report, also saw the "infinite patience" of computers as a negative effect in his classroom. That is, when a program would endlessly repeat the same question, the students often found it to be "infinite frustration," rather than "infinite patience" to be con-tinually asked a question to which they were unable to give the answer. This response presumably arises from poor program design, and is not confined to the special education classrooms, but does indicate that claimed benefits of com-puters cannot always be accepted at face value.

Finally, one last observation from Carmichael et al. (1985) may help to put the computer needs of special education students in perspective. In describing the emotional adjustment teacher, they note, "Mr. Veley had a great attachment to his 'boys' [the class was all male]. At the beginning of the school year, until it was taken over by the P.T.A., he made breakfast for the boys each day. He fre-quently gave them money to buy lunch or took someone out to dinner" (Car-michael et al., 1985, p. 395). Many teachers show dedication to their students in this or similar ways. In assessing students' computer needs, we must continue to remember the importance of the human context.

What then can be concluded about equity issues in special education? In gen-eral, the practice of most educational authorities is to give high priority to pro-viding disabled students with assistance to help them overcome the consequences of their disabilities. In this respect, the use of computers should be no different. However, if computer as novelty is seen to be an important benefit, the novelty effect will have to be obtained from other sources as years go by. Perhaps the special education class will be the first to have 3-D television and other novelties. Such a policy might also allow the teachers more opportunities to learn with their students, another benefit computers are seen as providing. Beyond these more obvious features, the next consistent benefit seems to be rate individualiza-tion (as discussed earlier in this chapter).

In many instances, special education students are at the extreme in their need for a slower rate of instruction. Associated with an inability to work quickly, or with concentration, go the effects of diminished self-esteem and lack of pride in success. An equitable distribution of computer access would give higher priority to these extreme needs of rate and concentration flexibility.

What is less obvious are the other dimensions in which special education students have strong needs for computers. In considering the implications of computers for special education, or technological aids for the handicapped in general, Goldenberg (1979) expresses a concern about the relative use of what he calls the "exercise model" and the "substitution model." The distinction seems to be similar to that made by O'Donovan (1984) in comparing "compensatory" and "curative" approaches to human problems, but Goldenberg favors a synthesis of the approaches while O'Donovan puts his priority on the curative (or exercise) model. These two views are not necessarily incompatible and can be seen as complementary, even though the two approaches are strikingly different in terms of the values underlying them. The views can be seen as complementary in that, rather than substituting technology for disabled human functions in cases where "exercise" or "cures" will not restore the function, a combination of the two approaches might be preferable. Thus, the synthesis view of Goldenberg can be seen as a way of using a partial "curative" approach when the complete cure is not available. (O'Donovan's observations are considered again, and in a bit more detail, in Chapter 4.)

Under any approach, one would expect that computers used as tools, particularly as tools to aid learning, would be a class of applications deserving close attention. These tools would not be restricted to the use of computers for programming (nor even emphasize them) as O'Shea and Self (1983) do, but would include word processing, graphics, music, and spreadsheet programs, plus others of this sort of "helping" tool.

Thus, one might expect that special education applications of computers for nonphysical disabilities would be primarily focussed in the therapeutic category, with learning tools being an example (though some of them might also be seen as prostheses). The main considerations would be in terms of specific needs of special education students. Where these needs were no greater than in the general student population, greater access for special education students would not be a goal of an equitable distribution of computer access.

SEX EQUITY

Ample evidence exists to show that girls spend less time with computers than do boys, particularly when the activity is programming or the computers are used before or after school (Becker, 1986). What remains to be determined is to what extent this is an equity problem. Specific questions include the degree to which boys benefit (or are harmed) by their increased exposure to computers, and the degree to which this difference is symptomatic of the effects on girls' self-images, brought about by cultural expectatioms. This is not intended to give the impression that the sex problem does not exist, for it almost certainly does. Rather, it is to suggest that the solution is much more complex than simply requiring that boys and girls spend equal amounts of time using the same computer applications.

Lockheed and Frakt (1984) indicate a number of factors that they feel are responsible for some of the differences in computer use between boys and girls. The first factor in their eyes is sex segregation, the tendency for students of both sexes to choose to participate in activities with other students only when they are of the same sex. Thus, when a school has a computer laboratory, the continual presence of boys in the computer laboratory tends to discourage girls from using computers, while in regular classrooms, with both sexes present, girls are more likely to use computers on an equal basis with boys.

A teacher once described an experience with the computer laboratory in a grade 7-8 school which tends to confirm this suggestion. She found that girls were unlikely to visit the room and use the computers there unless other activities brought them there. The most successful other activity was a crocheting class, which brought so many girls into the computer activities that the crocheting class was eventually cancelled. An unusual incident perhaps, but supportive of the notion that girls need some socially acceptable justification for beginning to use computers, while boys generally do not.

The cause of this difference in justification-need seems to be in the social context, Lockheed and Frakt's second factor. The strongest examples of this cultural component can be seen in the advertising (or in the movies) picturing of typical computer users and the common link within most schools of computers and mathematics. Another component of the social context, as seen by Lockheed and Frakt, is the lack of software directed at females, compared with almost half of the software directed specifically at male users. This problem may be more difficult to correct than it first seems, for Imhoff (1984), in reviewing an interactive adventure game designed specifically for 7-12-year-old girls, found that the most enthusiastic users of the program were boys in the 8-10 age range.

On the positive side, the link between computers and mathematics seems to be diminishing in introductory courses as the demand begins to exceed the mathematics department's ability to offer the courses. Even though the addition of teachers with different backgrounds is helping, this is not an adequate response to a mathematics bias, which should be eliminated even if it had no relationship to the sex equity issue.

Lockheed and Frakt make interesting observations about the relative "indirect costs" for boys and girls using computers. Since high school girls are known to spend more of their free time with their friends than do boys, choosing to invest their time in computer-related activities means a greater indirect cost, in terms of friendships and social standing. This may be a new factor, or it may just be a combination of the previous two factors. Boys can spend time with computers *and* their friends, while girls usually cannot, with both of these effects strongly influenced by cultural expectations about behavior.

Carmichael et al. (1985) also provide some insights into differential effects of male and female students from the results of their two-year study. Most of their evidence comes from one of the 13 classrooms studied, probably indicative of the strong roles teachers can play in increasing or decreasing sex differences. This class of grade six and seven students had the largest difference between the boys' and girls' performances on the LOGO test at the end of both years of the study. This difference cannot be attributed entirely to differences in time spent with computers, since students had some choice as to how their time would be spent, choosing to work with either LOGO or word processing. However, at the end of the first year, the *highest* girl's score was 70 percent, while the *average* boy's score was 70 percent. An interesting sidelight is that all (four) boys who were in this class for both years had a lower score the second year, while several of the (eight) girls increased their scores in the second year, a year in which the teacher was a less active participant in the computer activities.

The boys in this class were generally more active in their computer use than the girls, including their ability to dominate the free-time use of the (up to five) computers. Because the boys were often able to sign up for the free-time use shortly after 8:15 in the morning, the girls asked that an equal rotation system be set up, but the teacher disagreed. Although the computer manuals were locked away during the two years, one of the boys was the keeper of the key in the second year, allowing most boys to access the manuals freely. Boys were also more interested in the competitive challenges the teacher set each week. In addition, boys who were new to this classroom in the second year were quickly incorporated into the computer culture, while the girls had no similar culture to join.

Although the boys in this class spent more time with computers, the results of their spending more time were not always pleasing to the teacher. During the second year of the study he noted that "girls appear to be more consistent, following a pattern more carefully, completing programs with precision. . . . The boys however jump from idea to idea; their learning is quick, not solid" (Carmichael et al., 1985, p. 111). He was also "floored" when a girl who had let her boy partner control the computer interaction, though he appeared less competent than her, said, "He needs to feel he is in control" (p. 115).

The second year of the study created a different environment in this classroom, with the number of computers increased from two to five, but the students required to spend half their day outside the classroom, taking other courses from other teachers. During the first year, the classroom teacher had been able to reduce the load of the regular curriculum, but now much of it was beyond his control. Most of the girls responded to these new conditions by cutting down on their computer activity, while the boys were more likely to continue their computer work. The teacher saw it this way:

I am convinced that the boys and girls work equally hard but I do see a difference in their nature. When hassled and pressured the girls tend to bow to the pressure, whether it be the volleyball coach or history teacher, but the boys continually choose computers over the pressure and just accept the punishment of the teacher concerned. (p. 118)

The teacher also commented, in his log book, after talking to the parents of his students during the second year, "All boys have several games at home. Some girls have games, but all have word processing" (p. 122). Both of these observations should raise serious questions about the value of the increased computer activity for the boys. The boys were choosing computers over the rest of their curriculum and choosing games over word processing. An indicator of computer equity must certainly take into consideration something more than time spent with computers.

The link with word processing is one avenue that seems to require further exploration. McKelvey (1983) suggested that word processing be emphasized in schools, not only because of its beneficial effects, but because girls were more likely to become involved with computers when the activity was word processing. Wong, Uhrmacher, and Siegfreid (1984) described a pilot program for computers and equity which featured word processing. Collis (1985) reported that survey results from grades eight and twelve indicated that boys were consistently more positive in their attitudes about computers, but girls were consistently more positive in their attitudes about writing. Small wonder that the classrooms in which students were offered a choice between LOGO and word processing (and a teacher who favored LOGO) found the girls doing poorly in LOGO achievement.

The battle for sex equity in computer use is not without its victories, but the exact meaning of these victories may not be totally clear. New materials, such as *The Neuter Computer* (Sanders & Stone, 1986), and new techniques have been used to increase girls' participation in computer courses. Goldenberg speculates that this may not be the total solution if girls are motivated by a desire for business and secretarial skills (Wilton & Rubincam, 1985). Menzies (1981) supplements this view by documenting not only the decline in those jobs traditionally taken by women, but also the decreasing opportunities for advancement which these jobs offer. This may mean that the increase in girls' participation with computers is aimed at the wrong goals.

On a more positive note, although boys heavily outnumber girls in programming activities, both Linn (1985) and Goldenberg (Wilton & Rubincam, 1985) report that while the very best programming students are almost always boys, the better programmers are more likely to be girls. That is, they report that boys are more likely to be the ones who are very good at learning programming, but on average, girls are better programmers than boys. Johnson (1987a) also reports encouraging findings, that at four sites using computers for social history study (grades 7–8), although boys were more active in exploring software packages, girls were persistent in obtaining access to computers when a specific product was required. That is, girls had an overall participation rate (in computer work, not exploration) that was at least equal to the boys', while at one site, where the teacher gave more frequent computer access to students who were more productive in research, girls produced more final projects with a major computer component. Johnson's observations are in harmony with Gochenouer's (1985) that women (in a business setting) seemed to be more task-oriented than men when using a financial planning program.

The results of the preceding selective discussion should illuminate two aspects of sex equity that are not always part of the discussion. Both of these aspects have to do with the type of computer activity in which students might participate. It has become increasingly obvious that the type of activity offered has a differential effect on the participation rates for boys and girls. What seems to have been less obvious is that the type of activity offered also affects the benefits students are likely to receive from taking part. Taken together, the common element of these two aspects is student need. Once it is recognized that students need some computer activities more than others and that students may need some other curriculum components more than unlimited computer use (and that both of these needs are in competition with strong wants), the computer equity question may become more complex to analyze, but without this realization it is not likely to be solved.

SOCIOECONOMIC EQUITY

Socioeconomic factors affect students' opportunities to access computers in two major ways. The factor felt first is the level of school funding, based usually on the relative wealth of the community, district, state, or province. In the case of computer purchases, school funding can be either direct or indirect, since many schools have had computers purchased for them by parent or community groups. This means that although a government may use a process to equalize funding for all the publicly supported schools in its jurisdiction, such as is done by the Province of Ontario, public interest in computers may conspire to eliminate the equitable distribution the government has planned. Of course, the effects of local wealth are not only evident over large areas, but are also felt within towns and cities.

Anderson, Welch, and Harris (1984) provide evidence of socioeconomic inequities to support their concern that opportunities to acquire computer literacy are not fairly distributed. A major concern of theirs is that if schools do not provide these opportunities for the children from less affluent families, computers will serve to further increase the relative advantages of the "haves" over the "have-nots." The results they cite are from the United States National Assessments of 1979 and 1982, with indicators of computer courses and computer use related to school environment characteristics. For example, the percentage of students taking programming courses in high school was essentially unchanged

for "Title I" schools (those having a large percentage of parents with incomes below the poverty line), while sharply increasing for other schools. Similarly, the
1982 assessment showed almost twice as high a percentage of "urban/rich" students were using computers or terminals as compared to students in either rural
or disadvantaged urban areas. Another result showed that programming enroll-
ments were sharply increasing in suburban and small city schools, while remaining relatively stable in big city and rural schools.

In viewing these and other similar findings, it might be useful to recall a large-
scale survey which was done in the early 1960s and one of its results. In this survey, one of the factors that had the highest relationship with average school
achievement was the number of books in the school library. That is, schools with
large numbers of books in their libraries tended to have higher achievement by
their students than did those with smaller numbers of books in their libraries. It
doesn't take a great deal of reflection to conclude that this is not just a simple
cause and effect relationship and that greatly increasing the number of books in
the libraries of those schools with low achievement is not likely to solve their
achievement problems. The situation is probably much closer to what Lincoln
and Guba (1985) call mutual simultaneous shaping, with many factors affecting
any particular result. It is clear that the number of books in a school library is
dependent on many factors reflecting the relative advantages of the students
attending the school. One can also draw the same conclusions about the number
of computers in a school, at least in general terms, with many of the factors
again being related to the students' already advantaged position. The nub of the
socioeconomic equity issue is not that computers are the (sole) cause of some
students achieving more than others, but that if computers do provide a benefit
for students, this benefit is helping to widen the gap that already exists.

It is also useful to keep in mind that a considerable amount of information
may be hidden below the level of the statistics that have been gathered. For
example, in a Canadian school board with more than 70,000 students, in 1985
the schools had over 1,800 computers and terminals, or one for every 39 students. At a slightly more detailed level, the secondary schools averaged 29 students per computer, the K-8 schools averaged 36 students per computer, and the
K-6 schools averaged 75 students per computer. Of course, each of these figures
hid enormous variation, with one secondary school having a computer for every
15 students, a K-8 school having one for every 9 students, and a K-6 school
having one for every 12. At the other extremes, one secondary school had only
one computer for 339 students, a K-8 school had one for 124 students, and a
K-6 school had one computer for its 410 students. This is as much detail as was
available from these figures, but we can assume that within the schools an
additional source of variation could be uncovered, with some classes having
ample access to computers and others within the same school having little or no
access. We should also assume the possibility of considerable error in the individual school figures, since one school which to the naked eye appeared to have
fifteen computers, was listed as having only seven.

Equity of access to computers in schools is indeed affected by socioeconomic factors, but the computers in a school can only affect those students whose teachers encourage, or at least tolerate their use. In addition, computers benefit students in varying amounts, depending on the uses to which they are put and the instruction which accompanies the uses. Without information about these two factors, the statistics on computers per school are incomplete.

Adding to (and complicating) the picture of socioeconomic equity with regard to school use of computers is the factor of computers in homes. Some have suggested that the problem of differential access to computers, due only to the use of computers in schools, may be of short duration. Their explanation is that computers will soon be so pervasive that they will be as common as television sets and found in almost all homes. Already, Chancellor (1985) reports that home computers may be found in over 25 percent of British homes (though 42 percent have more than one television set), but at least two problems arise from this argument. The first is that although computers may decline in price to be comparable with television sets (less in some cases), the values of the consumers may not be such as to make them ready buyers. The problem is similar to that of the number of books in the school library. The fact that parents are sufficiently concerned about their children's education to buy them computers may be more important than the educational benefits of increased computer access. However, if a survey finds that students who have computers at home have higher achievement in school, it will be music to the ears of the computer marketing managers.

The second problem with the home purchase solution to the school computer problem is that the mere availability of a computer does not mean the availability of all relevant computer applications. That is, the difference between a minimal system and one suited for a variety of appropriate applications may mean a 50 to 1 (or more) ratio in price. The latter system could include disk drives, letter quality printer, graphic input device, telephone communications equipment, and most of all, the appropriate software. As the teacher from the Queen's University study (Carmichael et al., 1985) found out, all of the boys had multiple games to use on their home computers, while all the girls with home computers had word processing programs. This is another entry point for parent values. The commitment has to be just a bit higher to extend the simple purchase of a home computer into some intervention as to how it is to be used (analogous to the use of television). Parents who are unable (or unwilling) to be involved in their children's education will likely find the computer to be a poor surrogate parent (Brod, 1984).

Some school authorities have made efforts to cooperate with parents, not only through joint purchases of hardware, but also through coordinated purchase and use of software. These cooperative programs are described in more detail in Chapter 9, but the essence of them is that parents are able to obtain equipment at lower costs (or possibly on loan from the schools), the children have the same equipment at home as in the schools, and the software applications are also coordinated. Komoski (1984) believes that schools have a responsibility to provide guidance for parents in the selection of software. Certainly, this form of guidance also has benefits for the school, since it in effect multiplies the purchasing power of schools, making them a more potent force in influencing the products created by software developers. However, the more important aspect of this guidance is that it deals with the equity question in terms of the productive uses of computers, not merely in terms of a count of the computers in homes.

RACE (ETHNIC) EQUITY

Ethnic background is another factor that is hard to separate from other factors, such as socioeconomic status. Also, the individual factors may sometimes tend to cancel each other, such as the oft-reported factor that the cultural values of orientals tend to emphasize school achievement, with news stories describing the high achievement of recent Asian immigrants, even though they are relatively poor in terms of income and wealth.

One of the most obvious components of ethnic background is that of language differences. In Canada, for example, a substantial minority of the population has French as a first language and is taught in that language. But the availability of software, particularly educational software, is much more limited in French than in English, hence the opportunities for effective computer use may be reduced (games are often more easily available, or free of language). Also, even if one were to use a word processor for the French language, or even use one intended for English, the proper French keyboard and character set (with accents) are usually not easily found. Yet this is only a part of the Canadian problem, for the number of Canadians who have a first language other than English or French is substantial, varying between 30 and 50 percent of the provincial populations from Ontario westward to the Pacific Coast.

The presence of large groups of students with culture and language backgrounds different from the founding society has led to the provision of instruction designed to preserve and encourage this variety of cultures, also known as "the cultural mosaic." Two of the implications for computer use arising from such a policy are that it is more difficult to integrate computer use into instruction in a variety of languages and that the addition of this new curriculum material also makes it more difficult to include computer studies as a separate topic.

Some schools have an enormous task in trying to cope with the variety of nationalities in their charge, with at least one school having students who spoke a total of 38 different languages. The danger to many of these students is that their inadequate facility with English and a lack of translation services may cause them to be classified as low in ability when this is not the case. Such a classification can lead to exclusion from a number of desirable educational activities, including the use of computers.

Language ability is not the only distinguishing factor of other cultures, of course, and recognition must be made of the social stigma that usually attaches to recent immigrants and native students. Both of these groups, but especially native North Americans, are often also living within a homogeneous subculture, where values in many areas, including the access to computers, may be quite different from that of the general community. What facets of computer use are likely to be of value to students in such situations?

In many cases, the mastery of computer techniques brings with it a certain amount of prestige or increased self-esteem. Those applications most appropriate for students with limited ability in English would be those with low language requirements. Fortunately, outside of word processing, most applications of computers require relatively little language ability. Graphics and music applications often require hardly any language at all, while programming has been the avenue to employment for many immigrants because of the limited languages that are used. Most computer uses, including games, also give the user a feeling of control over the environment, limited as that environment might be, another potential boost to the self-image.

It should be noted that the proposing of computer use because of its low language requirements is a two-edged sword. The danger is that the students who lack language ability will spend so much time with their computer applications that their acquisition of English will be delayed even further. However, it is just such questions of student need that an equity assessment must address.

OTHER EQUITY DIMENSIONS

Equity considerations should not be seen as limited to the areas already discussed, for other dimensions could easily be more important in different environments. For example, we have Becker's (1986) finding that high achieving students often are given greater access to computers in schools. The important rule would be to consider any factor that affects a student's need for computer use as a potential equity dimension. Some factors that might be in this category include personality, age, geographic area, and motivation.

The personality issue is often raised with regard to social skills, with evidence pointing in both directions as to the social benefits which computers might bring. On the positive side, Turkle (1984) and Carmichael et al. (1985) both point to examples of students whose social status rose on the basis of their acquiring computer skills. However, Turkle also paints a picture of the "hacker" culture, a picture that has become a stereotype, of those who bury themselves in their computer activities and only communicate with others of their kind. Obviously, with those who tend to be introverted, the use of computers can either help to remedy or exacerbate the problem. It is when the use of computers becomes focussed on the control of other people, such as through intrusion into other computer systems, that the hacker can become a menace to others' privacy and possessions. It must be stressed that "prescribing a computer cure" for personality problems must be done with great care, more care than is usually evident.

Age also seems to be an important factor on which the ability to learn about computers varies, possibly because our teaching methods are not often well structured or developed. In the usual environment for learning about computers, the premium seems to be on a willingness to explore and experiment. In this type of behavior (sometimes known as the hands-on approach) children usually excel. Children also have the advantage of being able to spend much more time than adults usually have available to learn the intricacies of their computer systems. It should then come as no surprise that it is commonly accepted that one must be young to learn about computers and use them effectively. To a certain extent this is true, but an uncritical acceptance of this folklore may place an unnecessary strain on teachers trying to learn to use computers and their relationships with their students. More emphasis needs to be placed on the child's greater availability of time so that teachers and other adults will not be overly intimidated by the students' apparent ease of learning.

Many of the early predictions about the potential uses of the telephone dealt with the positive effects it would have on rural life (de Sola Pool, 1983). The introduction of computers as communications media might lead to similar predictions, or one might believe that isolation of the individual is more of a problem in large cities. In schools, one might see computer communications networks as vehicles for students with special interests to locate and communicate with those who have similar interests. In rural areas, students taking advanced level courses may have few classmates (or none) with whom they can share their study. However, students in large urban areas may have similar problems if they are taking courses for which the demand in their school is low. On the basis of this cursory examination of geographical differences, no significant pattern of need has arisen, but a more thorough investigation may prove this to be a dimension of divergent needs.

Motivation is a popular term, but one that is difficult to define in a noncircular manner. That is, things that are motivating are called such because of the effect they cause, not because of their inherent characteristics. At the moment, the motivational capabilities of computers are being stressed, with little regard given to the proportion of this effect that is due to novelty alone. Different methods of computer presentation do seem to have motivating effects, however, they appear to be effects which can differ from student to student. In some of the most obvious examples, motivational aspects are a part of other computer equity issues, as in sex equity where boys are more highly motivated by shooting-type video games than are girls, while girls are more highly motivated by word processing applications.

Motivational effects might be a part of equity concerns in at least two ways. The first is that new techniques of motivation (via computers) may be discovered for certain subsets of the student population. For students who have general motivational problems, this then becomes a potential benefit and an addition to their need for computers, possibly leading to an equity argument that these students require greater computer access than others.

The second question had to do with the possible consequences of the general use of motivational techniques to increase student interest and achievement. One part of this is the obvious result that could come about from the prolonged use of violence, as in many video games, one example of the danger of appealing to the baser instincts of people. The second part is more subtle, having to do with the nature of the reward which is used to motivate. Morgan (1984) points out what seems to be a consistent finding that rewarding someone for merely *participating* in an activity actually *decreases* their motivation for further participation in the activity, while rewarding them for their *achievement* in the activity *increases* their motivation for further participation. This can be interpreted to mean that the use of fancy computer graphics (or other reward) as compensation for using a mathematics program, regardless of achievement in the program, makes it less likely that the student will be motivated for further work in mathematics, while the use of rewards only for specific achievements is likely to increase the motivation for further mathematics study. That is, having students study mathematics, or any subject, via computer rather than with regular curriculum materials, because of motivation problems, may in fact lead to lower motivation to study mathematics in the long term. Whether these findings are precisely correct is not the main point, but rather one must use motivating features with great care.

CONCLUSIONS

It is difficult to draw strong, definite conclusions from such a mixed collection of possible factors and speculation. The main theme seems to be that equity depends on matching the features or strengths of computers to the weaknesses or needs of people. To identify the features, strengths, or even the benefits of computers alone is not likely to be sufficient. Neither is the identification of human needs or weaknesses, by themselves, likely to be sufficient. The successful search for equity, and the determination of its attainment depend on the careful use of needs assessment and evaluation techniques.

Specifically, this chapter and the one preceding can interact in at least two significant ways. One is in the evaluation of equity, a problem that requires substantial amounts of naturalistic inquiry to fully define the issues as well as systematic study to determine the effectiveness of proposed remedies. In addition, a less obvious interaction, but probably more important, is the question as to how equity does (and should) affect the evaluation of computer applications in education. That is, less emphasis might be placed on the average effect of computer programmimg on logical thinking skills in a classroom and more emphasis given to the varying needs of students. These needs would include not only those for increased logical thinking skills, but also the means (computers, or other approaches) that will increase them most effectively. Without consideration being given to the ways in which evaluation and equity can and should *affect each other*, the equity questions cannot be described completely, much less solved.

4   *Artificial Intelligence*

If faith in computers leads enthusiasts to see them as solutions for a multitude of society's ills, then proponents of artificial intelligence (AI) may be the hyper-faith movement of the technology era. AI is a hot topic not only in the media's interest in it for feature stories, but also on the stock markets in the form of investments in AI firms, and in academic circles where AI research leads to grants and fame. For the media, the source of interest seems to be based on a fascination with uses of computers as substitutes for functions usually performed by humans, with robots being a strong example. For example, a "Dinosaur-size robot with laser eyes" is described as "sure-footed as a camel, stronger than an elephant and a *good deal smarter than the insects* [emphasis added] on whose mode of locomotion it is partly based" (Browne, 1985, p. 8). Topics which fascinate the press are not necessarily unimportant, but may have more influence on human thought and behavior than they deserve.

THE DEFINITION OF AI

Part of the problem, or the threat in artificial intelligence, lies in its name and the promises that name implies. Yet the name cannot be ignored, for it is part of an image and concept being sold by those who propose the use of AI. Much of the problem in dealing with what AI means to society in general is in its ambiguous definition, like the concept of intelligence itself.

Intelligence became a more precise technical term when Binet created the first intelligence test so that people who had been classified as mentally deficient would have an opportunity to demonstrate their mental ability and thus be released from an institution. His test still forms the basis of much of the technical use of the term intelligence, but the general public's concept of the term is often quite different. Of course, even official use of intelligence testing has led to confusion, with the U.S. government's use of intelligence tests to screen immigrants in the early 1900s being a prime example. Those immigrants who did not score high enough on these tests were not allowed to enter the United States. That huge percentages of people should have been classified as "feebleminded" on the basis of tests that were not written in their language is a blot on American history.

Although the public may see intelligence as encompassing social skills, creativity, moral standards, common sense, learning ability, and memory (and perhaps more), the intelligence tests commonly used today would probably be better described as tests of "academic aptitude." That is, intelligence tests are quite good at determining a person's ability to do well in an academic environment. However, the term intelligence continues to be used in these different senses with no indication that a consensus definition will emerge (probably because what is currently measured by intelligence tests is the easiest part to measure).

Artificial intelligence, as a concept, suffers from a similar ambiguity of definition, but this time the ambiguity is not restricted to different views held by the general public and the technically informed. The *New Webster's Computer Dictionary* builds on the confusion residing in the definition of intelligence by defining AI as "computer processes and techniques that simulate human intelligence" (New Webster's, 1984, p. 14), but goes on to add that AI "is studied (1) to learn more about human intelligence itself, or (2) to improve the operation and increase the independence of computers" (p. 15). This sets the pace, with other definitions differing not so much in direction as in scope and distance. That is, Fredkin says modestly that "Artificial Intelligence is the next step in evolution" (Turkle, 1984, p. 242). Roger Schank, while avoding a direct definition in his book (Schank, 1984), does declare, "We are very much modern-day philosophers. We're addressing the same question that Aristotle addressed, and everybody else in between. We have different methods of doing it" (Turkle, 1984, p. 259).

AI ASSUMPTIONS

The range of definitions for AI (and other facets of this range will emerge in the discussion) is not only the major difficulty in trying to discuss AI and analyze its potential, but also the main component in the danger of AI. The danger of AI comes, both directly and indirectly, from what is often called "strong AI," the views held by its strongest proponents, that AI can be used to turn computers into "minds" that "understand." A typical, but not overly strong example of the strong AI view is that of Stonier who said, "The question is not whether machine intelligence will surpass human intelligence at some future time, but what will be the relationship between human and machine intelligence" (Stonier, 1984, p. 254).

The strong AI position creates a potential danger in two different forms, depending on whether its foundation, "machine intelligence will surpass human intelligence," is true or not. The first danger stems from the consequences of it being true, the logical implications of the strong AI assumptions, which have been seen in a general form at least as far back as C. S. Lewis. Some of his thoughts that capture the image are "Man's power is, in reality, a power possessed by some men which they may, or may not, allow other men to profit by. . . . For the power of Man to make himself what he pleases, means as we have seen, the power of some men to make other men what *they* please" (Lewis, 1978, pp. 34, 37). These lead up to his ultimate conclusion, "Man's final conquest has proved to be the abolition of Man" (p. 37). The first danger of AI is then, that if it is true, although it presents a fascinating intellectual challenge to create it, the results for humans will be no more liberating than the assembly line, but rather an even stronger tool for some humans to use in dominating others. (More will be said about this later, particularly in relating Weizenbaum's position.)

The second danger lies in the effects that acceptance of the strong AI view, even if it is false, might have on human thought and behavior. Some people who work in the AI field reject the strong AI view, agreeing that it has undesirable consequences and/or unreachable goals, but at the same time arguing that one can use the benefits of the general AI approach without worrying about strong AI ever coming into existence. Whitby (1984) likens these AI researchers to political parties who stand on principle when out of power, but revert to "the art of the possible" when in power. For those who believe the strong AI position is vastly overstated (as Dreyfus and Weizenbaum will be seen to argue in the next section), this rationalization can be comforting. At least two aspects of strong AI prevent this rationalization from being totally comforting, both based on the difficulty of separating strong AI from other AI applications.

First, and most obvious, is the commonality of name. Just as with intelligence, when we hear someone use the term AI, the natural tendency is to expect that their definition corresponds to ours. Or even more likely, when one hears many people speaking about AI, one is likely to assume that they are all speaking about the same concept. As long as this assumption is held, along with some people predicting and describing the strong AI position, while an increasing number of people (while not necessarily endorsing strong AI) are proclaiming the inevitability of AI, it is natural that the view "machine intelligence will surpass human intelligence" will continue to grow. As a result, even though the truth or falsity of strong AI may not be known for years or decades, the destruction of humans' self-image can begin immediately. For "Things a machine can do will be seen as insignificant, precisely because a machine can do them," in the view of Roger Schank (1984, p. 236), himself an AI researcher and strong AI proponent.

However, even beyond the commonality of name, a second defect in the rationalization of strong AI arises even when gentler terms such as knowledge engineering are used. This is the problem of assumptions, assumptions which are common to all forms of AI, whether they bear the name or not. These assumptions will be looked at more closely in the next section, but suffice it to say that when one sees minds and machines as functionally equivalent, certain harmful effects are assured. Whether the link between mind and machine is made for a greater understanding of the human mind, or greater independence of computers, the result described by Schank will occur, regardless of the name applied to the machine process.

The remainder of this chapter will provide additional information about these possible dangers as well as the potential benefits seen for AI, particularly in education. Throughout, the reader should keep in mind the role of needs, benefits, and side effects, as discussed in Chapter 2. One should also remember the central role of values, as discussed in the first two chapters, particularly as seen in Ellul's (1964) analysis of "la technique" or technology. That is, one should look at values in two ways, the way in which our values might be changed through the effects of AI, as well as the way in which our use (or nonuse) of AI will be determined by our values. Support for this view of the interaction between values and technology can also be seen in O'Donovan (1984), Florman (1981), Bolter (1984), Turkle (1984), and Davis and Hersh (1986). O'Donovan and Florman emphasize that technological change is the result of popular demand, not the plotting of scientists and engineers. That is, they see new technology being shaped by our value base (itself shaped by existing technology), not an independent creation of technical minds. Bolter and Turkle, on the other hand, provide support in the form of evidence of the ways in which computers (in the case of Davis and Hersh, mathematics and computers) are changing our understanding of ourselves and how we think. Both of these aspects are important in the further investigation of artificial intelligence.

ARGUMENTS AGAINST AI

It Can't be Done

Dreyfus (1979), in a revision of a book first published in 1972, discusses the limitations of AI from the viewpoint of "what computers can't do." He uses this phrase as the title of his book, though it is perhaps stronger than the contents warrant. He actually argues that it is very unlikely or improbable that AI researchers will be able to simulate human intelligent behavior using programming techniques. As a philosopher, he focuses on four erroneous assumptions that he believes are the cause of their unwarranted optimism: biological, psychological, epistemological, and ontological.

Dreyfus's first edition was motivated by a growing public acceptance of the magic of AI, even though little proof of its potential existed. Specifically, he pointed to a statement which Herbert Simon, later to win the Nobel Prize in economics, made in 1957. In it, Simon stated "there are now in the world machines that think" and "their ability to do these things is going to increase rapidly until—in a visible future—the range of problems they can handle will be coexistensive with the range to which the human mind has been applied" (Dreyfus, 1979, p. 81). Simon continued with a set of predictions of AI goals to be reached in the next ten years. Writing 14 years after the predictions, Dreyfus pointed out how far they were from being realized, how little attention the AI community was paying to this lack of success, and remarked, "It is essential to be aware at the outset that despite predictions, press releases, films, and warnings, artificial intelligence is a promise and not an accomplished fact" (Dreyfus, 1979, p. 85). Despite strong rebuttals from the AI community, Dreyfus's position was essentially unchanged in 1979, nor was it changed by the mid-1980s.

Biological assumption

The first erroneous assumption of AI, according to Dreyfus, was the biological assumption. This assumption, that the human brain functions like a digital computer, seems to be based on an earlier assumption that neurons could be simply described as having only two states—firing (a burst of electrical energy) or not firing—and that these two states were all that was needed to describe the functioning of the brain. The firing of neurons is now known to be a much more complicated process, with the firing of a single neuron possibly depending on the firing patterns of thousands of other neurons, but the belief that brains are simple electrical devices seems to live on. It should not, however, be seen as offering any support for the development of artificial intelligence.

Psychological assumption

The psychological assumption operates at a higher level, assuming that the mind can be viewed as a device operating on bits of information in accordance with a set of formal rules. The consideration of this assumption is also more complex. Dreyfus considers empirical evidence based on cognitive simulations (using a computer to simulate human thought) and finds serious anomalies (acknowledged by the researchers) in the results. This is a beginning of a vicious circle, for one can tolerate anomalies in a theory known to be generally true (as with Newton's inaccurate calculations of the moon's perigee), but this means assuming AI is true in order to validate an underlying assumption. Dreyfus does go on to examine arguments for making the psychological assumption on an a priori basis, but finds that they all hinge (sometimes implicitly) on the assumption that the relevant properties exist, moving to another vicious circle. The analysis may not be clear, but the burden of proof should be clear. That is, it is up to AI researchers to demonstrate that the psychological assumption is true, not for anyone else to demonstrate that it is false. As it stands, it is not at all obvious that it is true, and quite likely that it is false (to use one of Dreyfus's examples, think of the formal rules you use to decide if an object is a square).

Epistemological assumption

The epistemological assumption is also one of formalization. In this case, it is assumed that all knowledge can be expressed in terms of logical relationships between defined objects or events. Another way of looking at this assumption is that although one may not be able to *explain* intelligent behavior in terms of formal rules (the psychological assumption), all such behavior might still be formalizable. One example given by Dreyfus is bicycle riding, which can be formally defined in terms of laws of physics, but the formal description has nothing to do with a child's learning to ride a bicycle. The essence of the epistemological assumption is that not only does the formal description exist, but it can be used to reproduce the behavior.

Dreyfus sees acceptance of the epistemological assumption as being based on unjustified overgeneralizations from physics and linguistics. From physics, the success at simulating physical processes seems to suggest that the brain, being a physical object with physical processes, can be simulated. However, this is only true when one knows how the brain functions, and since this is not known, the results from physics do not apply. From linguistics, the success in formalizing linguistic competence seems to hold the hope of success in formalizing all knowledge. However, Dreyfus points out that linguistic competence, the ability to distinguish between "well-formed" and "ill-formed" sentences is only half the story, and the wrong half at that. What AI needs is a formalization of linguistic *performance*, not competence, the ability to create well-formed sentences, not recognize them. Not only does the linguistic generalization not support the epistemological assumption, but our ability to create and understand sentences which break the formal rules of linguistics ("I ain't done nothin'") seems to weaken, rather than strengthen, the arguments.

Ontological assumption

The ontological assumption is that all the data on which a mind (mechanical, or not) must operate are discrete, explicit, and determinate. That is, any object, event, or relationship can be described in terms of a limited number of definable characteristics, independent of other objects, events, and relationships. This is in some ways the opposite of Lincoln and Guba's (1985) mutual simultaneous shaping, where everything affects everything else. Another way of stating the assumption, which is hardly ever made explicit in AI research, is that the characteristics of the relevant data can be completely described, independent of their context. Dreyfus argues just the opposite view, that not only is everything dependent on context, but that it is also impossible to predict the ways in which context is going to be relevant. To illustrate that complete knowledge of context may be needed to arrive at a total definition (or understanding) one can use the sentence, "The box is in the pen" as being dependent on (and predictable from) context (baby, pig, convict, etc.). However, the creation of "James Bond" provides a new context, and the possibility of a miniaturized box in a fountain pen, not predictable from the other contexts. Dreyfus claims that the only solution to this dilemma is to restrict any nonhuman definition to a limited context, with defined relevance for observed data, which is what many practical applications of AI (particularly "expert systems") have done.

In considering alternatives to these assumptions, Dreyfus proposes that the human body is crucial to the intelligence of our minds, that in moving around with the body, the mind acquires the contextual information it needs. Descartes had proposed that the mind can cope with an infinite number of contexts, while a machine cannot, only because the mind has an immaterial soul, but Dreyfus gives this short shrift. He feels that the growing size of modern computer memory capacity renders Descartes' argument obsolete.

The soul was also discussed by Alan Turing, a brilliant mathematician who created an important part of the foundation underlying the modern use of computers. In 1950, he wrote a paper considering the question, "Can machines think?", in which he anticipated some of the objections which might be raised to an affirmative answer. In his Pulitzer Prize winning, *Godel, Escher, Bach*, Hofstadter says that Turing "proceeds to pick apart, concisely and with wry humor" and calls the responses "humorous and ingenious" (Hofstadter, 1979, p. 597), but only reproduces the objections, not Turing's responses. In a later book, *The Mind's I* (Hofstadter & Dennett, 1981), the responses are given. In them, Turing's response to the "soul" objection is that an omnipotent God can give a soul to any creature, including a machine—case closed. Ingenious perhaps, but hardly convincing.

Hofstadter also runs afoul of the soul in trying to explain how an intelligent machine might have consciousness, or an awareness of what it is doing. In order to give a "non-soulist" explanation, he proposes the existence of a "self symbol" or "self-subsystem" of enormous complexity. Later on, he declares that "A very important side effect of the *self*-subsystem is that it can play the role of "soul" (Hofstadter, 1979, p. 387). From this, he is able to assert that such a system could declare itself to have "free will." An interesting conclusion, but derived primarily from his initial assumption, in line with the *Humanist Manifesto's* (Kurtz, 1973) emphasis on the scientific over the spiritual, that the human soul cannot exist.

Given his assessment that the assumptions underlying AI are shaky and its accomplishments are few, how does Dreyfus account for the optimism which pervades the AI community? To do so he quotes Bar-Hillel, who made the following comments in 1966.

There are many people—in all fields but particularly in the field of AI— who, whenever they themselves make a first step towards letting the computer do certain things it has never done before, then believe that the remaining steps are nothing more than an exercise in technical ability. Essentially, this is like saying that as soon as anything can be done *at all* by a computer, it can also be done *well*. On the contrary, the step from not being able to do something at all to being able to do it a little bit is very much smaller than the next step—being able to do it well. In AI, this fallacious thinking seems to be all pervasive. (Dreyfus, 1979, p. 147)

Bar-Hillel's assessment is still true today, if not an understatement of the optimism. Schank (1984) acknowledges the low level of AI performance, describes some current approaches as dead ends, admits that the techniques that will pro-duce "true AI" are unknown, but still makes supremely confident statements about what is going to be accomplished. "Some day, intelligent machines finally will arrive. Machines that understand natural language will allow people access to information that they never had access to previously" (Schank, 1984, p. 227). In this, he not only solves the currently impenetrable problems of understanding natural language, but also discovers a new class of information which computers cannot give us access to until they understand natural language.

Evil Applications

Weizenbaum's case against AI is based not so much on what computers are unable to do, though he sees important limitations, but rather on what they shouldn't do. He would argue "that if computers could imitate man in every respect—which in fact they cannot—even then it would be appropriate, nay urgent, to examine the computer in light of man's perennial need to find his place in the world" (Weizenbaum, 1984a, p. 12). Weizenbaum sees his major argument as being not so much with computer science, but with "clever aggrega-tions of techniques aimed at getting something done" (p. 268), a description which seems to make them part of "la technique" (Ellul, 1964).

Weizenbaum focuses on two types of computer applications which he feels should be avoided, or at least approached with utmost caution. One type, which he feels are simply "obscene," are those which represent an attack on life itself. In this category he would include a proposal to combine an animal's visual sys-tem and brain with a computerized mechanism to create a thinking machine, as an obvious example. However, this category is also broad enough to include any proposal "to substitute a computer system for a human function that involves interpersonal respect, understanding, and love" (Weizenbaum, 1984a, p. 269). It is this belief that caused him to react with horror when a psychoanalyst suggested that his ELIZA program (Weizenbaum, 1966) might be the basis for developing a program to replace a psychoanalyst, a quest still being pursued by some psy-chologists (O'Dell & Dickson, 1984). Weizenbaum appears to have correctly seen this as a case of "la technique" leading to the "abolition of man."

The second type of application that Weizenbaum feels should be avoided is an even greater source of disagreement than the first type, requiring more subtle analysis. They are applications likely to have serious negative side effects. Since side effects are by definition unintended and usually unanticipated, predicting them is a difficult task at best. Weizenbaum uses automatic recognition of human speech as an example, saying that governments are likely to use such a technique to monitor telephone conversations. He wonders why computer tech-nologists should lend their support to such a project, but probably realizes the reason is their not seeing, or not wishing to see, the possible consequences.

Roger Schank provides the other side of this argument about computers understanding language. As an AI researcher, one of those whom Dreyfus feels are overly optimistic, Schank states "that there is a real prospect of creating intelligent computers that can understand and respond to almost anything we might say to them" (Schank, 1984, p. 21). In an advertising brochure from a company founded by Schank, the claim is made that "We give our computer programs the same kind of knowledge that people use, so our programs understand a sentence just the way a person does, and respond in conversational English" (Winograd & Flores, 1986, p. 128). Winograd and Flores believe that this claim would be seen as a gross exaggeration even by those who believe in the success of AI. Yet on the other hand, Schank does ackowledge that "a man with a low IQ is . . . incredibly intelligent compared to other animals and present day computers" (Schank, 1984, p. 30).

In his book, Schank attempts to answer

three important questions for anyone who now uses or who will someday use a computer: 1. What do we have to know about computers in order to live in a world that is full of them? 2. What can we learn about what it means to be intelligent through our development of computers that can understand? 3. How will intelligent computers affect the world we live in? (p. x)

Weizenbaum, given his view on the need for computer literacy, would certainly answer "not much" to the first question and Dreyfus would no doubt answer similarly to the last two. The issue, however, is not what is contained in these questions, but what is omitted. Although they delve into what we should know about computers and what we should learn from them, plus how they will affect us, the explicit needs they will satisfy is not made clear. This statement of need is only made implicitly, when Schank provides a rationale for his plans for computers and AI, by identifying the appropriate needs of his audience.

We want our computers to be able to do more than simply display a table labeled "Bills Outstanding" when we type *List bills outstanding.* We want the computer to know why we are asking so that it can get at the heart of our question. . . . A computer must know what it means to owe money, to pay money, and to need money . . . it must know enough about owing to be able to respond to . . . *Who owes us money?* or *Can we meet this month's payroll?* To do this means we must provide computers with the same knowledge that people use to answer these questions. (p. 111)

The logic proceeds from "we want" to "computer must," but leaves unanswered the questions about how much we need this, or what it will cost us to get it.

Dangerous Concepts

As indicated earlier, the AI concept can be dangerous, even if it cannot work, when people accept the associated predictions and/or assumptions, resulting in a change in their attitudes toward human beings, both themselves and others. Accepting the inevitability of AI seems to be the first step, followed by the total (not just physical) replacement of humans by machines, leading to the changes in values that these imply. All three of these stages are discussed in this section, but it should be noted that one stage doesn't actually have to be true before it has an effect. That is, AI doesn't have to be truly inevitable for its inevitability to be felt, nor do humans have to be replaced by AI for this concept to have an effect. Thus, the change in values can occur whether the first two assumptions are true or not.

Inevitability of AI

If anyone is going to reject the inevitability of AI, a Christian, believing in the creation of man by God and in His own image, would certainly be a leading candidate. That is why it is surprising to find a leading Christian publication, *Christianity Today*, featuring an article to answer the question, "Intelligence separates people from animals. Very soon it will not separate people from machines. How should Christians respond?" (Emerson & Forbes, 1984, p. 14). In case you feel that the heading may not represent the contents (as often happens), the authors state "What we have is a creature not made by God in his image, but made by us in our image. We will stand to this creation as God stands to us. At the same time, the machine mind will in certain ways far surpass our own—even surpass those minds that originally created it" (p. 14). Except for the insertion of "in certain ways," it seems to buy the AI line almost entirely (including parts that will be presented later in this chapter). It is surprising, but at the same time an expected result of assumptions, a reflection of the thinking by those Christians who accept others' assumptions while questioning their own.

The point at this time is not to argue the relative (and absolute) merits of Christianity versus AI, but merely to show that the assumption of AI's inevitability is widely held.

Replacing humans

At the present time, the replacement of humans by computers is being most highly touted in the form of "expert systems," programs designed to solve particular types of problems in a specific limited domain. Dispute continues, even within the AI community, regarding the appropriateness of this claim. For example, Schank is very cautious in his remarks about expert systems.

The words "expert system" are loaded with a great deal more implied intelligence than is warranted by their actual level of sophistication. The popular use of the term by the media also tends to give people the impression that an expert system is equivalent to a human expert in a given field, or that all AI is concerned with the construction of expert systems. Neither of these is the case. . . . Expert systems are not innovative in the way that real experts are; nor can they reflect on their own decision making processes. (Schank, 1984, p. 33)

Although the makers of expert systems attempt to deal with the ontological assumption by severely restricting the context of the system's operations, the results are in some ways even more disappointing. That is, if AI cannot surpass all human behavior in a restricted domain, such as the 8×8 world of chess, one's faith in super-intelligent AI is sorely tested.

Expert systems often have their knowledge of the problem domain stored in either the form of deep structure or surface structure. Deep structures are usually in the form of cause and effect relationships, abstractions, or analogies, while the surface representation is more likely to be based on empirical observations. Michaelsen, Michie, and Boulanger (1985) suggest that the best approach is to use deep structure in expert systems when it is cost-effective, otherwise using a surface representation. Duda and Shortliffe (1983) provide an example of the effects of these two structures in describing how MYCIN, an expert system for antimicrobial therapy, has a rule to prevent giving tetracycline to patients under eight years of age, but does not have the underlying reason for the rule in its knowledge structure. Because MYCIN contains only surface knowledge for this rule, it is unable to make the exceptions a human doctor would make (in severe cases).

The major problem with expert systems appears to be that human experts seem to be able to identify the critical components of a problem in a way that they and AI researchers have been unable to formalize. An example of this is seen in chess masters who are able to ignore most of the potential moves which a chess program must consider. The program's strength is in the detailed analysis of a move's consequences, while the expert's strength is in knowing, *in advance*, which moves are worth considering.

Reactions to the use of expert systems in business seem to be mixed. Predictions that the AI market, with expert systems as a major component, will grow from $148 million in 1985 to over $28 billion by the 1990s is one source of optimism, with laudatory articles, such as Kinnucan's (1984) "Computers that think like experts" being another. The basis for the articles' positive view is primarily on research systems' results and the extrapolation of these to the business settings. As Martins (1984) points out in an article entitled "The overselling of expert systems," the lab results are often not repeatable in the field setting. One factor he cites is that the researchers did not use the same tools which are available for commercial systems. Even Kinnucan's praise rings hollow when he reports that "A prototype system for diagnosing telecommunications network failures . . . matched the performance of intermediate-level technicians" (Kinnucan, 1984, p. 37). If this result is worth reporting in a national publication, the title of expert system may have to be replaced, perhaps with a new goal of "super expert" systems.

The use of expert systems in education is advocated by many, among them O'Shea and Self, who use expert systems as their main focus in a book devoted to the use of artificial intelligence in education. Their approach is specific, beginning with four premises and a conclusion:

Premises

1. Computers will be widely used in education.

2. Most present programs are unsatisfactory.

3. The main reason for 2 is that the programs lack knowledge of various kinds.

4. Artificial Intelligence is concerned with making explicit the kinds of knowledge mentioned in 3.

Conclusion

The designers of computer systems to be used in education should take account of the subject of artificial intelligence, and the users of such systems may expect them soon to provide facilities considerably more sophisticated than those available today. (O'Shea & Self, 1983, p. 6)

It is quite likely that Weizenbaum would dispute the first premise (at least whether computers *should* be widely used in education), while Dreyfus would undoubtedly dispute their later description of a computer's properties: "It understands, i.e. it can in principle be programmed to understand a student, just as a good teacher does, and to use this understanding to determine its teaching actions" (O'Shea & Self, 1983, p. 60).

As an example, O'Shea and Self refer to Brown and Burton's (1978) computer-based tutoring/gaming system, which was used, among other things, to teach student teachers how to recognize and identify students' procedural bugs in basic math skills. That is, it gave the student teachers examples of mathematics problems in which certain systematic errors were consistently made, until they were able to identify the systematic error, or bug. O'Shea and Self report that "The revelation that errors which appear random are the manifestation of systematic bugs is a breakthrough for many student teachers, and all those involved in the BUGGY game felt they gained something valuable" (O'Shea & Self, 1983, p. 241). Two points are not dealt with by most people who cite the BUGGY example: the extent to which these techniques can be generalized, particularly to nonmathematical content, and the extent to which this type of system merely treats the symptoms of poor instruction, rather than improving instruction itself.

Overstatement of results is often a feature of the description of expert systems, with Larkin's comment being a good example. "The intelligent performance of the BUGGY and DEBUGGY programs is at a level far beyond that of even experienced teachers of arithmetic" (Larkin, 1983, p. 54). This statement gives the impression that AI is well on its way to replacing teachers, especially since her article contains no description of the BUGGY and DEBUGGY programs. If these programs only do something that teachers *don't* do, rather than something they *can't* do, as Brown and Burton's description seems to say, Larkin's remark is another example of the overly optimistic overstatement described by Dreyfus and Bar-Hillel.

Changing our values

Ellul (1964) pointed out that "la technique" not only changed values as a result of its being used, but also required that certain values be changed before it could be used. The mechanization of bakeries, described in Chapter 1, required changes in the nature of bread and human taste before it was implemented successfully. O'Shea and Self also acknowledge that their proposed use of computers must be preceded by changes in human values.

The computer-brain analogy seems to be becoming culturally acceptable as evidenced, for example, by advertisements which make use of it. Perhaps by 1992 we shall be sufficiently far along this road for it not to seem inherently objectionable to a parent (as, on the whole, it does today) that his child be taught by a computer and not by a man or woman. (O'Shea & Self, 1983, p. 246)

This expectation is ominously similar to one expressed by Francis Crick, one of the discoverers of DNA.

We've just seen that the discussion as to how many people there should be in the world has now, as it were, become quite acceptable. It is not acceptable, *at the moment* [emphasis added], to discuss who should be the parents of the next generation, who should be born, and who should have children. (Schaeffer, 1972, pp. 21-22)

Some of the AI researchers are well ahead of what the public is willing to accept. Turkle gives an example of their advanced thinking on the replacement of humans by machines.

When MIT's Edward Fredkin talks about AI as a natural step in evolution he is taking this kind of reasoning a step further. Most of us feel a loyalty— sentimental, moral, or religious—to our species. But from a position of confidence about the artificial intelligence of the future, Fredkin casts a cold eye on our human limitations. "Basically, the human mind is not most like a god or most like a computer. It's most like the mind of a chimpanzee and most of what's there isn't designed for living in high society but for getting along in the jungle or out in the fields." . . . "We're tuned," says Fredkin, "to dealing with local not global situations, and our biggest problems turn up when global problems emerge." . . . "But we are in the process of creating entities that will do it far better than we." (Turkle, 1984, p. 262)

His belief in the superiority of machine thinking has allowed Fredkin to devalue human thinking to the level of chimpanzees. The somewhat magical attributes he seems to ascribe to machine thinking will be discussed in the next section.

Turkle also reports that Gary Drescher, also of MIT, has several proposals for new ethics. Isaac Asimov is the creator of "Laws of Robotics" which would prevent robots from injuring humans, require robots to obey humans (when not in conflict with the first law), and require robots to protect themselves (when not in conflict with the first two laws). Drescher turns the tables, proposing that machines with "consciousness" be given protection from a new form of murder, pulling the plug. This can inspire some obvious comments about the value system which would generate "machine rights," but one perhaps less obvious comment also seems appropriate. Asimov's laws have long been regarded as a standard for robot behavior, but the claims of strong AI proponents would seem to put their viability in jeopardy. Specifically, if one really could create a mechanical intelligence with free will and consciousness, a reasoning capability far surpassing that of humans, how would such an intelligence be convinced that it should sacrifice its "life" for any human's? Even a human mind should be able to answer that question. You can't value machines above humans and expect the value of humans not to be diminished.

Magic and science

Our usual practice is to see science and magic as completely different in terms of both means and ends, as competing forms of the struggle between humans and nature. C. S. Lewis (1978) disagreed, and put forth the following argument.

> You will even find people who write about the sixteenth century as if Magic were a medieval survival and Science the new thing that came in to sweep it away. Those who have studied the period know better. There was very little magic in the Middle Ages; the sixteenth and seventeenth centuries are the high noon of magic. The serious magical endeavour and the serious scientific endeavour are twins; one was sickly and died, the other strong and throve. But they are twins. They were born of the same impulse. . . .

> If we compare the chief trumpeter of the new era (Bacon) with Marlowe's Faustus, the similarity is striking. . . . Bacon condemns those who value knowledge as an end in itself, this, for him, is to use as a mistress for pleasure what ought to be a spouse for fruit. The true object is to extend Man's power to the performance of all things possible. He rejects magic because it does not work; but his goal is that of the magician. (Lewis, 1978, p. 46)

Magic has been abandoned because it does not work, but in AI, when science is unable to provide adequate answers, aspects of magic begin to reappear. The appeal to magic is most often seen when AI is straining against the assumptions explained by Dreyfus (1979), or against the "Lady Lovelace objection," first voiced by her more than 140 years ago. Lady Lovelace, a financial supporter of Babbage's quest to build the "analytical engine," cautioned him that the engine would be able to act only according to the instructions given to it and would not be able to create original thoughts. An example of the struggle against the specificity of today's analytical engine can be seen in an excerpt from Turkle.

> I attend the Boston premiere of the Walt Disney movie *Tron*, advertised as "taking place inside of a computer." ... *Tron* shows the insides of a computer as a community of programs, each personified as an "actor" with a history, a personality, and a function within a complex political organization. ...
>
> When the film is over and the lights go on I see Marvin Minsky. Minsky has been charmed. "That was great," he says, "That's a whole lot better than bits! I am in the middle of writing a paper which proposes to outlaw the whole idea of bits. It's no way to think about what goes on inside of a computer."
>
> If you are trying to use the computer as a model of mind, the bit and Lovelace models are unsatisfying. ... I ask Minsky what he wants to put in place of the bits. He answers, with a look that makes it clear that the answer should be evident, "A society, of course, just like in *Tron*." "Society" is his mnemonic for multiple, simultaneously interacting programs within a complex computer system. In the *Tron* landscape, Minsky has found an image, however fanciful, for what he has in mind. (Turkle, 1984, pp. 276-77).

Minsky has been battling against the Lovelace model for more than 20 years, as his views from 1966 show.

> Now, there is a common superstition that "a computer can solve a problem only when every step in the solution is clearly specified by the programmer." In a superficial sense the statement is true, but it is dangerously misleading if it is taken literally. Here we understood the basic concepts Evans wrote into the program, but until the program was completed and tested we had no idea of how the machine's level of performance would compare to the test scores of human subjects. (Minsky, 1966, pp. 249-50)

Minsky had been describing a program by Thomas Evans, designed to solve a type of intelligence test item involving the recognition of analogies between geometric figures. After labelling the Lovelace model as a "superstition" and "superficially true," he argues against it by saying the results of Evans's program were not known before the program was completed and tested. His argument is also superficially true, in that one normally writes a program for precisely that reason, otherwise it isn't necessary to write the program. But his implication that the program did something beyond the instructions Evans gave to it is as "dangerously misleading" as the "superstition" he attacks.

This is not to say that Minsky is entirely wrong, but rather to reject the one-sided optimism of his logical analysis. The difference may be seen more clearly by contrasting Weizenbaum's (1984) view that a loss of understanding of machine processes (as they become more complex) leads to a loss of control over their outcomes, with Minsky's interpretation that this means machines are becoming more intelligent. Minsky's interpretation seems to be based on faith, a trust that machines will in some way continue to improve in spite of, or possibly because of, our growing inability to completely understand exactly how they work. If this is the case, it is important to replace the notion of computers doing definable operations with binary digits by a vision of overwhelming complexity.

Lenat (1984) also stresses the positive aspects of unpredictable program results, citing instances in which EURISKO (his own program) developed unexpected, but winning strategies for a war game. The program may have been successful because of the ways in which the game environment differed from the real world. That is, its strategies of using a fleet of almost all small ships and having disabled ships sink themselves, though successful in the game, contradict the real world experience of humans, of which (fortunately for it) EURISKO had no knowledge. The tone of this *Scientific American* article is enthusiastic, and as Martins (1984) notes, not as candid in its analysis of the results as a report given the previous year at an AI conference.

Hofstadter pursues the same goal, that of increasing the complexity level of machine processing, as he describes how the "self-symbol," as a part of this processing, would make it unnecessary for an intelligent being to have a soul. Having introduced the notion of a self-symbol, he describes the complicated ways our minds handle symbolic representations. This ultimately leads him to conclude that "We plainly lack the vocabulary today for describing the complex interactions that are possible between symbols" (Hofstadter, 1979, p. 387). Later, he announces that the self-subsystem can as a "side effect" function as soul, but warns that this should not be seen as bringing consciousness to a magical or nonphysical level. The reward from the creation of complexity comes next.

> Certainly, one can see that the complexity here is enough that many unexpected effects could be created. For instance, it is quite plausible that a computer program with this kind of structure would make statements about itself which would have a great deal of resemblance to statements which people commonly make about themselves. This includes insisting that it has free will. . . . (p. 388)

Not surprisingly, he concludes this paragraph by referring the reader to Minsky.

It is interesting to note the similarity of Hofstadter's and Minsky's arguments. Hofstadter opposes the use of the magical and nonphysical, just as Minsky opposed superstition and misleading. He seems to see nothing magical in a computer getting free will through our developing a computer program so complex we can neither describe it nor understand it.

Papert completes the picture of the "society of the mind" by bringing the reasoning back in the opposite direction, describing the mind in terms of computational "agents" (Papert, 1980b). He had been discussing theories that might explain Piagetian conservation phenomena, that young children insist, up to a certain age, that the amount of liquid can change when it is poured from one vessel into another of a different shape. He posits a theory, based on computational methods, in which three "agents" in the child's mind each judge the amount of liquid in a different way, one on the basis of height, another width, and the third on history (no change over time). As the child views the liquid, each agent voices its opinion, with the loudest one winning. As the child grows older, the relative loudness of the agents' voices changes through processes speculatively described by Papert. Finally, he concludes,

> I have said that this theory is inspired by a computational metaphor. One might ask how. . . . As long as we only think about these agents as "people," the theory is circular. It explains the behavior of people in terms of the behavior of people. But, if we can think of the agents as well-defined computational entities . . . everything becomes clearer. We saw even in small programs how very simple modules can be put together to produce complex results. (Papert, 1980b, p. 169)

Thus, the circle is completed and although Papert denies the circularity, it remains. Having proposed the existence of computational agents to justify the concept of machine intelligence, using these same agents to explain the human mind does not offer any new insights. Both concepts continue to rely on the magical properties attributed to the agents.

One bit of magic some AI researchers do acknowledge comes from Rabbi Loew, who died in 1609, and the Golem (a clay giant which he could bring to life) he is credited with creating. The legend of the Golem has the moral that a human being who succeeds in fabricating himself will be destroyed by his invention. Turkle (1984) reports that a number of MIT AI researchers, including Marvin Minsky, grew up with the family tradition of being descendants of Rabbi Loew. This puts an interesting twist on the prophecy of Rabbi Loew that the Golem would rise again at the end of human existence, but in quite a different form.

THE THEOLOGY OF AI

Having seen the faith and optimism that many AI researchers possess in such abundance, it remains to determine the tenets underlying this faith, the theology of AI. Another way of stating this is, "What are the important human needs addressed by AI that make it so necessary for its adherents to believe that it will come to pass?" Associated with this question is an examination of the value changes that are likely to occur as a result of such beliefs.

During the preparation of this book, two events took place which led to additional insight into the interaction between human needs and computer technology, particularly AI. One took place in Norway, where my talk on the possible interactions between computer applications and human values prompted several people to initiate further discussions on this topic. During these discussions, it became apparent that these people were upset by the possibility, or growing probability, that computers were not the answer to the need for meaning in life. Turkle's (1984) observations indicate that such responses are not uncommon, but firsthand experience with this reaction is still surprising.

A second incident took place at the American Church in Paris, where the speaker was discussing the inadequacy of the word "love" to cope with all the meanings we want to attach to it. Since the topic of artificial intelligence was on my mimd, it led me to speculate that "artificial love" would be every bit as ambiguous as AI. However, after further consideration of the two terms, the areas of research in AI, and particularly the goals and aspirations of AI researchers, it seemed clear that AL (artificial love) is at least as appropriate a description for some of this work (or at least the motivation for some of the work) as artificial intelligence.

For example, Weizenbaum's (1966) ELIZA program is probably more remarkable for its appearance of *caring* about what people type in ("Tell me more about . . .") than for its understanding. This is probably consistent with the emphasis in the therapy being modelled—caring precedes understanding. Computer-assisted instruction's strong points of infinite patience and nonjudgmental correction are also more closely related to caring rather than intelligence. Similarly, Schank's (1984) quest for programs that understand humans may or may not be based on his need to be understood, but the human need for understanding and the need to be understood can't really be satisfied without caring, which is based on love.

Lewis (1978) and Ellul (1964) have described the human race as pursuing the conquest of nature to the destruction of itself. Dreyfus (1979) puzzles over what he sees as the unwarranted optimism of AI researchers. Yet when one sees AI as promising the fulfillment of deep, but *unstated* emotional and spiritual needs, the picture becomes more consistent.

For example, some of Schank's statements seem to be puzzling because of their apparent lack of consistency. It is not clear how he can acknowledge that current AI techniques are totally inadequate to produce the systems he foresees, but yet confidently state, "Someday, intelligent machines finally will arrive" (Schank, 1984, p. 227). The basis for this statement becomes clearer when viewed in the light of an excerpt from Turkle. "Don Norman says, 'I have a dream to create my own robot. To give it my intelligence. To make it mine, my mind. To see myself in it. Ever since I was a kid'. Roger Schank is listening to our conversation. 'So who doesn't?' he interjects" (Turkle, 1984, p. 260). Thus, just as some people have their bodies (or heads) frozen for future resurrection, so AI offers the possibility that Roger Schank's mind (or Don Norman's mind, etc.)

might have eternal life. Moravec describes a process in which "Though you have not lost consciousness, or even your train of thought, your mind (some would say soul) has been removed from the brain and transferred to a machine (Moravec, 1984, p. 13). Although they have no evidence to show that this will come about, they have faith in technology.

Some might object that the motivation of AI researchers has little relevance to the usefulness of the products they create. However, O'Donovan points out that "the primary characteristic of a technological society is not the things it may *do* with the aid of machines, but the way it *thinks* of everything it does as a kind of mechanical production" (O'Donovan, 1984, p. 73). Thus we could say that the beliefs we have about computers are more important (as side effects) than the actual uses we make of them (the intended effects).

One of the value changes one would expect from such beliefs and their associated achievements has already been noted. "Things a machine can do will be seen as insignificant, precisely because a machine can do them" (Schank, 1984, p. 236). Two examples based on areas of AI research, chess and language understanding, can illustrate this point. (Campbell [1984] refers to chess research as one of the discarded areas of AI, claiming that it has produced no insights into human thinking and is most optimistically described as establishing what human intelligence is not.)

Suppose the ultimate and infallible chess playing program were created. That is, the program would never lose a game when playing white (it might lose to itself when playing black, or it might always draw against itself). If such a program were available to all chess players, to carry in their pockets, or implanted in their brains, what would be the value of chess or being able to play chess? Except for the challenge of creating it, the "ultimate chess player" has no value, for achieving it would eliminate the value of chess, an activity which has given many people pleasure. (A similar concept, "Idiot-proof Scrabble sets" was described in *MAD Magazine* in 1965.)

On a different level, we might want to consider the consequences of a program which could understand written material, a "reading comprehension" machine. What would the consequences of developing such a machine do to the value of humans in terms of their reading ability? Probably something very similar to what calculators have done to the value of humans in terms of their arithmetic abilities. It is important that we note that the devaluing of reading comprehension (or any other AI function) does not have to wait for the creation of the relevant program. The promise that such a program will exist, if believed, is in itself a direct attack on the value of the activity it is to replace.

Two examples illustrate the way in which our expectations about computers can not only affect our use of computers, but also the experience of others in using computers. The first, given in more detail in Chapter 1, has to do with the secretary who quit her job, not because of technology, but because her two bosses had conflicting expectations about her use of word processing technology. The second example is presented fully in Chapter 3, having to do with the teacher who emphasized computers as challenges and puzzles, competition for the first solution to a computer problem, and competition to use the computers on a first-come, first-served basis. The teacher's attitudes and beliefs about competition and computer use seemed to have strong effects on his students' use of and attitudes toward computers.

Rogers (1984) sees AI as being dehumanizing in theory as well as in practice. He lists the conception of man as a "cognitive entity," a dehumanized view of knowledge, and neglect of the emotional and spiritual (or nonmaterialistic) aspects of humans as examples. Boden (1984) is more optimistic, claiming that our use of psychological terms and "intentional language" in describing AI machines can counteract the dehumanizing effects of mechanism, by providing a "richer image" of machines.

A more extreme example of the influence of AI beliefs on our values comes from *Microman*, a creative and entertaining book on "Computers and the evolution of consciousness." Near the end of the book, the best and worst possible outcomes of the use of computers are described. The following is part of the "best" possible world in the year 2120.

> We have, for example, overcome the almost obsessive and damaging tendency to give names only to heads and bodies (one reason, we suspect, for our species' early preoccupation with dancing figurines and humanoid robots). Riding on the technology of 2120 (not so different from the technologies latent in 2000), the average person is usually distributed across the information environment. Anne, Jo or Bill may literally inhabit many places at once; many people may also be in the same place—for instance in one brain—at once. But what is more important is the absence of an imperative. No individual is obliged to be splayed across his or her friends. No one is forced to concentrate their being in one head, either their own or any other. (Pask, 1982, p. 206)

Pask's goal ostensibly was to describe the developing relationship between computers and humans, and the ways computers are shaping us and our environment. However, the message in this and other sections of Pask's book is strongly permeated by thinking of the New Age, a religious movement which stresses the evolution of consciousness, with a strong component of Hinduism, emphasizing that "everything is one" or that "oneness" is the ultimate goal. Pask's future world builds on one of the AI assumptions, that the mind is not confined to the brain, and carries it to provocative conclusions, similar to those found in *The Mind's I* (Hofstadter & Dennett, 1981), another New Age book. One difference is that examples in the latter volume are more clearly labelled science fiction. Pask's conclusions are in some ways logical, however. If your brain can be duplicated or extended in a mechanical environment, then your brain can be in many places at once, and share its space with other brains. One should look at this and other logical consequences of assumptions, before agreeing with the assumptions.

AI IN EDUCATION

Needs Assessment

In looking at the possible uses of AI in education, it is important that such an investigation begin with needs assessment. In particular, it seems necessary to begin with human strengths and avoid unproductive duplication of them, putting the major effort into products that compensate for human weaknesses. It might be useful to review some AI efforts aimed at human strengths, before going into more productive applications.

Schank sets a goal of building computer systems which will understand natural language, but acknowledges that this is an area of human strength. "The power of the human mind is much more impressive than the power of the computer" (Schank, 1984, p. 27). "People who are not considered to be very bright can talk, learn, understand, or explain their experiences, feelings and conclusions. Talking is incredibly complicated . . . [people] intelligently produce far more sophisticated algorithms than we have yet been able to figure out how to give a computer" (p. 30).

Human need is also given as the rationale for the use of robots in hazardous environments (though the case for intelligence built into the robots is less convincing), but robots in general are aimed at an area of human strength. Dreyfus quotes an MIT AI Progress Report as saying, "Consider that a normal human can place an object on a table, turn about and make a gross change in his position and posture, and then reach out and grasp within one or two inches of the object, all with eyes closed! It seems unlikely that his cerebellum could perform the appropriate vector calculations to do this" (Dreyfus, 1979, p. 25). Although the matter of vector calculations is debatable, a mechanical arm under human (remote) control seems like a plausible alternative to the use of robots in hazardous areas.

Similarly, recognition could be made of human abilities to distinguish sound and visual patterns, even when they are distorted or masked, to retrieve vast amounts of description about previous experiences, and to create new forms of expression, thought, and meaning. This recognition will not be unanimous, however, for Minsky refuses to recognize some of these human attributes. While some researchers attempt to create AI programs that "daydream" as an approach to developing artificial creativity (Mueller & Dyer, 1985), Minsky says, "I do not believe in a 'faculty of creativity' as a special entity or component of mind; I see the word as concerning certain social judgments about novelty and about differences between individual thought-systems" (Minsky, 1979, p. 401). Perhaps he won't mind if this is called a creative solution to the problem of AI researchers being unable to develop creative machine intelligence.

O'Donovan (1984), in discussing ethical questions arising from developing techniques for artificial human fertilization, provides a framework which can be used in assessing the need for AI techniques in education. He puts part of his discussion in the form of a fairy tale, in which a woodman and his wife, currently childless, are promised a child by the wife's fairy godmother. The method chosen is in vitro fertilization with embryo replacement, which leads O'Donovan to ask questions about the choice of technique.

> Why was it necessary to adopt a compensatory approach to tubal infertil-ity, instead of a curative one? Magic, after all, like scientific research, must be assumed to know no limits. . . . To such a doubt we must concede this much justification at least: if at any time there was a straight choice to be made between two approaches to a problem, equally likely to be effective, one curative and one compensatory, it would be highly improper not to choose the cure, even if the other course offered gains for research not easily attainable otherwise. (pp. 68–69)

Viewed in the AI setting, O'Donovan's directive would favor developments aimed at curing the shortcomings of human performance, rather than providing com-pensatory help, or alternatives to the human functions. In short, if the mind does not perform certain needed functions, what can be done to help it do these needed functions?

Ellul's (Vanderburg, 1981) suggestion that we need to become mutants in order to survive in a technological world can be seen in the same light. He is say-ing that we should be motivated by the needs of our own survival and reject the challenge of technological achievement (a false need) in favor of the needs which maintain our humanness. Thus, by mutant he means that we should be "in the world", but not "of the world", using technology to meet our own needs, but not adopting the values of technology which are based on the needs of technology.

The principles which underlie the use of AI in education, or in general, could be similar to those for prostheses, or other physical aids. That is, in some con-texts they are of little value, such as crutches for someone with normally func-tioning legs. Physical aids can even have a negative effect, as in the case of a wheelchair for a child who should be learning to walk, or for an elderly person who may lose the ability to walk. One could look at the effect of artificial mobility, the automobile, on our ability to walk and fear that "Computers will do for thought and language what the automobile has done for legs" (Smith, 1983, p. 12). (The preceding points are discussed further in Chapter 3.)

Some of the work in machine translation of languages might be seen as an example of the violation of this principle of valuing human strengths. Human translators usually have no problem in understanding the two or more languages being used, so a prosthesis that understands human language is not only very difficult to create, but also redundant. In practice, the prosthesis is even less use-ful, since it doesn't understand either of the languages. A Canadian translation project, eventually limited to the domain of weather reports, was able to pro-duce text at less than two-thirds the cost of human translation. Unfortunately, correcting errors in the machine text raised the cost to almost 30 per cent above that of human translation. This might seem to call for a solution of increasing public acceptance of badly written weather reports, as in the solution to mechanizing the bakeries (see Chapter 1). True to form, however, the AI community views the results optimistically. "TAUM-METRO has translated some 2.5 million words each year with *only* [emphasis added] 20 per cent of the sentences requiring revision. *This success* [emphasis added] was followed with TAUM-AVIATION for the translation of maintenance manuals" (Science Council of Canada, 1983, p. 39).

A positive instance of the computer as prosthesis can be seen in the solution of the "four-color-map" problem, as described by Bolter (1984). The theorem states that no more than four colors are necessary to color a flat map so that no two countries with a common border have the same color. Though simple to understand, it had resisted proof from its origins in the nineteenth century until Appel and Haken solved it in the 1970s. They used traditional mathematical techniques to prove that 1,500 types of maps had to be considered, then used computers (1,200 hours on three computers) to verify that four colors were sufficient for every type. Thus, this proof was achieved because the use of the computer as prosthesis was complementary to human strengths, not competitive with them.

Pea seems to be in accord with the concept of filling human needs, while valuing human strengths, as he says, "Perhaps only by joining the strengths of human intelligence with the strengths of the computer can the potential of either be realized" (Pea, 1985, p. 91). This is close to the same message, but not as harmonious as saying, "only by meeting the needs of the weaknesses of human intelligence (by computer strengths, or any other method) can the potential of human intelligence be realized." This near miss is perhaps indicative of his entire thrust. The title is "Integrating human and computer intelligence," and the sentence preceding the previous quote is "The most speculative but also the most spectacular possibility is that human and computer intelligence will co-evolve" (p. 91). This is not to say that Pea focuses on the assumed ability of our mind to live outside our brain, though he does accept it. Rather, it is important to note that he begins with a review of computer strengths in solving problems, expert systems, and the like, instead of beginning from an analysis of human needs. His analysis of the AI role in child development and education emphasizes tools, but often as a substitute, "providing the set of computational tools necessary for intermediary cognitive work, which usually goes on in the child's mind and strains age-related memory and processing limitations" (p. 88). The problems he foresees don't seem to include the possibility that one could prevent necessary growth by providing this sort of prosthesis too soon. Although a glimmer of hope can be seen in Pea's discussion, his interest in the continued development of machine intelligence seems to inject a strong element of bias.

Bring People Together

A second aspect of the possible beneficial uses of AI in education is that of encouraging cooperative work among humans, not just human-machine interaction. AI and other computer systems could be used to help bring people together, or at least not work to keep them apart.

In proposing that cooperative work be encouraged, particularly if it requires that the participants be in the same physical location, one probably has to assume that education will continue to involve students attending schools. Many who propose the use of AI or other educational computer applications assume that traditional schools, despite their rugged resistance to change, will cease to exist. Two reasons to believe they will continue (in addition to their resistance to change) come to mind. One is based on the millions of preschool children in the United States who are already left at home alone by working parents, which, among other factors, suggests that a home learning environment may not even be available, much less desirable. The second reason comes from Goodlad's (1984) detailed study of schools in the United States. He describes an environment where, particularly at the secondary level, students are willing to tolerate the educational process because it facilitates the social process of meeting their friends. Continuing the educational process while eliminating the social process may not only be undesirable, but strongly resisted by students.

The strong appeal of computers used as communications media might be seen as the basis for bringing people together, particularly for society in general. But, for education, though the purposes are more specific, the applications may be more varied. The basis for the improvement of instruction is often that of individual (or very small group) tutoring, the motivating force for years of research done by Benjamin Bloom and his students. Bloom (1984) describes this as the "two sigma problem," since the average achievement of tutored students is usually two standard deviations higher than the average of those taught in classes of 30 students per teacher. That is, the average tutored student is above 98 percent of the students in large group instruction in terms of achievement. A framework for possible uses of AI in education might be derived from Bloom's work in trying to find methods of group instruction that will yield achievement gains equivalent to individual tutoring (Bloom, 1984).

Their efforts, most of which have involved more effective ways of bringing people together, have concentrated on investigations in four areas. These are the learner, the instructional material, the home environment and peers, and the teacher and the teaching process. Their results indicate that using combinations of variables can produce results equivalent to those produced by tutoring.

In the area of the learner, results indicate that student support systems in which groups of two or three students study and review together can produce an achievement gain almost half that of tutoring. Results in this same direction also come from Levin, Glass, and Meister (1984) who report that 20 minutes per day of peer tutoring (students tutoring other students) has been shown to be not only more effective than 10 minutes per day of computer-assisted instruction in raising achievement, but is also considerably more cost-effective, or greater gain per dollar (since very little of the CAI cost is due to computer hardware, decreasing equipment costs are not likely to change this results). In the language of

Chapter 2, it can be said that peer tutoring is a "critical competitor" for CAI and other computer applications to instruction. AI used in education should be consistent with these kinds of findings.

For example, Brown and Burton describe a limitation of the BUGGY gaming environment as "... it simply provides an environment that challenges their theories and encourages them to articulate their thoughts. The rest of the learning experience occurs either through the sociology of team learning or from what a person abstracts on their own" (Brown & Burton, 1978, p. 186). Their next step is to implement an intelligent tutor in the program, while a more effective alternative might be to further exploit the power of team learning, as did Johnson, Johnson, and Stanne (1986), who found cooperative CAI led to higher achievement than competitive or individualistic CAI.

Bloom's second area, instructional materials, is one in which the use of AI techniques is already considerable. Bloom observes that some students achieve as well with CAI as with tutoring. One area of research is aimed at making these gains available to a larger proportion of students. The AI attempts to model the student, to analyze what the student is learning and how, are aimed at this goal, but it has not been achieved.

A number of objections might be raised to the ways in which AI is seen as being applied to the development of instructional materials. A common problem is that many of them are just not well thought out, as in many applications of LOGO, a language whose roots are in AI. For example, Schank enthuses that "LOGO challenges the children to draw a picture or solve a fun problem, and compels them to think carefully about what is going on" (Schank, 1984, p. 206). Such a statement is simply not true, as the discussion in Chapter 7 should make clear. However, Schank was not involved directly in the making or use of instructional material at the time this was written, so one hopes his optimism is restricted to those who have not used LOGO in teaching.

A more serious charge against AI-based instruction, sometimes called ICAI (Intelligent Computer-Assisted Instruction), is that it tends to treat symptoms rather than causes of instructional problems. This could also be described as taking a compensatory rather than a curative approach, as seen in the work described by Brown and Burton (1978). Their use of the BUGGY and DEBUGGY programs centers around the identification of systematic errors in children's math skills and the training of teachers to find such errors. None of their work addresses the question of how one goes about correcting these "bugs" after they have been found, or more important, how one would structure the initial instruction in these skills so that these systematic errors would be less likely to occur.

A second serious charge against the AI-based instructional approach is that it has a tendency to put "old wine in new bottles," dressing up old knowledge in new terminology. Skinner levels this charge against the entire field of cognitive science, defined by Wilkinson and Patterson (1983) as being at the intersection of linguistics, psychology, and artificial intelligence (Schank [1984] describes artificial intelligence as being at the intersection of linguistics and psychology).

In commenting on a cognitive psychologist's statement about "recent findings in cognitive science," Skinner asks, "If these are *recent* findings, where has cognitive science been?" (Skinner, 1984, p. 949).

Anderson, Boyle, and Reiser demonstrate an ability to rediscover knowledge in describing their "intelligent tutoring systems." These systems were developed on the basis of "The ACT-Based Approach to Intelligent Tutoring," where ACT stands for their theory of cognition. They state that

> Implications of this theory for tutoring include making the goal structure explicit, minimizing the working-memory load, and giving instruction in the problem-solving context. *Another important implication* [emphasis added] of these principles is that students should be given immediate feedback about their errors. (Anderson, Boyle, & Reiser, 1985, pp. 457-58)

Psychology has long been an arena for competing theories which describe the same concepts using different terms, so these statements are not surprising. The important implication should be that in order to make use of the principles stated as coming from the theory for tutoring, useful as they appear to be, one should not have to subscribe to an artificial intelligence view of the instructional world.

A similar packaging of known techniques into the AI format can be seen in the description of the SOPHIE program (Brown, 1977). The use of SOPHIE, an ICAI program designed to teach understanding of electronic circuits, includes its use in a gaming scenario. The gaming use allows two students, each at their own terminals, to take turns creating and locating faults in the electronic circuit simulated by the program. Faults are found by making a series of measurements at various points in the circuit, each measurement having a "cost" that is used in determining the players' scores. To this point, the preceding description contains nothing which would require the use of AI techniques, so the question arises, "What is the added value of using AI techniques in what could be a relatively straightforward simulation?" The SOPHIE program allows the users to communicate in natural language, such as "Let R22 have the wrong value," but this does not seem such a significant advantage that one need change the instructional orientation to that of AI. To be sure, the uses of SOPHIE are not limited to the game described, but to include what seems to be a useful simulation package as though it depends on AI, when in fact the use of AI is barely relevant, can easily mislead those not familiar with computer uses in education.

O'Shea and Self (1983) offer another view into the lure of AI as well as illustrating conflicts within the community of those advocating AI applications in education. Although their book is subtitled "Artificial intelligence in education," the content is firmly grounded in a knowledge of, and appreciation for, the history of developments in CAI. O'Shea and Self also acknowledge the shortcomings of current AI programs and are cautious in the claims they make about its use, at least in the near future. Their leaning toward AI does affect their presentation, however, for the chapter on "computer as tool" is almost entirely based on programming in LOGO and Smalltalk (two AI-related programming languages), with the only entry under "word processing" in the index being its mention in the glossary. Thus, although their view of AI is a cautious one, their commitment to it does seem to restrict their view of instructional applications of computers.

O'Shea and Self's reference to the work of both Papert and Brown (and other developers of AI tutors) brings attention to a conflict that Papert's views of computers in education seem to make inevitable. As discussed in Chapter 7, Papert opposes the use of CAI, which he calls "the computer programming the child," in favor of "the child programming the computer" using LOGO. In this he emphasizes the choice that students will have, not only in how to solve a problem, but also in which problem to solve. Brown (1977), on the other hand, while favoring learning by doing, and giving students substantial freedom to solve problems in their own way, also advocates developing systems to help students solve defined problems in ways that have previously been anticipated.

Although the conflict between AI control and student control may not be serious, and is usually not deemed worthy of mention, it does illustrate the bias that can come from espousing a preferred technique. If one does research in ICAI, it indicates a belief that CAI must have AI techniques to be effective, while working with CAI often implies that delivery of instructional content via computer is preferable to human instruction or tutoring. This "bias of preferred method" may be the explanation for the choices made by Anderson, Boyle, and Reiser (1985) in their evaluation of a LISP (an AI programming language) tutor program. They found that in the first study, ten students tutored by humans took 11.4 hours to complete the material, while computer-tutored subjects took 15.0 hours and students on their own took 26.5 hours. The three groups performed equally well on tests of LISP knowledge. Note that the ambiguity about the relative effectiveness of the methods only seems to be between the two forms of tutoring, not between the tutored and untutored groups. The significant point of this research is that in their next test of the LISP tutor, *the human-tutored group was omitted.* Only if the goal of developing a machine tutor is more important than developing effective learning methods would it be logical to drop the most effective method from the evaluation.

To return to Bloom and his four categories of reserach, the quest for more effective instructional materials needs to have its goals redefined. These goals should be in terms of helping people to learn what they need to know; they shouldn't be confused with the pleasure of working with exciting machinery, nor the challenge of trying to get inanimate objects to masquerade as humans.

Bloom's third area of research interest, home and peer environment, has probably received the least attention and offers great opportunities for computer applications, possibly involving AI. Bloom (1984) reports that attempts to change home environments have been effective but costly, involving regular communication between parents and educators. Peer group influence is also a powerful factor and a matter of communication, in this case to help students with similar interests reinforce their mutual achievement. The use of data banks as "serendipity machines," a concept discussed in more detail in Chapter 7, is one method of bringing those with similar interests together. Pask's (1982) description of CASTE (Course Assembly System and Tutorial Environment) also suggests this possibility, though it does not seem to be an explicit goal of the system.

Levin, Boruta, and Vasconcellos (1983) favor the AI cognitive science approach and describe a system linking children in San Diego, California, with other children in Alaska, broadening the range of peer interaction for both groups. However, it is not clear that either group of children would need such a long distance link for the interaction to be beneficial. Similarly, these connections do not have to have narrowly defined education as their goal. A project conducted by the Centre Mondial in Paris was designed to connect cancer patients, via home terminals (already distributed without charge by the telephone company), with both a data base of relevant information (vertical link) and with each other (horizontal links).

The role of AI, if any, in such communication systems is to help the appropriate people communicate easily with each other, not to substitute for the communication. The need, for cancer patients, the recently bereaved, etc., is for someone who can understand, someone whose similar experience provides them with the necessary credentials. It is hard to imagine this kind of need being satisfied by an AI program, even if it "has cancer," or responds as though it does.

Bloom's last area, the teacher and the teaching process, is one in which some AI work has been done, but the efforts generally seem to be compensatory rather than curative. This objection may not be appropriate for Brown and Burton (1978), but the intelligent tutoring systems of Anderson, Boyle, and Reiser (1985) seem to be examples of competitors, rather than being complementary. Larkin (1983) also appears to be saying that better methods of presenting science knowledge (better than teachers are now using) exist, but an AI program to present these concepts is preferable to a teacher presenting them.

In their research, Bloom and his students have found that the average achievement in a class rises dramatically when teachers are given specific feedback on their differential treatment of students. Their studies have shown that students can observe themselves to provide this information. Another area of possible AI application is to provide an interface between students and teachers to facilitate this process of feedback for the teacher.

It is, of course, possible for computers to be an unintentional cause of improved teacher-student interaction. Eaton and Olson, in a study described in more detail in Chapter 8, describe a group of elementary teachers who "did computers" with their students for the purpose of increasing problem solving skills, by means of programming in BASIC (not LOGO or any other AI-linked language). By "doing computers" they mean the teaching of what are often called computer literacy or computer awareness skills, with the teachers often learning with (or from) the students. The interesting result was that although the stated goals of increased problem solving skills were not achieved, the teachers planned to continue because of the "new relationship with students through . . . a shared learning experience" (Eaton & Olson, 1985, p. 6). Rather than trying to replace the teacher, AI applications should be aimed at developing this new relationship deliberately, rather than as a side effect. A combined (formative) approach, designed to build on human strengths, seems likely to be more productive than continuing to compare human systems with machine systems (summative approach).

CONCLUSION

The word evolution seems to be ubiquitous in the AI literature, the concept of evolution seeming to be an important part of the AI movement. One of Minsky's uses is when he is considering the origin of new processes, and ventures that "in thinking, just as in evolution, entirely new things are very rare" (Minsky, 1979, p. 416). Stonier is even more poetic in pondering, "Might not the emergence of machine intelligence with in [sic] human societies be as important in the near future, as was the emergence of complex self-replicating molecules within that primordial slime in that distant past?" (Stonier, 1984, p. 254). Hofstadter (1979) explains the operation of the human brain through a description of how ants developed their abilities by evolution. Schank (1984) has a chapter on "Revolution or evolution," with a section on "The evolution of artificial intelligence," while Pask (1982) includes "evolution of consciousness," a favorite phrase of the New Age movement, in the subtitle of his book. Yazdani and Narayanan refer to "Darwin's discovery of the relationship of man to other species" (Yazdani & Narayanan, 1984, p. 64), rather than Darwin's hypothesis, or theory.

This penchant for evolution is probably indicative of a belief that chance processes have generally beneficial results, that poor systems tend to get better, or that good side effects are more likely to endure than bad side effects. It is interesting to note that some people who adhere strongly to a philosophy in one domain, as with John Cage's belief in randomness as an ideal in music, find they are unable to tolerate the philosophy in other domains, as with Cage's refusal to follow the ideal of randomness in mycology, identifying and eating mushrooms. The same result can hold for evolution, as the life of Darwin illustrates. In his autobiography, he laments that in his later years, he had lost his love of poetry, art, and music and the pleasure these had given him up to the age of 30. This loss is not only a source of unhappiness to him, but he speculates that it "may possibly be injurious to the intellect, and more probably to the moral character, by enfeebling the emotional part of our nature" (Darwin, 1958, p. 54).

Now it may not be surprising that one who is responsible for the origins of evolution on a grand scale should find the results of his personal evolution so distasteful, but the AI view seems to be proposing the short-term benefits of evolution in the form of systems which will evolve to a better form. Unfortunately, this view may be catching on outside of the AI community, for Bereiter (1985) has proposed "chance plus selection" as a principle for helping students to learn, suggesting that student writers be given random access to strategic moves.

Ignoring the fact that a belief in the long-term truth of evolution is contradicted by scientific evidence (as with the ostrich's calluses described in Chapter 2), it is probably naive to see evolution as a dependably beneficial short-term process.

Even more distressing is the future that AI proponents hold out for us. Schank sees that "We may be able to have intelligent companions who can advise on matters social and intellectual, spiritual and emotional. What happens to the people who do not have the courage or hope that it takes to write letters to Dear Abby?" (Schank, 1984, p. 246). Are these the benefits that evolution can bring? If people are so deprived of spiritual and emotional support, and so alienated from other humans that they must turn to "Dear Abby" (itself a product of "la technique"), they need spiritual and emotional healing and reconciliation, to be brought into meaningful relationships with other people. What a cruel joke to offer them a machine companion to complete their alienation.

Surely, the goal of satisfying human needs while respecting human values would not lead us to the preceding suggestions for the use of AI. In considering the use of AI in education, one must look carefully at the probable consequences and not succumb to the allure of the technological challenges.

5 Courseware Development and Evaluation

DEFINITIONS

Educational computer users like to create new terms, a characteristic which seems to be common to most of our culture. The hope may be that some of the deficiencies of both the old term and the practice it defined (say, Computer-Assisted Instruction) may be eliminated through the use of a different term (Computer-Based Instruction, Computer-Assisted Learning, etc.). Much of the same process seems to be happening to the term courseware, but in this chapter it will be used to represent what seems to be its original definition, while taking into consideration some of those other terms that have sprung up to replace and supplement it. O'Shea and Self (1983) define courseware as "the set of programs and associated materials for a computer-assisted learning course" (p. 269), tying it to the concept of course as a measure of length. This link has led to the use of other length-oriented terms, such as "lessonware" and "unitware," but no such requirement of length is intended by the use of the term courseware in this chapter. Rather, the intended use is closer to that given by the *New Webster's Computer Dictionary* (1984), "computer programs used for instructional purposes" (p. 78).

Courseware, in this chapter, then, refers to computer programs and their supporting materials that are intended to deliver instructional content to students, whether as initial presentations, reviews, or remediation. The process of using courseware is often called Computer-Assisted Instruction (CAI), or CAL, or CBI, or CBL, etc. The choice of which three letter acronym is used is not important, and no particular process will be assumed here. It is probably necessary, however, to point out Computer-Managed Instruction (CMI) as a distinct variant, for it may or may not include courseware and other aspects of CAI. CMI differs from CAI (and its siblings) in that instruction itself does not have to be presented through the computer in CMI. That is, a CMI system would not have to (but could) include the delivery of courseware, but would maintain the records of students, monitor their achievement, and might even prescribe their next unit of instruction, but the instruction itself could be delivered by a teacher, a book, a film, etc. Since CMI systems do not necessarily involve courseware, and their function is primarily one of teacher support, they will be discussed further in Chapter 8.

CAI and the use of courseware has a long history of optimism associated with it. In 1966, fully developed CAI was seen as being only a few years away. "One can predict that in a few years millions of school children will have access to what Phillip of Macedon's son Alexander enjoyed as a royal prerogative; the personal services of a tutor as well-informed and responsive as Aristotle" (Suppes, 1966, p. 207). Suppes, one of the early leaders of CAI work, saw CAI as being composed of drill and practice, tutorial, and dialogue modes of instruction. In 1967 he wrote that the first of these modes was well established, the second was being worked on, and the third was in the future. This 1967 article was one of two Suppes's selections from the 1960s included in Taylor's (1980) *The Computer in the School: Tutor, Tool, Tutee*. It is interesting to note that his assessment of the stages of development for the three CAI modes (drill and practice, tutorial, and dialogue) was as "state of the art" then as it had been in 1967, or indeed as it is today. Self validates this assessment in a self-referential manner, describing his own belief in 1972 that interactive dialogue would be a part of CAI by 1977. "Of course, I was wrong. We are little nearer today to knowing how to write such a program than we were in 1972. In fact, today nobody seems to think it actually matters that we do not know how to write such programs" (Self, 1985, p. 150).

Because of the slow development of CAI, relative to the early glowing predictions, a certain amount of scepticism has been seen on the part of potential users. Control Data is reported to have invested more than $900 million in its PLATO CAI systems, without yet making any profit, though their hopes are for billions in return (Friedrich, 1983). The entrance of the microcomputer onto the educational scene, however, has been a tonic for the CAI movement, restoring much of the original enthusiasm. For a more complete picture of the historical development of computers used in instruction, see O'Shea and Self (1983). In it, one can see that drill and practice techniques are well established, tutorial techniques are being developed, and full interactive dialogue is still in the future (*Plus ça change, . . .*). Moreover, what is available is expensive to produce. A. B. Arons (1984) estimates that even limited dialogues take 100 hours of expert teacher time and 500+ hours of programmer time to create a program a student could use for one hour.

ASSUMPTIONS

Although the purposes and definitions of CAI and courseware may change over time, they are usually explicit, while the assumptions underlying this activity are often disguised, implicit, vague, and/or hidden. In order to discover the assumptions, it is necessary to use several sources, since assumptions are most easily seen in the light generated by heated disagreements.

The beginnings of CAI came from the work being done in programmed instruction and Skinner, for one, believes that it should stick to these roots (Green, 1984a; Skinner, 1984). He believes that the most powerful reward that can come from courseware is the knowledge that the student is learning something and that dressing up instruction with fancy graphic designs and game formats is self-defeating. This view seems to be supported by Morgan (1984), who points out that rewards for participating in an activity decrease motivation while rewards for achievement increase motivation. Lepper (1985) can be seen to support this view as well, in pointing out that the spectacular nature of courseware can have the effect of making all other materials, and the teacher look less interesting. Lepper also attacks the process of individualizing instruction to the student's ability by increasing the difficulty of the material as the student progresses. He observes that this can be quite disturbing to children if they are not informed that this type of sequencing is taking place. As one child said, "Every time I think I've got it, I just miss more of them" (Lepper, 1985, p. 5). On the positive side of the argument, Skinner's approach does emphasize clarity of objectives, sequencing of instruction, individualizing of rate, and "priming" the students through the programming of instruction.

DISCOVERY LEARNING

The last is an important point, for it puts Skinner in opposition not only to Papert and other current advocates of discovery learning, but also a long line of educational philosophers, going at least as far back as Plato. Most opponents of discovery learning seem to agree that learning in this manner is more satisfying and may lead to better retention, but the dispute usually centers around the question of efficiency. Skinner feels that a discovery approach to science, as an example, merely delays the acquisition of skills which would be needed to make a "real discovery." Discovery learning plays a large role in the typical use of LOGO, but may also be a factor in more "traditional" courseware, though usually in the form of guided discovery, a compromise between the extreme positions.

Salomon (1986) offers another objection to the discovery approach in terms of the lack of "mindfulness" it requires of the student. His comments are based primarily on the context of LOGO, but can apply to any environment in which the student is not required to exhibit mindfulness—attention to details, careful examination of problem characteristics, generation of hypotheses, etc. Its opposite, mindlessness, can be seen in the use of any instructional program where the limited alternatives guarantee a right answer if you will only type long enough. Courseware encouraging mindless behavior would include those that allow un-limited responses to multiple-choice questions, as well as those presenting an indefinite goal (draw an interesting design). Even traditional programmed instruc-tion can be at least partially mindless if the required answer can be obtained without paying attention to all the written text.

The most complete look at the assumptions of CAI comes from Dreyfus and Dreyfus (1984, 1986). Their analysis is similar in important ways to the Dreyfus (1979) treatment of the assumptions of artificial intelligence, assumptions which flow together in the increasingly popular area of ICAI (Intelligent CAI). The first common assumption is often what Bar-Hillel called the first-step fallacy in artifi-cial intelligence (see Chapter 4), the assumption that initial successes can be extended indefinitely. A second assumption is that all human thought can be put into a form that can be stored in computers. This can appear in the form stated by Taylor (1980), "Despite the extensive innovation in computing, much re-mains the same—particularly in the way computer logic structures are related to human thought structures" (p. 1). As Dreyfus and Dreyfus point out, since this assumption is rarely discussed or critically examined, it has become widely ac-cepted as a fundamental truth to guide the use of computers in education, par-ticularly in instruction. As the authors also explain, the issue is not new. Socrates asked Euthyphro for what we would call a heuristic rule for recognizing piety and Plato felt that those who could not formalize their knowledge did not have true knowledge, but merely belief.

In order to illuminate the strengths and weaknesses of CAI, Dreyfus and Dreyfus describe their own five-stage model of skill acquisition, a process for moving from novice to expertise, using as examples automobile driving and chess playing.

The novice begins by learning rules and the recognition of features. For the student driver this means features such as speed and distance, rules for shifting, etc. The chess neophyte may learn numerical values for pieces and rules for ex-changes, defining center squares, and the like, a memory load which makes them very slow players.

In the second stage, advanced beginner, the student begins to add some *situational* knowledge to the rules and features. The driver may begin to use engine sounds in addition to the speed given on the speedometer as a cue for shifting gears, while the chess player may begin to recognize an overextended position.

The third stage of competence marks a distinct difference in the goals set by the learner. In the first two stages following rules was the overriding considera-tion, while the competent driver may set a goal of arriving at a certain time, alter-ing driving behavior to meet this goal. As a result of this change in the type of goal, emotional involvement is increased, depending on the success or failure in reaching the overall goal. A common pattern is seen, that of emotionally detached planning, followed by assessing the relevant, ignoring the irrelevant, rule-guided decisions, and an emotional reaction to the final result.

Detached planning is no longer a feature of stage four, proficiency. The learner now begins to "see" without analyzing, in the manner that a proficient driver may sense that the speed is too high when approaching a curve on a rainy day. This would be followed by a more conscious determination of appropriate speed based on a number of relevant factors. The contrast is that the competent driver would make the conscious determination first, in order to decide if the speed was too fast. In the case of chess players, they may sense that they should attack, but be deliberate in deciding how this should be done.

The final stage is expertise, one of almost total unconscious performance, such as the driver who changes speed until the "feel" is right. This is a result of an enormous amount of experience, such as master chess players who can distinguish approximately 50,000 different types of chess positions. Experts may be so unconscious of their performance that the experience of consciously analyzing specific actions, such as shifting gears, may actually disrupt and diminish their performance.

To supplement the description of this model, Dreyfus and Dreyfus also provide an example based on experimental results from Air Force pilot training research. In the United States Air Force, beginning pilots are taught specific rules for the ways in which one must scan flight instruments. Yet, research has shown that the instructors who teach these scanning rules do not in fact use these rules, nor any other observable rule. Their conclusion is that any method of training (CAI or any other) which enforced the scanning rules would prevent the students from moving on to the more situationally appropriate scanning used by the instructors and other experienced pilots.

One implication which Dreyfus and Dreyfus draw from their model is that a drill and practice form of CAI is appropriate for some students, particularly those in the novice or advanced beginner stages of learning. However, they reject the implicit assumption of CAI, that the success of drill and practice programs should be extendable to those areas which require understanding on the part of the computer program, both in terms of the domain to be taught and the students' knowledge and conceptualization of the problem. Although AI researchers have recognized the representation and utilization of knowledge as a key issue in their field for more than a decade, progress has been lacking in this area. This leads Dreyfus and Dreyfus to suggest that the lack of progress is due to the limitations of the "rule-and-feature" model of knowledge, that one can determine the rule to be applied in a given situation on the basis of a finite and predictable set of features.

The most serious difficulty for the rule-and-feature model seems to be in its handling of images. Computers do not generally store images or pictures, though they can access devices which do store images. Because they store descriptions rather than images, they don't have the human facility for recognizing situations as being similar unless the descriptors of similarity have been defined in advance.

In order to recognize the 50,000 chess patterns that chess masters do, a computer program would have to be given the specific components which defined the various patterns, then when given a new pattern, analyze it into components in order to look for matching patterns in its memory. To put this in more common terms, when we see someone who looks familiar, we may not know who they resemble, and can only pick out why they look familiar after we know who they look like. A computer program would have to work in the reverse direction, categorizing features, then looking for a match, etc., so that it would know the "why" of resemblance before it determined the "who."

Dreyfus and Dreyfus flatly state, "The computer can be used as tutor, all right, but only for drill and practice" (Dreyfus & Dreyfus, 1984, p. 591). Their fear is that in attempting to use CAI beyond these levels, we will only be limiting the learning of students to rules, not helping them to achieve greater levels of understanding.

In review, we seem to find an array of conflicting assumptions in addition to those considered and rejected by Dreyfus and Dreyfus, and the assumptions based on their five-stage model, which they proposed as replacements. It is often assumed that the entertainment value of courseware is crucial, but also assumed that entertaining courseware has long-term negative consequences. It is assumed that learning by discovery is more powerful, while learning by discovery is assumed to be less efficient than specifying what is to be learned in advance. Other assumptions are that deliberate increases in difficulty can be harmful unless students are informed of the process in advance and that "mindfulness" is a necessity for effective learning.

In considering these conflicting assumptions, it would be helpful to have research results to which one could turn. Research results on CAI are not abundant, particularly those which involve the extended use of CAI. Even more discouraging, those results which are available lead proponents of differing views to both see them as support for their respective positions. For example, a number of studies have been done at the University of Michigan using the techniques of meta-analysis (a method of combining the results of many studies into one summary statistic) to analyze CAI used in various environments, such as different grade levels. One article summarized these results by stating, "In general, students learn more, retain more or learn the same amount faster using computers" (Bracey, 1982, p. 52). However, another article, basing its claims on the results from the same set of meta-analyses, stated that "Consistent evidence is found for the generalization that there are no learning benefits to be gained from employing any specific medium to deliver instruction" (Clark, 1983, p. 445). How could one author make such a positive statement about CAI while another claims that no medium (including computers for CAI) offers any learning benefits?

In fact, both authors were correct. Consistent effects are found which favor the use of CAI, but Clark has drawn his conclusions from a more detailed look at the results (Clark, 1985). One factor which decreases the importance of the consistent difference is that the difference between CAI and conventional courses is drastically reduced when the same person is responsible for planning and teaching both courses. That is, if you remove the difference due to different people being involved, the effect of using CAI is less than a gain of 2 points on a 100-point final exam. It is the distinction between statistical significance and behavioral significance that allows both authors to be correct. As discussed in the Appendix, statistical significance can be a misleading source of information for decision making.

COURSEWARE AND NEEDS

The preceding assumptions give some indications of the needs which courseware might address, but they are more in the form of hopes, rather than assessed needs of the type discussed in Chapter 2. Some of the proposed harmful effects have a stronger research basis, but since the reactions of individuals to the use of computers can vary greatly, and since research can be so flexible in the causes it is used to support, this is of little comfort. A satisfying determination of needs will probably have to await a discipline-oriented search. In the meantime, it might do well to review the seven possible potentials and limitations of computers in education as described by Walker (1983), one of the few to be at least quantitatively evenhanded, before going on to consider the process of developing courseware.

Many of Walker's potential benefits are in the form of solutions to needs, some implied and some explicit. He begins with the concept of "more active learning" as a potential, the notion that computers are usually programmed to demand some response from the learner, the implication being that this demand will also require their attention (or perhaps, mindfulness). His second feature is that of more varied sensory and conceptual modes, based primarily on the variety of devices for the display and reception of information. This is a possible plus, but must be tempered by the warning that the compulsive use of variety to dazzle the student can be counterproductive. His third potential is learning with less mental drudgery, largely a characteristic of tool applications (discussed in more detail in Chapter 7), but also often a part of CAI programs. In the latter case, the tool component might be used to display results of a learning exercise in the form of a graph, or bar chart, for example.

Walker's fourth benefit, learning nearer the speed of thought, addresses the individualization of rate, which is possible with computer learning, but is also a feature of other self-study materials, including books. His next point is on the same theme, but slightly further in the future, and is the general individualizing or tailoring of instruction. His discussion is based on the BUGGY program (see Chapter 4) and he forecasts a time when computers will compose tailored lessons on the spot (a prediction that Dreyfus and Dreyfus would no doubt dispute). He also includes aids for the handicapped under this point, a benefit which would be more generally accepted. More independent learning, the sixth potential, seems to be in the same vein as the previous two, but focuses on the consistent verification which CAI can provide for the learner. His final benefit is better aids to abstraction, including the use of interactive graphic image displays, fantasy simulations, and the use of programming to put an abstraction into a more concrete form. In summarizing these strengths, Walker views them as the "raw materials" out of which one would create not only the CAI courseware, but also instructional word processing, data bases, and all other educational applications of computers. This is a useful perspective, but missing the important ingredient of a needs assessment to determine where all of these identified computer strengths should be applied.

Walker then goes on to list what he sees as the seven most serious limitations of today's microcomputers, beginning with the assertion that computers can only supplement conventional learning, not replace it. This claim is backed up with evidence from a study in which Patrick Suppes supplied 26 very bright students (with IQ of 165 or higher) with unlimited access to CAI versions of two courses, but found that even those students who were interested in the material found it difficult to complete the courses on their own. Walker believes that this limitation of CAI will hold for the next decade (Dreyfus and Dreyfus would probably extend the period).

His second point is that computers are too hard for teachers to use and that it will be years before they will be as simple as a movie projector, a device which is still too complex for many teachers. Lack of standardization, his third limitation, also leads to difficulties for teachers trying to learn to use computers, since they may have to contend with more than one model.

Courseware development is the focus of Walker's fourth cautionary point, the scarcity of good programs. He sees the tools for courseware developers becoming more sophisticated, but the task of software design as still being a craft that few will be able to master. His fifth limitation may be at least a partial explanation of the fourth, since in it he asserts that nobody as yet understands how computers should be used in education. By this he means that the limited use of computers for short periods of time does not give us insight into how they should be used when they are available to all students throughout the day. His suggestion that "we will simply have to try different ways of using computers and carefully assess the results" (Walker, 1983, p. 106) is a bit nondirective, but essentially describes the need for information from actual classroom use.

Walker's sixth limitation is in harmony with Dreyfus and Dreyfus, the fact that computers can handle only rule-based procedures, though he leaves the door open for future developments which could remove this obstacle. His final limitation is that computers will not solve current school problems and might make some of them worse. This can be seen as a clear indication that computers are not being used to attack the most serious problems of education, but are often used to solve problems which appear to have been created specifically for computers to solve.

Walker's conclusions are "a complex and qualified vote of confidence for computers in education" (p. 107). He believes that today's microcomputers are not appropriate for some schools, but that other schools, communities, and teachers should wholeheartedly embrace computers, though he doesn't seem to define how these two classes are to be distinguished. One hopes that needs assessment would be a part of the decision as to whether a school was a part of one group or the other.

COURSEWARE DEVELOPERS

A number of questions arise in beginning a discussion about courseware developers. One that requires immediate attention is the reason why the term courseware developer is used here in preference to that of courseware author. The primary reason for this distinction is that the process should be seen as a continuous interaction, both within the developmental team and between the team and the potential users of the materials being developed. A second reason, implied in the first, is that courseware development is not an appropriate task for an individual, but for a team of people with a variety of complementary skills.

It is not surprising that many individuals assume that they can create completely acceptable courseware without additional assistance. One factor is the increasing presence of widely advertised authoring systems, which promise the potential authors that all the significant external obstacles standing between them and satisfactorily completed software have now been removed. A second factor may be in the obvious nature of the flaws that are present in so many present day programs. This can lead the unwary to believe that because these flaws are so easy to see, it is easy for them to create programs which are better, rather than understanding that it is easy for them to do just as bad.

Roblyer (1982) has commented on how many people have expressed an interest in "getting into the courseware business." When she cautioned them that the development of good courseware is more difficult than developing any other kind of materials, their reaction was often one of disbelief. She felt that this might be due to the fact that good courseware often *looks* easy to do, just as a well designed haiku may appear too simple to be difficult. Her focus, however, was not on the reasons why courseware appears so easy to do, but on why it is, in fact, so difficult.

One of the persistent problems in creating quality courseware has been the reliance on checklists of good authoring, rather than a more analytical approach to courseware development based on an instructional design theory. One consequence of this choice can be seen in courseware which presents learning opportunities (*allows* learning to take place), but does little to promote learning. Some of the best examples of an increased emphasis on instructional design and an decreased emphasis on "authoring tips" are provided by Roblyer (1981). She concludes that the main cause for the lack of quality in much of the courseware being produced is that many of the people involved in courseware development efforts have viewed the process as programming and the product as merely applications software. This view, as with the authoring view, tends to result in an inability to recognize the need for special expertise in designing the instruction itself.

One of the consistently mentioned differences between casual authoring of CAI programs and the production of educational courseware is the very serious nature of the latter. Bork (1985), a developer of large amounts of science courseware, stresses that curriculum material development is a serious and difficult business, regardless of the media involved, whether in the form of courseware or textbooks. In fact, he begins his description of the courseware development process by describing how textbooks are produced.

The first major distinction that Roblyer (1981) sees as distinguishing between instructional courseware design and an authoring approach is the use of a theory-based model in the former. The benefits of using such a model begin with the necessary assumption that the design must be based on knowledge of the many different ways in which humans learn. As a result of this assumption, the model should contain step-by-step procedures for designing the materials. A further benefit of using a theory-based model is in the recognition that creating individualized instruction is a complex process. In this process, the structure of the model can serve as a management device to help bring structure to the development activities.

Although an increasingly large number of instructional design models exist, their common elements usually include a statement of behavioral objectives, a specification of testing methods, and a specification of learning events. The degree of specification may vary, but the goals which students are expected to achieve should be known and stated.

Case's (1978) instructional design model can be used as an example. His is a developmental model, in that it takes into account developmental differences that make children learn in different ways than adults. In particular, he begins with two common limitations of young children's cognitive learning: their tendency to apply reasonable but oversimplified strategies and their relatively small memory capacity. In response to this, his model emphasizes analyzing the strategies which children spontaneously use, including learning activities to show the limitations of these strategies, and minimizing the information the child must remember at any one stage. Overall, the approach is to identify where children are initially, where the instruction should take them, and the directions that children are likely to go on their own. As can be seen, some of the emphasis in this model is in the forms of needs assessment.

Lepper and Malone (1986) also present a theory-based model, though a more specialized one for the design of instructional games. Their focus is on the various features which can be used to increase the motivational aspects of such games, particularly the potential trade-offs between motivation and learning. Their major categories of motivational variables are challenge, curiosity, control, and fantasy, with each analyzed in terms of its instructionally relevant and irrelevant characteristics.

The second important component of the instructional design process is the emphasis on a written design document, in contrast to a brief written, oral, or nonexistent description which might precede the typical authoring process. The value of this document is similar to the value of the planning process before programming or writing, as described in Chapter 6. Written documents at this stage help to ensure that the planned product is matched to an instructional need and that the purpose is clear to everyone, including (or particularly) the programmer. A design document also helps to check on the match between the definition of an instructional problem and the planned solution. A third value of this document is that it serves as a blueprint to the programmers, which may be followed as they build the courseware.

Consistent with a theory base, components of the design document should include statements of goals and objectives. This should be supplemented by a learning map indicating the skills to be covered and those prerequisite to instruction, the hierarchical and prerequisite relationships among the skills to be taught, and a suggested sequence for presenting the skills. A third component of the design documents is the description of the learning events which are to take place, such as those proposed by Gagné, and the ways in which they will be accomplished (inside or outside of the courseware). The final component would be composed of flowcharts, storyboards, or key screens, with a storyboard or mock-up produced for every important screen that is to appear in the courseware.

In the courseware development process used by the Ontario Ministry of Education, strong emphasis is placed on the use of "key screens" in design documents. The key screens are those which offer the student important information and/or choices of the activities which will follow. One key screen might be the general introductory menu to the program, with each important section having one or more key screens of its own. In general, the organization of these key screens is in the form of an outdoor marketplace, with the main key screen indicating the links between booths (other key screens) in terms of prerequisites, sequences, exits, etc.

The third distinctive feature of instructional design is an emphasis on the team approach to development. Roblyer feels that the term authoring carries with it a strong implication that the task is to be done by one person. She cites practical evidence which suggests that a team of two or more specialists is needed to develop effective courseware. The expertise represented in the team must include a content matter specialist, an instructional designer, and a programmer. In addition, other skills will probably be essential, such as a graphics artist, music consultant, etc. It is possible that some combination of these required skills will be present in one person and that a very small team might have them all. The advantage of involving more people in the team is not only that it makes it more likely that all areas of necessary expertise will be adequately covered, but also provides insurance against the errors and biases of one individual dominating the final product.

It is important to have adequate procedures for coordinating the activities of the team members and providing communication among them. Yourdon's (1979) "structured walkthrough" is only one example of such a technique, but one which is discussed in more detail in Chapter 6.

Structured walkthroughs are most important as a peer review process, leading to the final difference between instructional design and authoring, which is based on the fact that authoring seems to describe only a creation process, whereas instructional design methods usually provide for formative review, or validation by users, and revision. This is a most important distinction, since this stage is probably essential to assuring that the courseware actually accomplishes what the developers intended it to do. The actual formative activities should include the checking of accuracy and appropriate sequence by subject matter and design experts, plus a variety of activities involving the intended audience. The latter can include observing students individually (with or without accompanying interviews), small group use, and more extensive field testing. The important point of this activity is that the emphasis is on performance, what actually happens with students, rather than on the appearance of the product, or the opinions of those who have seen it.

Roblyer believes that a better understanding of the differences between instructional design and authoring is necessary to counter two unproductive trends. The first is the perception of courseware as merely another type of applications program, rather than instructional materials from which students learn. The second trend is the view that courseware can be developed successfully through isolated, unsystematic efforts of individuals. Both of these trends must be reversed if courseware is to become a useful part of the instructional process, particularly if this means large volumes of courseware will be necessary to meet the needs of both teachers and students.

Although the use of instructional design is well accepted in business settings, the view of courseware as just another applications program seems to be well entrenched in education. Teaching computer programming to teachers is receiving heavy emphasis in many in-service activities and a relatively small emphasis on instructional design is only beginning to emerge. Signs around the second trend are a bit more encouraging, with team efforts becoming more nearly the norm. Unfortunately, the tendency still exists for educators who are new to the use of computers to feel that they have been called to the splendid isolation of a life of unassisted courseware development.

COURSEWARE DEVELOPMENT PROCESS

Assuming that the choice has been made to follow the principles proposed above, difficulties still arise in carrying out this decision. One part of these difficulties is the matter of personal and corporate resolve, for producing mediocre courseware is relatively easy, while producing effective courseware requires substantially more effort. The problem of resolve can be compounded by the fact that those who produce mediocre courseware often seem to be completely unaware of how much their efforts could be improved, or in what ways, and are therefore quite oblivious to the difficulties in producing good courseware.

Needs Assessment

The starting point of successful courseware development lies in needs assessment, beginning with the determination of the instructional problem requiring a solution. A possible form of this process has been described in Chapter 2, but an additional word of warning may be in order. An example reported by Pepper (1981) can serve to emphasize the importance of determining the actual needs of students in a direct manner and not merely recording teachers' perceptions of student needs.

Pepper described an experiment in which he varied the type of text material used in an introductory level university programming course. In the first stage of the experiment, students were asked to read excerpts from one text, answer comprehension questions, then read excerpts from another text (the order of the texts was randomized) and answer opinion questions about the text material. To their surprise, the text which the experimenter and instructors greatly preferred did not fare any better on the comprehension items, and the other, more "verbose" text was preferred by most students. Thus, the first part of the experiment showed that student perference was the opposite of teacher preference (on the selected texts), but no difference was found in effectiveness.

In the second part of the experiment, along with excerpts from two existing textbooks in computer science, a set of new excerpts was created according to the student opinions of what they preferred. The main characteristics of the new material were an informal style, many examples, simple examples, and the use of graphical and textual aids. The results were a confirmation of the students' preferences, with the subjects scoring higher in achievement after reading the experimental chapter and also rating this chapter highest in all seven categories of preference.

The significance of these results for this discussion is not in the area of textbook writing, though important applications do arise there, nor in the suggestions this makes for courseware design and development. Rather, the important point is that the perception of the instructors about what the students needed was exactly the opposite of what the empirical results showed the students needed to improve their learning. This is not to say that teachers never know the needs of their students, nor that students are always aware of their true needs. However, to have confidence in a needs assessment, the needs must be confirmed by two or more sources, not to be based only on the expressed opinion of students, only on teachers' opinions, or for that matter, only on those of parents. The HOTS (Higher Order Thinking Skills) program is a case in point, often utilizing software in ways which seem contrary to developers' intentions and teachers' practice (Pogrow, 1987).

The process of needs assessment is also applicable to the creation of a development team, with similar cautions applying here as well. Courseware development requires a greater variety of skills than may be obvious from examining related activities such as teaching, textbook writing, or computer programming. Although this may seem to be an obvious statement, teachers or programmers, given the urge to create courseware, often underestimate the additional skill they require in order to develop high quality courseware. Even if the developer is a rare person with all the necessary skills, or especially if this is true, the needs of the development team for a variety of views within the team must be recognized.

Communications

Although a team approach is more likely to assure the presence of the necessary skills and a variety of perspectives, it should not be seen as a panacea in itself. In particular, problems of communications can occur within the team. Successful group work requires a group that can express their expectations in a form that other group members can understand easily. This may require that the members with an education background will have to learn some "computerese" and the computer people may have to learn some "educationese" in order to make sure they are working toward the same goal.

One frequently proposed suggestion, at least in advertisements, is the use of a nonprogramming authoring system which is designed to permit people without programming experience to create courseware units. Lipson and Fisher (1985) are among those who propose such an authoring system, though one of their goals for the facility is to allow teachers to modify centrally produced materials. For either type of application, authoring or modifying, this solution is unlikely to be successful in the long run, due to the constraints which such a system tends to impose on the types of courseware which it can be used to develop. It is inevitable that such a system will involve a trade-off between ease of use and flexibility. Just as an automatic camera can be limiting (unless it has a manual override), so the use of an authoring system is initially convenient, but becomes confining once the user gains experience. The experienced user of an authoring system is likely to want to try alternatives which the system creators decided not to implement (or of which they had never thought).

Related to this question of constraints is a second area of need for the developers, namely the limited system support (such as editing, or other utility programs) offered by most microcomputer systems. The use of microcomputers creates a considerable amount of flexibility in terms of how, when, and where they may be used, but the lack of support can counterbalance this freedom. Some of the support system problems that were caused by the lack of memory in early microcomputers have now been reduced, but the problem of software and other forms of support still give strong advantage to some form of centralized courseware development process. The most important of these advantages is in the informal communications network that brings the necessary information to all members of the development teams. One of the problems noted at the University of Illinois large-scale PLATO CAI development project was that these informal activities became too large and the authors were too dispersed, both in terms of time and space (Francis, Goldstein & Call-Himwich, 1975). In some cases, it may be that administrative decisions are made which restrict the amount of communication between developers, particularly when long distances are involved, even though this communication may be crucial for the development of quality courseware.

The Ontario Ministry of Education, in funding the development of courseware by teams of individuals and small companies, has provided a communications structure among the teams through the creation of a Software Development Assistance Centre (SDAC). The SDAC serves as a link among Provincial authorities, computer manufacturers, software companies, and the development teams, as well as helping the development teams to maintain contact with each other. A telephone hot-line, a regular newsletter (including responses to hot-line questions), and a monthly (or more frequent) forum for discussion of relevant topics are some of the methods used by the SDAC. It also provides a test site where developers may bring their programs for viewing and comment, test the works of other developers, or sample previously completed products. These and other functions of the SDAC will be discussed in later sections of this chapter.

FORMATIVE EVALUATION

Many developers do not recognize the importance, nor the difficulty of carrying out, appropriate formative evaluation activities. Formative evaluation can be distinguished from summative evaluation through Bob Stake's definition, "When the cook tastes the soup, that's formative; when the guests taste the soup, that's summative" (Scriven, 1981a, p. 63). More formally, formative evaluation is used during the development of a product (broadly defined), to provide feedback to the product developers, enabling them to make improvements to the product.

In actual practice, the distinction between summative and formative evaluation may not be so clear. Since a particular evaluation may contain both formative and summative components, it may be better to think of them as defining a continuum. It is unfortunate that much of the current emphasis in courseware evaluation appears to be summative (information for potential buyers), while many of the questions being asked are really formative in nature (Does the program run? Does it make good use of graphics?).

Some developers attempt to avoid recognition of the formative evaluation tasks by marketing materials which have not been tested with potential users (field testing). Because of this, one can find courseware sold as being appropriate for all grade levels (from grade one upwards), when actual use demonstrates that most students in grade six find the program to be beyond their capabilities. Results such as this indicate that the programs were probably never used, at least in the form in which they were marketed, with students as low as the grade six level. In fact, Bialo and Erickson (from EPIE) reported that 80 percent of a group of popular instructional programs were developed without the benefits of field testing for formative feedback (Hassett, 1984).

The Ontario Ministry of Education has defined a formative evaluation plan for their courseware developers which contains three stages. The first of these is an intensive review of the design document produced after the original developer proposal has been accepted for funding. The reviewers are appointed by, and are usually part of, the Ministry of Education, which funds the development. The second phase of evaluation occurs (assuming successful passage of the first stage) when a working prototype, a preliminary, but functionally complete form of the program, has been completed. This evaluation is conducted by the developers, using a small number of potential users, possibly in a laboratory setting. The final phase of evaluation is carried out after all obvious problems, discovered in the second phase, have been corrected. The final evaluation is carried out in the setting(s) in which the product will be used, with potential users, and evaluated by experienced evaluators independent of the development team.

The SDAC also plays a part in this Ontario evaluation plan. In addition to holding workshops on formative evaluation issues, the SDAC also facilitates the exchange of formative reviews between developers, provides a test site where developers may test their programs, or those of other developers, and maintains a data base of Ontario schools and teachers who are willing to take part in field testing, the third stage of the formative evaluation process.

An unusual, but interesting, example of a formatively driven development process is described by Good, Whiteside, Wixon, and Jones (1984). Instead of beginning with a set of commands specified in advance, they created an "electronic mail task" for which the software was repeatedly revised to incorporate the commands which novice users attempted to use. They found that after processing 67 subjects, their system, which began with a success rate of only 7 percent of commands being recognized, was capable of recognizing 76 percent of the spontaneously generated commands in the final version. Formative development of this type may be needed if courseware is going to be easily used by the majority of teachers and students.

Without a formative emphasis in courseware development, the summative evaluation (advice to prospective buyers) is usually in the form of a recommended compromise. The fruits of this approach can be seen in the quality of educational software generally available. Even though an overwhelming proportion of software is seen to be of an inferior quality, the evaluation methods used are almost always summative in nature, inadequate to correct the problem of software quality. In summative evaluation of educational software, as currently practiced, the focus is on methods to select the software packages which might be good enough to purchase or use. This approach does little or nothing to remedy the problem of low quality, but merely sets up a procedure for determining the compromise in terms of how many undesirable features should be included.

What is needed, not only in the development of educational software, but also in other areas of instructional decision-making, is an emphasis on a formative approach to evaluation, in which deficiencies are identified and corrected. In this approach, certain goals and objectives are set and the process of revision continues until they are attained. For example, in the area of equity, such as access to computers and computer skills, the question is not "How much inequity do we want?" but "How do we reduce inequity?" The necessary process is to make changes to instructional settings, materials, and procedures as long as these changes bring about an increase in equity.

Side Effects

The focus of the formative evaluation process is on the attainment of stated goals, but at the same time, the detection of side effects is also critically important in this process, just as in the detection of media effects (see Chapter 1). In defining side effects, Scriven says they "are the unintended good and bad effects of the program or product being evaluated. Sometimes the term refers to effects that were intended but are not part of the goals of the program" (Scriven, 1981a, p. 145). The most complete discussion of the rationale and principles of this form of evaluation seems to be found in Scriven's (1974) discussion of goal-free evaluation.

Goal-free evaluation evolved out of Scriven's dissatisfaction with the use of a standard checklist for rating the goals of a project, the effectiveness of meeting these goals, etc. For him, the clinching evidence in favor of goal-free evaluation may have been the dramatic example of one of 70 products being rated in the top ten, even though it had zero results in terms of intended outcomes, because of the surprising results from unanticipated effects. (At the same time, one must be cautious that the unintended outcomes are really appropriate for satisfying true needs, not just surprising and interesting.)

Scriven's initial impression was that the goal-free approach would be confined to summative evaluations, but further reflection seemed to lead to the conclusion that formative evaluation, if it were to lead to favorable summative evaluation, must also include a goal-free component. The use of the goal-free approach might raise some problems for the project staff, since it would seem to require an external formative evaluation, with probable additional expense, but presumably greater validity in the results. In the Ontario courseware development process, this problem has been addressed through encouraging development teams to provide formative feedback, possibly goal-free in nature, for other development teams on a cooperative basis. The cost of this external formative input is in terms of a team's time, but the experience of viewing another team's prototype product critically should give them greater insight into their own product development, as well as developing their own evaluation skills.

The proposal for the use of goal-free evaluation has received considerable criticism from other evaluation experts, much of it reported in the Scriven (1974) article. One of the frequent remarks is that it is more appropriate to train evaluators to be unbiased, rather than keep them uninformed about the project's objectives. The usual response from Scriven is that he will withdraw all suggestions for the use of goal-free evaluation as soon as the training of unbiased evaluators is implemented. This is an important point for developers, who are likely to find it both more productive and less time consuming if they attempt to identify the biases of their users and evaluators, rather than attempting to locate unbiased opinions.

Roberts (1974) also speaks of observer bias and considers the values of the observer to be crucial in attempting to choose between competing hypotheses. He suggests that we should use our values to consider the cost of making a wrong choice and modify our selection process accordingly. That is, to use his example, we should require stronger evidence to reject the hypothesis of racial equality in mental function than to accept it. The reason is that accepting the view of racial inequality wrongly is more serious than if we accept racial equality when it is in fact false.

Another source of consistent complaint about goal-free evaluation stems from the persistent perception that Scriven is proposing goal-free evaluation to replace goal-based evaluation, when he is actually suggesting that they both be used, with goal-free (necessarily) preceding goal-based activities, which can be used as a double check of the goal-free results. It may seem odd that the desired outcomes are initially ignored, but the rationale is that you can always look for what you expect to find, but the opportunity to evaluate without expectations is extremely limited. If the goal-based evaluation is seen as a part of the goal-free process, the implementation should be less threatening to all concerned. That is, both developer and evaluator could be embarrassed if the evaluation failed to consider and detect the effects on some intended outcomes, thus the necessity of doing the goal-based study, if required, after the goal-free search.

Rather than pit goal-free and goal-based evaluation against each other, it is more productive to look on them as two of many possible approaches, or perhaps as points on a continuum. For an example of these approaches to evaluation in the domain of computer applications, one might consider *The Psychology of Computer Programming* (Weinberg, 1971), heavily loaded with anecdotes and case study material, as being toward the goal-free end of the continuum, while *Software Psychology* (Shneiderman, 1980) is an examination of evidence that focuses on the effects of intended outcomes. One interpretation of these two viewpoints might be to conclude that Weinberg offers interesting insights into what programmers actually do, while Shneiderman's evidence, particularly as seen by Sheil (1981), seems to indicate that we know very little (at least in a scientific sense) about what programmers actually do. It may be overly simplistic to cast this in the form of a comparison between goal-free and goal-based approaches since it is more properly a contrast between naturalistic and experimental methods. The important point is that our intentions, which generate the type of evidence discussed by Shneiderman, are often very poor predictors of what actually happens, as demonstrated by the anecdotal information in Weinberg's accounts. Equally important is the warning that we should not see these differing views as the only possible viewpoints. Shneiderman gives the results of only a few experiments out of the many which might have been done, while Weinberg describes only a few incidents out of the much larger number which actually happened. Thus, we can see the more recent descriptions of programmer behavior by Turkle (1984) as being complementary to those of Weinberg and others, not opposing them.

Moving to a setting more similar to courseware development, Crawford and Crawford (1984) provide an example of the difference between intentions and outcomes as they describe the production of distance education materials.

> The materials are produced using an ISD [Instructional Systems Design]-theory based model. There is an emphasis on written documentation, a team approach has been used extensively and provision is made for formative review and evaluation. However, there is an increasing resistance to the theoretical basis, particularly the behavioural elements and there are considerable pressures to forget the model and "get it done". Further, while written documentation is required, there is an increasing trend toward superficial and incomplete analysis and documentation. The team approach, which in the past, saw subject matter experts, instructional designers, editors and visual designers collaboratively producing courseware, is rapidly giving way to subject matter experts (authors) providing materials for instructional developers to "fix-up". Finally, while provisions are made for formative review and evaluation, it rarely occurs because of time pressures, physical production models and costs. (p. 345)

Their experience shows that side effects are not just something you search for in evaluating, but that the evaluation itself, instead of proceeding as intended, is detoured by the side effects of the development process, through the effects of time pressure, etc. In some ways, this is a fulfillment of Ellul's definition of "la technique" in terms of "*methods rationally arrived at and having absolute efficiency*" (Ellul, 1964, p. xxv). It illustrates the danger of viewing the courseware development process in a limited cost/benefit manner, for the most effective means of producing courseware (not necessarily learning) is to minimize such "frills" as formative review and evaluation.

A specific instructional example of side effects can be seen in one of the classrooms described by Carmichael et al. (1985). The incident is described in more detail in Chapter 3, but the essential element is that the teacher, in presenting computers as an environment for competition in the solving of "challenges" he posed weekly, occasioned a number of students' attitudes being based on the competition (which most of the girls disliked) rather than on other attributes of the computer environment which could have been stressed. It is not that this classroom necessarily became competitive because of computers being introduced (though it might have), but that the side effect of competition seemed to *dominate* many of the intended effects of computer skills, understanding, awareness, etc. Trumbull (1986) also reports on an increase in competitiveness, which she attributes to frequent use of game formats in instructional programs. These findings have greater import when considered alongside the observation that "Computer-assisted cooperative instruction promoted greater quantity and quality of daily achievement, more successful problem solving, more task-related student-student interaction, and increased the perceived status of female students" (Johnson, Johnson, & Stanne, 1986, p. 382).

Simulation and Microworlds

A more general instructional example of side effects (and the importance of assumptions) can be seen in the use of simulations or simulation games, which can be independent of computer use, but increasingly are a format for courseware production. Simulation or modeling is not only a popular, but a very useful application of computers in instructional settings. In this application computers are used to build systems which mimic the real world (to the extent we know it). However, in choosing the mathematical representation of a given process, the person(s) designing the simulation usually have to decide which are the most important aspects of the process and how they should interact with each other. This is because, except in the simulation of relatively simple processes, some of the features of the real world are intentionally (or unintentionally) omitted in order to make the simulation possible (or desirable). In the case of physical processes, such as a chemistry titration, the real world interaction is sufficiently well defined that an inaccuracy in the simulation (or incompleteness of the model) might be detected easily by the knowledgeable user. However, simulations in the social sciences or humanities, such as a program which simulates a classroom, allowing the user to make decisions about teaching strategies, are more likely to be influenced (perhaps unintentionally) by the designers' assumptions. Moreover, they are likely to be influenced in such a way that will be more difficult for even the knowledgeable user to estimate.

One of the advantages of simulations is that they enable students to investigate systems that they would otherwise be unable to observe, due to cost, time scale, or the resources required. In fact, the investigation of imaginary systems is another useful possibility, those systems which are unrealizable in the real world, such as a system in which ice is heavier than water, or other physical laws, such as the law of gravity, are altered. One of the hazards of these applications, and simulations in general, is the possibility of presenting an imaginary system, such as the world as the modeler would like it to be, as though it is an accurate description of the real system. Because computers are often seen as more authoritative than books or other materials, this misapplication, whether intentional or unintentional, offers potential for "thought control," which requires that simulation models be used with care.

In the late 1960s, a simulation study in the United States investigated, among other things, "the effects of urban renewal." In a study of this type, the assumptions made about the relationships among variables would be crucial, since they would completely determine (except for random fluctuations) the outcome of the study. That is, one could (and probably should) argue about the assumptions, but not the results, since they are completely determined by the assumptions. Consequently, one should accept the results if (and only if) one accepts the assumptions. It might be concluded, in fact, that if one knows only the results without knowing the assumptions (true of most media reports), one would know almost nothing.

The use of simulations, or simulation games to teach values (whether intentional or unintentional) is particularly likely in curriculum areas such as history or social studies. For example, if one creates a program that requires the user to make decisions for a mythical person, family, or group living in a historical period, including the present, it is quite possible, or even likely that the results of these decisions (in the simulation) will be strongly affected by the values of the simulation developers. Thus, we might expect a simulation of early North American settlers to reward the user for such currently valued traits as the seeking of prosperity and personal peace, while some of the most "successful" people of that era, in terms of reaching their own goals, might have had very different values and practices, such as those based on altruism and patriotism. Conversely, one might also find that the simulated values were those of the past and conflicted with those of the present.

Some specific examples may serve to sharpen the dilemma. If the goal were to create a simulation game based on the life of some "successful villian," such as Hitler, Stalin, or Napoleon, misgivings might arise over allowing the user to gain power through the use of duplicity, violence, or other socially undesirable traits. However, in the interest of historical accuracy, these rewards would probably be included, since many of the facts about the lives of the simulated people would be known by the users of the simulation. After all, who would be willing to believe a simulation in which Stalin attained even greater power by following the principles espoused by Gandhi? The options for simulation developers would seem to be limited to either choosing to model the life accurately, or else choosing to model only those lives which are admirable, thus not creating simulations that reward undesirable behavior and values.

The dilemma becomes more difficult and less obviously solved when we consider simulations that are based on the lives of mythical people. In this case, the simulation developers have considerably more freedom to impose their own values on the users of the simulation because any contradictions with actual conditions of the era are much less obvious, even when the simulation is based on current conditions. That is, if a government wished to influence its people to believe that personal satisfaction was more likely to be achieved when one lived in a high-rise apartment than in a single-family dwelling, such a simulation would not be obviously false (to most people) if skillfully done. This is not to say that the use of simulations to change values will be necessarily successful, but to point out that such effects, whether intentional or not, are possible and likely to be tried. In the long run, social simulations may be more useful if they are used to stimulate other learning activities, rather than being seen as environments in which to learn about society and/or history.

Simulation is also the technique that underlies the development of "microworlds," as proposed by Papert and others, the relatively constrained computerized domains which allow, but don't require students to explore, test, and generally learn by discovery (Papert, 1980b). Discovery learning is one pole of a controversy perhaps best defined by the opposing views of Papert and Skinner. Papert complains that the delivery of content material by way of CAI is "programming the student", while Skinner (1984) attacks the discovery method as inefficient, claiming that programmed materials can attain the same level of achievement in half the time. Malone and Lepper (1986) also point out that the intuitive appeal of the discovery approach has not received strong research support. However, they feel that computer-based simulations and microworlds are useful in that they can provide a better environment for encouraging discovery learning.

An unfortunate aspect of the dispute over discovery learning is that the opposing sides seem to see the alternatives as being mutually exclusive, not just in a particular instructional setting, but universally. The reason for this view seems to be that they see their methods not simply as preferred techniques for instruction, but as philosophies (or possibly religions) of education, if not for life in general. A better approach might begin with making two important distinctions about the definitions of school and students, rather than considering the methods to be mutually exclusive, or even looking for a synthesis of the techniques.

First, a distinction can be made between the global activity known as school and the many different learning stages and activities that comprise the total school experience. Just as an evaluation of computer use becomes clearer when specific activities are considered, so an analysis of specific learning needs of students should provide a more accurate evaluation of the benefits of discovery learning and programmed methods, or other alternatives. This can be particularly true when the stages of learning are examined. For example, Dreyfus and Dreyfus (1984, 1986) acknowledge the benefits of a microworld for the novice learner, but feel that this form of simulation can actually get in the way of learning by the time learners have reached the stage of advanced beginner. They argue that the learner needs to move from learning rules in a simplified microworld to acquiring a repertory of real-world situations, more complex than those modeled in the microworld. (See also Chapter 7.)

However, a second distinction may be even more important to the analysis, that of individual students versus the general notion of students. Although most efforts to create different individualized learning environments for individual students have been unsuccessful, indications that their needs differ continue to appear. For example, it seems to be found consistently that 20 percent of the teachers who are rated best by some students will be rated worst by other students, and vice versa (Follman, 1984). The fallibility of student ratings may be the source of this discrepancy, but the possibility exists that different students require different approaches. If the important goal is what they learn, it may be more important to focus on the facilitation of individual students, or groups of students, rather than the promotion of one's favorite theoretical position, be it discovery learning or programmed instruction.

It seems unproductive to suggest that discovery learning is appropriate in all contexts, with mycology (mushroom identification) being an obvious example. It is unlikely that anyone would be comfortable with a discovery approach to the identification of edible mushrooms, a 'Russian casseroulette'. If a division of effort is to be suggested, the learning of essential skills, such as how to use a computer (or pencil) to facilitate other learning, might be an area for more structured (courseware) content. Similarly, some of those areas where the objectives are less precise, such as the practice of the previously mentioned computer skills, might be done more appropriately in a microworld. That is, those students who possess a more complete array of learning skills have a real possibility of discovering something new and worthwhile for them, such as a new method of applying the skills to a particular problem. It must be remembered, however, that the range of possible discoveries is usually limited by the dimensions of the microworld (Roszak, 1986) and increasingly sophisticated microworlds may be needed as learners develop their skills. In any situation, the choice of instructional method must be influenced by the characteristics of the particular student's needs relative to the content being studied, with continuous monitoring for side effects of any mode of instruction. (It may be worth noting that the emphasis in side effects, or goal-free evaluation is on discovery, but it is a discovery aimed at finding things we don't know, not the replication of what has already been learned by other people.)

CONTROLLING THE DEVELOPMENT PROCESS

With a wide variety of government agencies, companies, and individuals involved in the development of courseware, the control of the process may vary depending on the identity of the players. In the case of a private, profit-making (or at least profit-seeking) company, the comparison of cost versus benefit would probably be paramount, with the benefit being defined mainly in terms of increased sales. That is, if an increase in cost can be seen to lead to an even greater increase in revenue, it is a desirable cost. As seen in the quote from Crawford and Crawford (1984) given earlier, this view of the courseware development process is not limited to private companies, with publicly funded bodies also subject to demands for increased productivity at a lower cost. In fact, since public funding of development often means that the normal "free market" feedback is removed, it may be even easier for these organizations to put quantity ahead of quality, unless serious attention is given to the formative evaluation process.

The Province of Ontario has entered into the courseware development process by means of direct funding (in the amount of millions of dollars per year) of courseware developers, including small and large companies, and groups of individuals (but not publicly funded institutions). The level of funding is not intended to cover the full costs of development, only the rights to use the courseware in Ontario's publicly funded schools. Payments are made to the developers after the completion of each of the stages of design, prototype, and field testing. The agreement to cover this process is detailed, with over 50 numbered sections plus ten appended schedules. The province also provides support in the form of (government) curriculum consultants, regular developers' meetings, and the Software Development Assistance Centre (described earlier).

By paying only for the Ontario rights to developed courseware, the province is able to make more efficient use of its development dollars. Moreover, because the developers retain rights to all use outside of Ontario (and nonpublic school use within Ontario), a potential conflict arises for developers. Although their initial source of funding is from the province, the astute developer realizes that a much larger potential market exists outside of Ontario. Hence, the cost-effective developers will be tailoring their courseware for the U.S. market, not for Ontario. This is an ironic result in a country concerned with cultural domination, but one that has tradition behind it. The province's authority for educational television is required to depend on program sales for a significant part of its budget, thus it develops television programs which often exclude Ontario and other Canadian content in favor of U.S. content, in order to increase the sales potential.

Two other goals of the Ontario funding program are of a more long-term nature and perhaps more solidly based. The first is the production of courseware that has demonstrable benefits for students' learning and the second is the development of a "courseware industry" in Canada (Canadian developers outside of Ontario are also eligible for funding). Both of these goals are supported by the formative evaluation requirements built into the development process and, as a result, both of them seem possible to attain. In both cases, the direct result is enforced by the contractual process, but the overall effect is probably even more important, the effect of this development model (and others like it) on the perception of what courseware can and should be. If the intentions of this model do not run afoul of the difficulties described by Crawford and Crawford (1984), or similar problems, the demonstration effect—presenting a process by which courseware with demonstrable benefits can be produced—may be the most important result for the educational use of computers.

SUMMATIVE EVALUATION

In order to discuss the role of summative evaluation in courseware development, one must distinguish between the current use of summative evaluation and the possible uses of summative evaluation when formative evaluation has been properly carried out during the development process. Currently, summative evaluation is often used to do the task that should have been done by formative evaluation. That is, it is used to identify problems and errors in the programs, such as poor displays and unclear instructions. This role for summative evaluation is only beneficial or required when formative evaluation has been ineffective.

When courseware is developed consistently through a process that incorporates formative feedback effectively, the role of summative evaluation should change. The future role of summative evaluation should be that of helping the teacher and other educators to match the content, objectives, and teaching strengths of courseware to the needs of students. This is not to say that such evaluations would no longer uncover defects in the courseware being reviewed, but merely to point out that the defects would no longer be the focus of the evaluation. Summative courseware reviews might then be more similar to the reviews of new automobile models, which still contain an indication of the defects found, but the emphasis is on a comparison of alternative features, not defects.

In developing the new style of summative evaluation, more attention should be paid to the needs of teachers who will use this evaluation material. In the past, summative evaluation forms have been created, tested, and modified using feedback from those who fill out the forms, the evaluators, rather than those who will use the information, the teachers as consumers. It seems only fitting that the reviews of courseware, those instructional programs validated on the basis of learner feedback, should themselves be validated on the basis of feedback from the potential users of the reviews.

Product Evaluation

Summative evaluation of courseware is really a form of product evaluation, which Scriven asserts is "at its best . . . the most satisfactory type of evaluation currently practiced" (Scriven, 1981b, p. 121). This claim is based primarily on the maturity of product evaluation, it having been done and discussed in serious and scientific ways much longer than most other types of evaluation. His discussion of product evaluation is in the form of a description of the ideal model, composed of seven checkpoints. These checkpoints are not to be considered as a linear sequence of steps, for the ideal product evaluation involves an interaction of the checkpoints and several iterations through the checklist.

The first checkpoint is the needs assessment or definition of the function that the product is to perform. This is complemented by the second checkpoint, an assessment of the product strengths, or inventory of resources. The comparison of these two points is essential in determining the match of needs to product characteristics, just as in the curriculum needs process described in Chapter 2.

The third checkpoint takes the data from the previous two points and does comparison shopping or identifies critical competitors (see Chapter 2 for definition and examples). The primary task is to identify the products that are available in the range defined by the relevant needs and strengths. In this context, the need for explanation of differences is minimized and the primary emphasis is on the "horse race" between critical competitors. The anecdote about locating a critical competitor for an elevator indicator (given in Chapter 2) illustrates that critical competitors may not be obvious.

In the fourth checkpoint, performance testing, the important aspect is to select the correct variables to be tested, the degree of accuracy, and the proper comparisons and assumptions about the user. The temptation is to select those variables that can be easily measured or can be measured with great accuracy. The use of listener tests in evaluating high fidelity components, rather than using instruments, illustrates a resisting of this temptation, a change analagous to substituting behavioral significance (those differences which are significant to the users) for statistical significance in evaluation.

Checkpoint five concentrates on locating the features and flaws of the products, particularly the secondary functions and characteristics they possess. The seaworthiness of large yachts (unusually unsatisfactory, but ignored) and the electrical safety of appliances (electrical hazards bring a rating of "not acceptable" by *Consumer Reports*, regardless of other achievements) are two contrasting examples reported by Scriven.

The estimation of operational costs is an aspect of the sixth checkpoint, price shopping and cost analysis, which is often overlooked. One demonstration of the importance of operating costs is the low selling price of safety razors, which can be given away because the company will make its money from the sale of blades. Operating costs are also often overlooked in the purchase of computers and other electronic equipment, along with the costs of coordinating people. This can be a tragic oversight, since both of them are often important aspects of adopting and implementing a new program.

The seventh and final checkpoint is that of setting standards and providing an overall synthesis. The most difficult decision involves setting the weights to be applied to the various criteria in order to answer the crucial question, "Which product is the best buy?" This can be a highly complex and frustrating process when one product is not clearly superior to the rest. If minimum levels of performance are required on some dimensions, eliminating those products which fail to do so may simplify the task. Also, whatever the weighting scheme used, the results should be compared with one's own intuitive feelings about what the rankings should be. For example, an initial weighting scheme might permit a pedagogically inferior courseware package to attain the highest weighted result because of points earned through technical excellence. Only when the evaluator is satisfied that the component scores and their weights are meaningful, leading to valid weighted totals, should the rankings be thought of as final.

Not all of the techniques of product evaluation can be applied to the evaluation of courseware, though the examples Scriven provides make fascinating reading. Nevertheless, the core of the process—particularly in determining the needs and product strengths, and their comparison—justifies the use of this checklist as a guide to thinking about the summative courseware evaluation task.

The strength of the summative process is its practicality, in that it deals with people's needs to compare programs and products which exist. Its major weakness is in its link to the improvement of courseware. The approach taken by the EPIE—Consumers Union consortium (MICROgram, 1983) is a possible answer to this weakness. Their reviews, though aimed at potential purchasers of courseware, also contain suggestions for courseware improvement aimed at the developer. This technique not only gives the developer a suggested path for product improvement, but also educates the consumer with an awareness of what types of features should be a part of courseware packages. This is in line with a focus on providing useful information to the evaluation consumer. That is, it may be good to know which product is better, but it is even more useful to know why one product is better and how all of them might be improved.

COURSEWARE RESEARCH

For more than two decades researchers have been investigating the uses of CAI, but many of the basic questions remain unanswered. For example, Grubb (1964) studied the possibility that pairs of students working together at a CAI terminal could learn more effectively than individual students. Twenty-one years later, so little progress had been made on this question that Roblyer, in listing important research questions, said, "[school personnel] have begun experimenting with pairing or grouping students for computer use. Studies are needed to indicate whether these approaches result in equal or fewer gains in achievement and accompanying student attitudes" (Roblyer, 1985, p. 42).

Chambers and Sprecher (1980, 1983) have made systematic reviews of the CAI research literature. They find that the few large-scale studies have failed to give evidence of clear superiority of CAI over regular classroom instruction. In the many small studies they find several consistent patterns of results. Generally, CAI produces either better or equal learning in a reduced period of time, when compared to the regular classroom. CAI also seems to produce more positive student attitudes toward both computers and the subject matter. However, in interpreting these findings, it is well to heed Calfee's (1985) observation that any CAI design can be misinterpreted or misused. That is, computer techniques for interpreting student explanation are not good and the general finding that CAI is helpful doesn't change that fact.

Many of the basic questions about CAI remain unanswered because much of the research and evaluation of CAI has been misdirected. A great deal of effort has gone into comparisons between the use of CAI and other forms of instruction. As Cronbach, et al, (1980) have pointed out, little satisfaction is derived from finding out which of two methods is better (a summative question). Our preference should be to discover how the methods can be improved, possibly through combining them (a formative question). The focus on the relative effectiveness of CAI versus teachers has left us with little insight into the ways both might be used most effectively in classrooms, or how peer tutoring and other human interactions might be linked with CAI. The complexity of determining a satisfactory integration of CAI is illustrated by contrasting the finding that CAI used to supplement classroom instruction appears to be very cost effective (Hawley, Fletcher, & Piele, 1986) with the observation that teachers seem to consistently (and greatly) overestimate the amount of time their students use computers for instructional purposes (Mathinos & Woodward, 1987).

Learner Control

One area of research which has received considerable attention, and most of it formative, is that called learner control, the ability of students to choose from various types of presentation formats, instructional techniques, etc. CAI is an excellent vehicle for implementing learner control, though CMI would be even more flexible, but the results from these studies have been generally ambiguous (Merrill, 1980). The most consistently found result seems to be that learners are often unable to (or unwilling to) choose the instructional method that will enable them to learn more effectively. Clark (1983) reports that students seem to choose the method that they believe will allow them to achieve success with the least effort. As a result, high ability students tend to choose structured methods that, in agreement with Dreyfus and Dreyfus (1984, 1986), actually limit the use of their already acquired skills, while lower ability students are more likely to choose discovery-oriented methods, though these deny them the structure they require.

Intelligent CAI

Perhaps the most popular area of CAI research is that of ICAI, or Intelligent CAI, which is the use of artificial intelligence techniques to improve the performance of CAI. Because of the popularity of AI, developers seem to be tempted to call their products ICAI, even when the techniques used were known before their "discovery" in AI (for examples, see Chapter 4).

Sleeman and Brown (1982), in reviewing the state of "Intelligent tutoring systems," observed that the frequent problems were that systems were inaccurate in assessing the students' level of knowledge, tended to accommodate only one conceptualization of the problem, used ad hoc strategies, and were too limited in their interaction with students. In the more restricted environment of "coaching" students playing a computer-based game, Burton and Brown (1982) characterized the major problems as knowing "when to interrupt" and "what to say." Beginning with an underlying and explicit assumption that it is best for students to discover as much as possible, and based on three years of investigation, they propose 12 principles of computerized coaching. The principles are intended to increase discovery, maintain interest, increase learning, and enhance the general game environment. They acknowledge the existence of subtle problems which resist general solution.

Implicit in Sleeman and Brown's observations and explicit in much ICAI work has been an emphasis on developing a model of the learner, so that the program can, through monitoring the learner's responses, determine, among other things, the specific "misconceptions" held by the learner. Correcting these misconceptions usually is not seen to be a part of the ICAI process. Unfortunately, this approach seems to ignore the experience of teachers who have found that it is much more difficult to correct students' misconceptions than to determine what they are. In the context of classroom needs, a more useful approach would be to develop instructional aids, possibly using AI in the form of an expert system for instructional design (Merrill, 1987), which would preferably prevent these misconceptions, or if not, correct them.

However, even if developing a model of the learner is an appropriate goal, Bruner (1985) for one, insists that one model of the learner is not sufficient to describe what actually happens in learning. He acknowledges that a model of the learner is necessary to improve education, but feels that choosing only one model is a reflection of political, practical, and cultural issues. In light of the discussion of artificial intelligence in Chapter 4, all three of these issues seem to be relevant in the desire of ICAI researchers to find a model of the learner.

Out of this short review of courseware research, limited though it is, some trends inhibiting the effective use of courseware can yet be seen. One of them is the apparently strong desire to avoid the use of human skills and strengths, to concentrate as much function as possible into the computer programs. A second is in responding to the lure of the challenge as being a guide to development, rather than it being shaped by the most pressing needs, while the third is a "horse-race" mentality, which sees the advance of knowledge as a competition between opposites which can never be combined, such as CAI versus teachers, or discovery learning versus programmed instruction. As a result, we have courseware designed to replace teachers, courseware aimed at unimportant but interesting problems, and courseware which sells only one form of instructional philosophy, such as discovery learning, to the exclusion of all others. Real instructional problems persist, but if the emphasis continues to be on a confrontation between mutually exclusive approaches, independent of urgent classroom needs, the progress will continue to be slow.

6   *Programming and Writing*

INTRODUCTION

One of the failures of the computer age has been the failure of those who teach programming and those who teach writing to realize that the skills they are teaching have a great deal in common. Early recognition of this fact was seen at least a decade ago in Kernighan and Plauger's (1974) *The Elements of Programming Style*, which took its form from the similarly named popular writing guide. Only a few writers have acknowledged the link since that time, among them Schneider (1984) who diagnoses faults in a piece of written documentation in terms of commonly found programmimg errors. When the documentation refers to sections that don't exist, he say's, "Its GOTOs get lost" (p. 164) and when it refers to "enclosed agreements," but doesn't indicate what should be done with them, he concludes that "Its IFs have no THENs" (p. 164). English and Edwards reverse the procedure, describing the process of successful programming in terms of the techniques of good writing. In their view, a programmer must "understand the subject, know the audience and organize the ideas into an outline or design. [He] must then revise until it works flawlessly" (English & Edwards, 1984, p. 47). Van Dyke (1987) illustrates the ways in which our understanding of linguistic literacy can enhance the teaching of computer literacy, including "programming as composition."

Common Elements

The fundamental similarity of these processes lies in their common origin, a need to communicate. Both of them involve the communicating of an idea which you understand to someone (or something) who does not understand. In this way programming is most like descriptive writing, particularly the description of some process, but the principles of clarity, sequence, and organization apply to both programming and most forms of prose.

One should not, however, get the impression that writing and programming are identical, for that is obviously not the case. The most important difference may be that the writer can assume a much greater degree of flexibility on the part of the intended audience than can the programmer. That is, the programmer is usually working with a relatively limited number of words and basic structures which have been predefined, and any additions to this list must be explicitly defined by the programmer. Thus, the programmer can create new words, if they are defined, but is not allowed to use nouns as verbs (to interface), or verbs as nouns (an intercept) as we do when writing or speaking.

The similarities between programming and writing are usually not seen because the accepted definition of programming, or more precisely, the interpretation of the definition, is narrow. The *New Webster's Computer Dictionary* (1984) defines programming as "the process of converting a problem specification into a sequence of instructions to be executed by a computer" (p. 253). Most people tend to view this as a highly specialized skill reserved for the elite. In the past this skill was necessary to get "control" over computers, but this is no longer true and it appears that programming can (and should) be defined more broadly. The problem can be seen as one of interpretation, for if your problem is a lack of money and a sequence of instructions to an automated teller (computer) solves the problem, then by the preceding definition, this is programming.

The new definition of programming might be viewed as a continuum, or multidimensional space, including a number of activities which share common elements with what is currently called programming. The most obvious continuum might range from highly specific computer tasks, such as coding in a traditional programming language, to more general skills of planning and scheduling. Another dimension might range over computer applications, moving from those requiring a great deal of computer expertise, typically individual or low volume creations, to those of extreme "user-friendliness," which completely protect the user from having to know any specifics about the computer being used. The common thread to these dimensions is the notion of user "control," which is now available from a variety of programming-like activities.

The expectations we have about the writing process also offer similarities and differences with those of programming. The major similarity is that of communication, with programming usually being a more precise form of communication. However, English and Edwards illustrate the converse by quoting a very experienced programmer, who advised new programmers, "If you cannot write it [your idea] in clear concise English, you can't program it" (English & Edwards, 1984, p. 46). The stage of planning is often another shared expectation of these processes, the belief that *effective* writing and programming both require planning. The key is effectiveness, best illustrated by the easily generated programs and texts, which glaringly display their lack of planning. The aspect of problem solving, written into the definition of programming, is also often a part of writing, with the problem frequently being in the form of a question needing an answer.

A greater amount of similarity is probably seen in the feedback received from written and programmed materials. In the case of writing, one needs feedback for revising, while the similar process in programming is called debugging. Programming is probably more like the specialized writing form often called school writing. In school writing, the primary goal is that of not making errors, with the communicating of ideas a distant second. In school writing, you leave out ideas that require words you can't spell, while in programming, features that require unknown commands or structures are similarly omitted (at least in the first version of the program).

Feedback for programs usually comes from the computer they are intended to run on and consequently it is more uniform in its results. The feedback to our writing differs in major ways depending on the readers and their expectations about what the text should contain and how it should be said. The computer, in the form of the programming language compiler or interpreter, will often reject our efforts entirely, demanding that we make certain corrections before implementation of our program can even be attempted. Human readers are not likely to be so severe and consequently their demands (or requests) for revision tend to lose their clout, since they have usually understood the message in spite of its errors.

Feedback for programmers can also come from humans, these data being more relevant when the computer no longer rejects the program as unworkable, but the results are not right. Just as teachers of writing put an emphasis on the role of constructive criticism, so Weinberg (1971) proposes "egoless programming" as the road to programming excellence through the seeking of peer criticism. In both cases, programming or writing, the human feedback can be part of a group process, with rules set out for maximum benefit with minimum distress. Knapp (1986) describes a group process for students to use in critiquing writing for group members, following a six-step model. A similar process, the "structured walkthrough" (Yourdon, 1979), is one of the techniques which provides the same sort of feedback for professional programmers. In both cases the emphasis is on maximizing the value of the feedback while minimizing the pain for the writer or programmer.

In the following sections, four major aspects of the writing and programming processes will be explored in more detail. The first is style, including the personality of the person, as well as the way this is seen through their work habits and final products. The second aspect has to do with planning, its importance and effects as well as the ways in which computers and other humans can help us with our planning. The third aspect is the actual creation step, the writing or programming of the first draft and the computerized aids for this process. The final aspect is that of revising/debugging, including personal differences in this phase, computer aids, and human assistance for the author-programmer. The chapter concludes with two positive-negative comparisons, one having to do with arguments for and against computer programming as a valuable activity for elementary and secondary students, while the second is a consideration of the possible benefits and drawbacks for an individual using word processing in the writing process.

STYLE

Although this discussion will be primarily in terms of the methods used by programmers and writers in creating their products, it could also be applied to the products themselves. More than two decades ago, Page (1966) described a computer program which simulated an expert's judgment of essay style with great success. The approach was based on the correlation between "countable" features of an essay, such as sentence length, number of commas, etc., and the rating by human experts. Partly because human ratings of essay style are notoriously unreliable, the results from the program were virtually indistinguishable from that of expert judges.

Analyzing the style of programs, mainly in terms of their complexity, has also been an issue in computer science. Redish and Smyth (1986) describe a system which provides an assessment of program style as a by-product of program compilation (converting the written program into a form usable by the computer). This feedback is provided for students doing programming assignments, but could also be used in other environments to improve the style of programs.

The image of the computer programmer is usually one of a distinct personality, often separated from the rest of the population in strange ways. This stereotype may be based on the actual personality of a small proportion of programmers who exhibit unusual behavior, just as some writers are unusual in their lifestyles. Matheson and Strickland (1986) found that even computer science students characterized computer scientists as less sociable, though they did not describe themselves as fitting into this stereotype. Weizenbaum (1984) distinguishes between the compulsive programmer and the professional programmer, primarily in the way they view the relative importance of the problem to be solved and the computer which will solve it. The stereotype of the "hacker" often comes from the compulsive programmer's overwhelming interest in contact with computers, their details of operation, and their operating systems software, while little importance is attached to the solving of problems, at least those with precisely definable goals. Weizenbaum sees them as being interested only in imprecise problems which can be solved (at least in their perception) entirely on the basis of knowledge about computers, and which are abandoned when it becomes apparent that some noncomputer knowledge is required. However, hackers are also seen as having produced significant achievements as a result of their persistence and skill (Elmer-DeWitt, 1984).

Turkle's (1984) view is somewhat different, with her categories of programmers being "hard masters" and "soft masters." The hard master sets out to achieve a definite goal, and although this may be slightly augmented or modified, this goal must be achieved for the program to be a success. The soft master is seen as more interactive, more likely to change goals on the basis of the computer response to the preceding attempt at a solution. She finds that girls who program are more likely to fit into the soft master category, being more accustomed to negotiation and compromise, while boys are more likely to show the strong will required for the role of hard master.

Turkle's categories are based on her observations of children, while Weizenbaum's are based on adults, though often young adults. Therefore, his observations that the professional is likely to have others do the actual interacting with the computer may be a stage to which some of the children Turkle observed will eventually progress. Unfortunately, some of them may also progress to be compulsive programmers, as seen in Weizenbaum's oft-quoted description.

> Wherever computer centers have become established . . . bright young men of disheveled appearance, often with sunken glowing eyes, can be seen sitting at computer consoles, their arms tensed to strike, at the buttons and keys on which their attention seems to be riveted as a gambler's on the rolling dice. When not so transfixed, they often sit at tables strewn with computer printouts over which they pore like possessed students of a cabalistic text. They work until they nearly drop, twenty, thirty hours at a time. Their food, if they arrange it, is brought to them: coffee, Cokes, sandwiches. If possible, they sleep on cots near the computer. But only for a few hours—then back to the console or the printouts. Their rumpled clothes, their unwashed and unshaven faces, and their uncombed hair all testify that they are oblivious to their bodies amd to the world in which they move. They exist, at least when so engaged, only through and for the computers. These are computer bums, compulsive programmers. They are an international phenomenon. (Weizenbaum, 1984a, p.116)

With the proliferation of microcomputers, the phenomenon is not only international, it is no longer confined to computer centers. Schools and homes are now the site for these consuming struggles between computer and programmer.

An important question is, "What is the role of the computer in this compulsive behavior?" It could be that the compulsive programmers and hard masters are those who in other generations might have been absorbed in cars, motorcycles, or amateur radio, and to the same extent. Or, it may be that computers actually promote compulsive behavior in those who would otherwise not show it, at least not in such an extreme form. Turkle sees it as a combination of the two, saying "the computer acts as a Rorschach, allowing the expression of what is already there. But it does more than allow the expression of personality. It is a constructive as well as a projective medium . . . it allows 'softs' . . . to operate in a domain of . . . the 'hards'" (Turkle, 1984, p. 108).

Weizenbaum's position may be the same, though he is less explicit in relating cause and effect. He describes the enormous risks the compulsive programmer will take in radically changing his program, particularly when time is short, in an attempt to discover the source of its problems. These hurried changes may undo weeks of work, since they are usually unrecorded and too numerous (and often illogical) to be remembered. Weizenbaum compares this frenzied risk taking to Dostoevski's description of compulsive gamblers who make huge bets on the last roulette turns before the casino closes, observing that "Dostoevski might as well have been describing a computer room" (Weizenbaum, 1984a, p. 122). The implication might be that programming is just another domain for those who otherwise would have become compulsive gamblers. However, the opportunities for compulsive programming, particularly for children, are more numerous than those for compulsive gambling (though many governments seem determined to make gambling equally accessible). Thus, we might conclude that Weizenbaum feels computers offer a persuasive, rather than a passive, environment for compulsive behavior.

Personality is an even more important component of most writing, where the greater flexibility of vocabulary and structure allow it to be seen more clearly. Dostoevski's passion for gambling can be seen through his writing in *The Gambler*, but would the availability of computers have turned him into a passionate programmer? More to the point, would a computer as word processor have allowed him to express his gambling passion even more strongly through the techniques of his writing style? Would he have experimented with wording, deleted large sections of text, and modified indiscriminately, all without saving the previous version on his disk, as he gambled to find the ultimate expression of his thoughts? We can only speculate, but the computer as a device to be "brought under control" is not only a challenge for the programmer, but also for the word processing writer, who specifies "a sequence of instructions to be executed by a computer" in order to solve a writing problem.

Those who teach the teaching of writing, such as Donald Graves (1983), stress the importance of the writer getting involved personally. Graves feel that "if the writer isn't getting into the piece, then you aren't teaching writing" (Green, 1984b, p. 28). His concern that technology is not being used to increase writer involvement is echoed by Frank Smith (1983), as both of them decry the use of computers to drill the particles of language without providing an opportunity for students to use language in real communications. If the use of word processing in writing instruction does indeed result in students writing more (though this usually means spending more time, not more words per hour), along with an increased ability to change their writing to more accurately reflect their thoughts, then this increased, more effective production should allow them to put more of their personality into their writing. Specifically, one might expect that student writers will be able to introduce more of their personality at an earlier age as the word processors allow them to ignore the mechanical aspects which would otherwise dominate their attention. Most people might assume that this effect of word processors, if it is true, would be good for student writers, but this may not always be the case, probably depending on the type of writing that is done. Certainly in the case of programming, computer scientists are greatly concerned that student programmers are freely expressing their personalities without acquiring any of the discipline which distinguishes the successful professional programmer. Similar concerns might eventually be expressed about the discipline of writing, in contrast to the current euphoria over increased productivity.

Work Habits

One way that all workers, including programmers and writers, express their personality and individual style is through their work habits. We may come to arrive at very similar results by way of extremely different paths. Morris (1985) comments on the variance in programmers' work habits in considering the possible large-scale use of artificial intelligence techniques in projects such as the Strategic Defense Initiative (SDI), sometimes known as Star Wars. He contends that the achievements of the AI world are based primarily on the work of "hackers," those compulsive programmers whose idiosyncratic work habits are strongly driven by the challenge of the seemingly unattainable (found in both AI and Star Wars). These work habits are generally contradictory to those of the Software Engineering (SE) approach, with its emphasis on reliability, maintainability, and documentation of products. It is in the prediction that SDI will involve the creation of 10 million lines of computer program, much of it AI-based, that the conflict takes on new dimensions. The size and importance of SDI demands that an SE approach be used, since the projection of a "reasonable" error rate of 3 errors per 1,000 lines of program leads to the presence of 30,000 errors in what is supposed to be a crucial defense system. Morris asserts that the AI hacker can submit to SE techniques such as "egoless programming" only "by trading his or her soul for money" (Morris, 1985, p. 161). (Note that Parnas [1985], who was more intimately involved with SDI, believes that SE techniques are inadequate for the task, regardless of the programmers involved.) If the availability of microcomputers for all students, and the growing infatuation with AI promises, leads to an even larger proportion of hacker programmers, the problem could be substantially more serious than Morris depicts.

At the other end of the sociability dimension, Greenbaum (1985) describes how one Swedish software company has been structured around the preferred lifestyles of the founding members. The changes apply not only to their offices in a restored Stockholm building, but to their biweekly dinners in members' homes, and the island cottage used for meetings and seminars. The atmosphere is emphatically convivial, but at least one member admits to working long hours at night to complete work which could not be done during the day in the friendly office.

But what of the computer's effect on the work habits of writers? Writers already vary greatly in the way they reach their writing goals. According to

Schwartz (1985), some writers are unable to stop revising, while Isaac Asimov never revises, writing faster than he can think of things to write. Similarly, some writers revise based on their own opinions, while others seek the opinion of others. And of course, they vary in their use of writing instruments, some writing in longhand (to retain 'the feel' of writing), others using typewriters (of varying capability), with still others using the full technological support of word processing. Arthur Haley is reported to have an unusual style of writing, each day producing a quota (perhaps 500 words) of final draft material, working from first to final draft all in the same day. When he began using word processing, his general work habits did not change, though he did double his daily output (the combined effect of word processing and open-heart surgery). Arthur Haley's work habits were obviously well entrenched by the time he adopted word processing, but this does not assure us that computers will have no effect on the work habits and writing styles of young writers. The effect could be liberating, through elimination of mechanical aspects, or confining, due to the devaluing of noncomputerized techniques, and will probably vary from person to person. At the moment, the evidence does not allow a clear view of the potential effects, but does indicate that the assumption that computers will have no effect is probably unwise.

PLANNING

Planning seems to be the component that separates the professionals from the amateurs, both in writing and in programming. Schwartz (1985) devotes over half of her book on interactive writing, writing with a word processor, to getting ready for writing. She provides justification in the form of statistics indicating that professional writers may spend as much as 85 percent of their time preparing to write, with most of the remainder spent on revision. This does not necessarily mean that all planning must be done before any writing can begin. Rather, planning may occur in the middle of writing, just as revising might be a part of planning.

Weizenbaum describes the professional programmer in much the same way. He stresses the lengthy preparations, writing, flow diagramming, diagnosing faults, and the documenting of the completed sections, with the actual sessions using the computer as relatively minor activities, possibly delegated to someone else. A similar emphasis can be seen in Yourdon's (1979) *Structured Walkthroughs*, a book entirely devoted to a peer group review process designed to improve the quality of computer programs. Walkthroughs can occur at any stage of product development so long as it is late enough for well-defined concepts to be discussed and early enough for improvements to be incorporated. The major stages where walkthroughs might take place are those of specification (defining the need), design (defining the solution), code (creating the program), and test (validating the solution). The planning of a writing project is most like the specification and design stages of program development, with the author defining the needs of the audience to be addressed and then designing the content and structure to meet these needs.

Though programming instructors usually stress the importance of planning, students rarely see the value of it, presumably because their programming problems are usually short, and ignore it as much as possible. Students are likely to create flowcharts (or equivalent diagrams) only if required, and then often after the program has been successfully completed. In cases where students actually do take the process of programming seriously, the results may take observers by surprise. Roger Casey, an OISE graduate student intent on collecting pilot data for a thesis project, presented programming problems to a small number of secondary school computer science students under different programming conditions, hoping to analyze the differences in results between conditions. Students were given the option of planning for a period of time or moving directly to the computer to create their program. Based on the results at one school, where one of the best students was unable to complete the problem from a standard programming text, he selected a simpler problem for use at a second school. However, in contrast to the first school, where the top student chose not to plan, students at the second school had been taught such an effective method of planning that they were able to create the correct program easily in their first attempt, completing two programming problems in the allotted time. This story may have two morals. The obvious one is that differences in programming techniques are of little importance when proper planning has been done. The second and less obvious moral may be that the successful use of planning techniques is much more likely to occur in a girls' school, which the second school was, because girls are often less fascinated with using the computer than are boys.

This anecdote leads to a consideration of the computer's role in the planning of writing. The planning of writing, including the jotting of notes, diagramming the links of story elements, and other informal or graphic techniques, is not as well suited to computer use as the writing and revision processes. Schwartz does refer to the possible use of a graphic input device (used to enter hand drawn material into the computer) to create preliminary jottings and branching diagrams, but the suggestion is unconvincing. At the moment, computers are much more likely to be used for planning only in the form of text, thus encouraging some forms of organization such as hierarchies and reorderings, while discouraging other alternatives, such as a nonlinear diagram. If this is the case, computers may serve more as an aid to incomplete planning, particularly for those who like to use computers, since most forms of planning and preparation can be seen as postponing the direct use of computers.

Summary

The use of computers seems to have a mixed effect on the planning process in writing and programming, partly dependent on the currently restricted availability of computers. Where access to computers is limited, whether in a writing or programming class, students are more likely to make use of planning time, provided they know how to plan effectively, than if access to computers is unlimited.

In some writing classes, it has been found that students told to plan for the first five minutes at the word processor simply begin with the first sentence of their writing, unless they have been given very specific directions on how to plan. In programming classes, the same is likely to be true, with elementary students, particularly those using LOGO in a discovery learning environment, more likely to be deficient in planning skills, trying out programming commands during their time on the computer.

WRITING

Although this phase of the writing or programming process should be the shortest, taking only one percent of the time of professional writers, it receives the most emphasis, particularly from students who enjoy creating products on the computer. Even though the lure of word processing is not as strong as the desire to control the computer through programming, students are reported to spend longer times writing and create longer products when they write using computers (Daiute, 1986). Part of this is no doubt due to the novelty of computer use and part is due to the ways in which computers facilitate the process, be it writing or programming. In the future, the novelty should decrease, but the facilitation should increase, possibly leaving the net effect at the same level.

At the moment, the facilitation effect of computers on programming is probably stronger than its effect on writing. The microcomputer has always been the "built-in" audience for the programmer, allowing the testing of the syntax of commands or the logic of the program at almost any time. This responsiveness of computers to programmers is increasing with the creation of more powerful programming tools, though they may not yet be widely available. An example of the new tool is the "smart editor," a programming environment which will not allow the user to write a program with a syntax error (or some other types of errors) in it. The editor prompts the programmer for the definitions of variables that are used and generally insists that the program be written in such a way that it can be processed without errors, other than those of logic or problem-solving technique.

The smart editors will certainly change the learning environment for both teachers and students. Current programming courses devote much time and effort toward the elimination of syntax errors, affecting the goals of students as well as the grading practices of teachers. A system that removes the concern for the details of program syntax from the learning process should allow more emphasis on the solution the student is trying to program. Some students never do reach the level of programming solutions to problems, but the ability to master syntax and other details is often enough to assure a passing grade. The smart editors can create problems for these students, as well as for teachers who will now have more difficulty in grading, having to deal with questions such as "what is elegance?" in program writing. If similar systems are developed for writing support, the same effect will be felt in writing, with questions such as "what is style?" becoming relevant at earlier grade levels.

Of course word processing has already affected the grading of written work by eliminating the handwriting factor, just as calculators have had an effect on how mathematics is graded. The problem for the teacher is a variation on the already familiar one of attempting to separate the message (or algorithm in programming) from the style (or elegance), a difficult task, particularly if the message (or algorithm) is considered wrong or incorrect. What the use of computers is doing is bringing this problem into sharper focus.

Bereiter (1985) has proposed a number of teaching activities that might help students to develop a more complex approach to writing, in the context of his discussion of the "learning paradox," how learners acquire more complex skills and strategies. Only the least promising of his suggestions, random access to strategic moves, seems to have any direct link to a computer implementation, but his analysis could provide a useful basis for developng future computerized writing aids.

Spelling Programs

Computer aids for writing, though enthusiastically predicted, are more difficult to come by because of the greater difficulty in determining what is an error in the more flexible writing environment. As an example, one might look at the possibility of spelling support for the writer. At the present time, spelling support is more likely to be available after a draft has been written, while the writer would usually prefer to have spelling assistance when writing the difficult word. In particular, elementary school students, following the rules of "school writing," are likely to drop any ideas that require the use of words with unknown spellings. However, assuming that the spelling assistance is available at the proper time, how can the program determine the word you are attempting to spell? In most cases, the program can suggest possibilities, usually those words in its vocabulary that differ from your tentative spelling by a small amount (typically one letter less, one letter more, one letter changed, or two letters transposed). Therefore, in order to get help from the spelling program, you have to have a pretty good idea of how the word is spelled (similar to what is needed in looking up the word in a dictionary).

What is often overlooked, however, is the probability that the spelling program will accept your spelling as correct even if it is wrong. That is, quite often the misspelling of one word ('from') results in the correct spelling of another word ('form'). An intriguing feature of spelling systems, similar to the logic systems of Godel's theorem (Hofstadter, 1979), is that the more powerful they are, the more likely they are to make mistakes of this type. That is, if a spelling program has a large vocabulary it is more likely to find that your misspelled word is in that vocabulary. Thus, we can choose between spelling programs which indicate more words as possible errors when they are in fact correct, or programs which accept larger numbers of words as correct when they are in fact misspelled. The tradeoff is inevitable, unless the spelling checker has an understanding of the meaning of the text.

Spelling programs may also introduce errors through increased sophistication of their techniques. One spelling program permitted both ACHIEVE and ACHEIVE as legal words. The first spelling was in its rather small vocabulary of 12,000 words, but the second was a result of techniques used to make the vocabulary appear larger. The program removed prefixes and suffixes from questionable words in order to find a match in the vocabulary list. When the suffix -IVE is removed from ACHEIVE, the result is ACHE, which was in the program's vocabulary.

This excursion into the idiosyncracies of spelling checking programs may have been enlightening, but one might ask what it has to do with the general use of computers to assist writers. One response is that it exemplifies the thought which Chris Hopper has often expressed, "The trouble with word processing is that you have to teach the students how to write." By this he means that word processing can clear away many of the mechanical problems for student writers, just as smart editors can clear away many details for programmers, but the result is that their lack of ability to write (or program) becomes even more obvious when it is not clouded by penmanship (or syntax errors). In the case of a spelling program, its paradox is that in order to make effective use of it the user needs to know how to spell, just as one needs to know how to write in order to make effective use of word processing.

The second feature which can be generalized from the use of spelling programs is that the use of computers to assist writing is likely to produce very "personal" effects. The size of the vocabulary is one example of the personal effect, with different users benefitting from different size vocabularies, though the effect is more subtle than that. It should be clear that "bigger is not necessarily better," for the word list from the largest unabridged dictionary would contain thousands of words we couldn't even recognize, much less use in our writing. What is needed, however, for the best personal assistance, is not a spelling program with our reading vocabulary, but our writing vocabulary, which is likely to be smaller. For example, I might use the word "prerequisite" with some frequency, but have probably never used the word "perquisite" (before this time), even though its meaning is clear to me. Therefore, in my personal spelling program, any use of the word "perquisite" should be flagged as a potential error (even though this time it is correct). McLean (1985) provides a description of a set of programs he has created to do exactly what has been identified here, allow students and other users to create and augment their own spelling programs. More examples of the personal effects of computers on writing will be given later in this chapter.

REVISING AND DEBUGGING

One could argue that revision and debugging are only necessary because of inadequate planning, that the works of Isaac Asimov and C. S. Lewis show that it is possible to write first drafts that don't require revision and programming can be done in the same way. This argument is not entirely true, but neither is it entirely false. That it has some truth can be seen not only in the work of extremely gifted authors (and composers), but in the relationship between the amount of planning done before writing (or programming) and the amount of revision (or debugging) which is later required. Planning does indeed reduce the demands for revision, and in the extreme, perfect planning should lead to the elimination of revisions. However, for a more revisionist argument one can look at the effect of the audience on the programming process. The programmer begins with a set of requirements (or needs) from the potential user and uses these to plan and create a working program. Some program design methods are aimed at more interaction with users to clarify their needs, but it is difficult to prevent users from changing their requirements once they have tried the first version of the program. As a result, one popular method of program development is called "prototyping," where the prototype created for user testing is a deliberately temporary program, designed to be totally replaced when user needs are more clearly seen. In some ways this is analogous to the needs assessment procedure described in Chapter 2. It can also be seen in the courseware development process used by the Province of Ontario, as described in Chapter 5.

The question of audience response is also crucial in writing, even though some authors create finished products without any external review, based entirely on their own perception of audience needs. This perception is more easily obtained by authors who write a series of similar works for a relatively constant audience. However, it is interesting to note that C. S. Lewis, noted for writing first drafts in publishable form, admitted in the third edition of *The Pilgrim's Regress* (Lewis, 1977) that "On re-reading this book ten years after I wrote it, I find its chief faults to be those which I myself least easily forgive in the books of other men: needless obscurity, and an uncharitable temper" (p. 9). His 12-page preface is an attempt to eliminate some of the obscurity, but he also notes that further clarification could be made. This admission implies that not only does he now see the obscurity more clearly, but he has also acquired a better ability to deal with it. Independent of these considerations, the important point for this discussion is that he realized the "reader's difficulties" ten years after the book was written, but these were not part of his "audience perceptions" when he was writing the book.

Weizenbaum (1984) described programmers, both compulsive and professional, as revising their programs on the basis of printouts, the image of their programs as written on paper. The advent of the microcomputer, along with increasing numbers of video terminals attached to larger computers, has drastically altered this form of revision. Although the written form of a computer program, the printout from the computer, often includes aids to debugging, such as a concordance of terms (usually called a "cross-reference" list), many young programmers prefer to "see" their program where it "really is," on the video display screen, rather than search for the faults in the printed version. The use of word processors may often be seen to have a similar effect.

The preference that some programmers have for viewing their programs on the screen seems strange in terms of the effectiveness of revision it is likely to produce. The microcomputer display is usually limited to 24 lines of program or less, with no support provided to show the referencing of variables in different parts of the program, or other aids often found in the printed form. Yet, a logical reason can be found for this preference, since in one sense, the version on the screen is the only "true" version of the program. When the program printout is created, it and the screen version are identical, although the paper version may contain additional information. But nonprofessional programmers are not in the habit of noting the changes they make to their programs (at least not all of them) on the printed version. As Weizenbaum noted, they are least likely to write down the most drastic changes they make at the end of their debugging session, thereby giving them little faith in the printout. What this says about their perception of printed information versus video displays in general is interesting, but the effect on their programming is bound to be negative if it leads to their ignoring potentially helpful information in the printed form. For both writers and programmers, such habits can lead then to a choice between an incomplete printed version of their program or writing and a partial view of the real program or document on the screen.

Computer systems have been, and are being developed to help bridge the gap between the screen and paper versions of both programs and writing. A common approach is that of allowing the user to "hide" parts of the program or text. That is, a smart editor may allow you to suppress the display of a section of your program, typically a part which is well defined and (probably) assumed to be correct, replacing it with a single title or summary of the part that is hidden. The smart editor might also permit you to suppress all of the lower detail of your program, displaying only the higher level components, the titles of the various parts contained in the program. Similarly, some text handling programs permit like operations, displaying the major headings, the full text, or some variation in between in response to the user's choice. In general, these features tend to work better for handling programs, since the structure of programs is more restricted than that of text and more easily anticipated by the tool designer.

One of the most fascinating features of word processing (and smart editors) is the ability to cut and paste, to move a section of text, of almost any size, from one part of the document to another. Students who have access to word processing often spend a considerable amount of time making these kinds of moves, but observations by their teachers and others indicate that they usually conclude the exercise by putting the text back in its original order. The common experience is that students rarely make revisions to their texts which require this kind of move, though they master the mechanics of the transfer and enjoy watching it happen on their screens, like the display of an academic video game. Students' actual revisions are much more likely to be in close proximity to the blinking cursor that indicates their current entry point for text, most frequently adding additional text, or making changes to the most recent word, or perhaps to the last sentence (Diaute, 1986). The conclusion for this function is the same as for the others, in order to make use of the word processor's extensive capabilities for revision, one must know how to revise.

If successful revision requires knowing how to revise, and knowing how does not come from the computer, where does the student get this information? Most programmers are aware of the following type of incident: A fellow programmer asks for help in discovering an error, begins to describe what the program is supposed to do, then stops when the error becomes obvious (to the teller, not necessarily to the hearer). This phenomenon can happen even when the hearer is not familiar with the programming language being used (it might even work when the problem is told to stuffed animals, but this is only conjecture). The important point is that obtaining feedback from others, either individually or in groups, can help to solve your programming or writing problem in one of two ways: through their opinions based on their different perspective, or through your new perspective that comes from hearing yourself describe the problem.

Based on the benefits of peer review, some formalized procedures have emerged to provide these in a systematic way. As mentioned above, the structured walkthrough (Yourdon, 1979) can be used not only for planning and test phases, but can also be particularly effective in the revision of programs. However, in order to be effective, a trusting, nonjudgmental, supportive environment must be created and maintained. As a result, Yourdon devotes considerable attention to these aspects, not only the psychology of walkthroughs, but also the importance of their being separate from the management function. The principles he puts forward might also apply to similar forms of peer review used in writing. For example, Knapp (1986) describes a six-step procedure for a group critiquing process, to be used as a demonstration for students who can then meet in small editing groups to carry out critiques on each other's writing. Graves puts forward "writing conferences" between teacher and student, a structured setting for specific feedback on a piece of writing, providing not only suggestions for immediate improvement, but also setting the tone for any peer review that might later take place (Green, 1984b; Graves, 1983).

Although formal structures are important in guaranteeing a minimum level of feedback for programmers and writers, the informal settings are often even more effective. Weinberg (1971), made an early plea for the concept of "egoless programming," actively seeking the suggestions of others as to how your program might be improved. He also provided examples of informal feedback settings in his discussion of what he called "programming as a social activity." Perhaps the best example is that of the role of the vending machines in a large university computing center. When two students complained about the noise level around the machines, located in a common work space next to the programming consulting service, the center manager had them moved to a remote spot, based on his brief observation of the revelry about them. A week later the manager had a more organized complaint about the lack of consulting service, which was suddenly overwhelmed with clients. Two weeks of investigation failed to reveal the cause until a graduate student in sociology was commissioned to interview those in line. Weinberg's description of how the vending machine functioned is that "Since most of the student problems were similar, the chances were very high that he could find someone who knew what was wrong with his program right there at the vending machines" (p. 50). Although informal mechanisms may sometimes be more efficient, they are not as appealing to the management point of view. The manager's response to the vending machine explanation was disbelief and an increase in the number of consultants. However, the consulting service was soon abandoned entirely, since few people could be found who were willing to answer the generally low-level questions. In some environments, only formal structures seem valid.

Discovery Learning

Papert places great emphasis on the debugging process as a powerful mechanism for discovery learning. His contention is that students will persevere to discover the information they require in order to achieve their goal of a particular LOGO program. He provides a hypothetical conversation to illustrate this process, in which two children use the LOGO turtle to draw a flower. He asserts that "These and other experiments can happen every day—and they do" (Papert, 1980b, p. 76). As the hypothetical students attempt to draw petals, they create something resembling a fish, after which, Papert has them say, "We could try some more numbers" and "Or we could try some mathematics" (p. 82). He then has them go on to discussions of the "Total Turtle Trip" until they create the desired shape. Such conversations undoubtedly do happen and it would be comforting to believe that they were a regular occurrence, but the results from Carmichael et al. (1985) indicate that other types of results are even more frequent.

The researchers in the Queen's study, in their two years of observation, reported not only successes, but also failures, as well as partial successes. One feature frequently observed was a difference between the intention of the child and the final result eventually obtained through an interaction with LOGO on the computers. The change in goal was often influenced by students' "favorite numbers." One example was that of a boy who wanted to draw a square as part of a house, but wound up with a crooked wall through the use of 43 degree angles. Since 43 was his favorite number, the crooked wall was acceptable to him.

Another example was that of two girls who wanted to move the turtle to a position from which it could make a square for the top of a house, but they made two false starts and then decided to draw lines inside their original square. Other examples deal with students who had no goal at all, but liked to use large numbers to see what would happen.

The researchers also comment that the technology allows students "not to be reflective" about some things. For example, a boy had drawn a "planet" as a circle that went around 360 degrees twice. When asked why, he answered that it was possible to draw it by going around only once, but that it didn't matter. Another boy is described as working without hesitation on his program. "He doesn't waste any time deliberating about whether or not his next move is right" (p. 276). At the same time, it is interesting that a teacher comments, "They are learning to be precise, to be accurate and the importance of specific consequences" (p. 278).

One consequence of these two features is that the students' skills did not necessarily transfer to other situations, including a test of LOGO skills. Students complained that tasks were confusing, or difficult to do without a computer. One intermediate level student put it in interesting language, "now you ask us to think with paper. You have to prepare us for paper and pencil" (p. 270). This student's teacher, just a few months before, had said, "I believe LOGO helps shape the way a person thinks. It teaches logical thinking, analysis, the ability to learn through deduction" (p. 280). It may be that these skills are more apparent than real.

These disappointing results may have come about because the students were not engaged in thoughtful experimentation, the "mindfulness" described by Salomon (1986), but were using what would more accurately be called trial and error, a process maximizing action at the expense of thoughtfulness. Carmichael et al. describe two grade three students' difficult struggle to create a square, including many false trials, then add one student's statement that "they had done the same thing yesterday" (p. 276), an indication that their previous day's work may not have had a foundation in "thoughtful" discovery learning. One frequent aspect of trial and error learning is called superstitious behavior, the retention of stereotyped, but irrelevant behavior. In practical terms, if you try a long sequence of LOGO commands to accomplish your goal (with some of them irrelevant) and *you do not know which of them are relevant*, your next try is likely to involve the same long sequence. This may be why the researchers observe that many grade one students "showed a preference for certain numbers" (p. 313). Three students always used RT 45 as the answer, no matter what the question, while others made extensive use of 12s, as many as 20 to 30 in a row. One girl showed a definite preference for small numbers, moving the turtle a total of 40 units in small increments in answer to an estimation question. She correctly answered "bigger" when asked about the relative size of the next interval, but then began a series of small increments for the answer to the next question. The effects of LOGO, discovery learning, and trial and error learning on students will be discussed more fully in Chapter 7, but it does seem clear that the debugging process does not necessarily lead to a deep understanding of the resulting program. With this in mind, it would be wise to approach the use of word processing in writing carefully, lest the effects of trial and error begin to appear in student writing.

Program Maintenance

An issue of program revision which is growing in importance, though less critical in writing, is that of program maintenance. That is, the effort required to keep completed programs functioning properly and up-to-date has become an enormous problem as the inventory of programs increases. It is estimated by James Martin that over $20 billion is being spent annually on maintaining programs written in COBOL, the programming language used in most data processing operations (Carlyle, 1985). Maintenance costs are estimated to be about 60 percent of total data processing budgets and from 50 percent to 75 percent of total program cost. Although some are looking toward artificial intelligence techniques to save the old programs, the root cause lies in the lack of coherence and structure in the original programs and the weaknesses introduced by careless debugging strategies. The problem is particularly difficult to correct since the high costs of maintenance act to reduce the funds available for new programs, making it less likely that the new programs will be properly developed and documented.

POSSIBLE COGNITIVE BENEFITS OF PROGRAMMING

Although the vocational benefits of learning programming are attractive to many, both through direct entry to the career of programmer, or as a supplement to other career skills, the less direct benefit of transfer to other cognitive skills is probably the most attractive lure for most educators. It is this hope that brings programming out of the technical curriculum and into the academic mainstream, including the elementary school tributaries. Although Papert's descriptions of the potential benefits of LOGO have fueled these expectations, he prefers not to see his writings as "promises" and views attempts to evaluate attainment of these goals as succumbing to "technocentrism" (Papert, 1987). His preference seems to be "that he would like [LOGO] to be judged as an instrument for teaching in the same way as how teachers decide what poetry to teach or what textbooks to use. He would leave it to the professionalism of teachers to make judgments of whether people are learning" (Solomon, 1986, p. 130).

The most extensive review of possible cognitive benefits to be derived from learning computer programming is by Pea and Kurland (1984). They examine two polar opposite beliefs relating to the possible benefits from learning programming, neither of which they feel is acceptable. One views the learning of programming as the learning of autonomous facts about a programming language and nothing more, while the other sees it as affecting everything about a student. The latter view, similar to previously held assumptions about the teaching of logic and Latin, among others, sees programming as promoting powerfully general cognitive skills at a high level, such as planning and problem-solving skills (Galanter, 1984).

Pea and Kurland begin by reviewing the claims that have been made about learning to program, beginning with the AI claims that it helps us to understand our thinking, proceeding through phrases such as "mathematical rigor," "heuristics," debugging as "constructive and plannable," and "problem solving." Their review indicates that the instructional environment generally produces rather poor results, with little understanding being shown by those students who claim to be able to program.

The core of Pea and Kurland's analysis has to do with their consideration of what constitutes skilled programming. They propose four levels of expertise, with most students functioning as program users and code generators, while the most likely transfer for cognitive skills is likely to occur at the highest level of software developer, or possibly at the next lower level of program generator. Although they go on to explore cognitive constraints to programming and the evidence for cognitive benefits, their conclusions are most strongly influenced by the magnitude of the experience gap between a student who may spend 30 to 50 hours programming and a programmer with only three years' experience who will have as many as 5,000 hours of programming. This leads them to suggest that the projected goals for programming instruction should be much more modest than has been the case.

Salomon and Perkins (1986) expand on the analysis of Pea and Kurland, putting their interpretation in terms of what they call the "low road" and "high road" transfer effects. They see low road transfer, which occurs through extended practice, as possibly being a factor when students acquire a great deal of varied programming experience, leading to a collection of skills which have become automatic without mindful effort. High road transfer, on the other hand, is seen as requiring mindful abstraction and could occur if a novice programmer deliberately analyzed the programming process in an attempt to apply it to other environments, such as general problem solving.

Salomon and Perkins feel that the high road, obviously more effective when used, is a possible avenue of cognitive transfer for programming, finding support for this belief in the results of Linn (1985). She found that "exemplary" programming classes (more experienced teachers, emphasis on design, etc.) not only led to markedly higher achievement, but that the correlation between programming achievement and general aptitude was lower in the exemplary classes. That is, not only did students learn more, but the achievement differences between the medium and high ability students were smaller in the exemplary classes. Salomon and Perkins assert that these differences can be attributed to a greater emphasis on "mindfulness" in the exemplary classes, leading to more effective use of the programming experience. In this way they complement the observations of Pea and Kurland regarding the experience difference between novice and professional programmers.

One path to increasing the programming experience of students, assuming that this is a desirable goal, is to consider the wider definition of programming as proposed earlier in this chapter (Ragsdale & McKelvey, 1985). Using a wider definition, many other computer application activities could be included, not only writing but also the use of spread sheet programs, editors, data bases, music composing programs, etc. One way of directing the focus of these activities would be to consider the prerequisites of successful programming, but as Pea and Kurland have recounted, this is not a simple task. Their review of mathematical ability, analogical reasoning, procedural thinking, etc. finds little evidence to substantiate the links which have been hypothesized between them and programming ability.

One element of a widened definition of programming might be increased emphasis on the programming aspects of noncomputer activities. Burns (1980) suggests a number of activities to prepare children in grades four through eight to get ready for computers. Since some of the tasks are directly related to programming, essentially programming without a computer, the probability of transfer to noncomputer tasks, as well as programming, should be enhanced. This approach also facilitates the extension of programming over age levels and activities. Robert Taylor (1982) has also suggested an approach to programming without a computer, based on an iconic language, FPL (First Programming Language). Although the decreasing price of computers might seem to make these activities irrelevant, the lack of support in the programming environments of the cheaper microcomputers gives the suggestion more merit.

Group Writing

One possible approach to the integration of both programming and writing is through group writing projects (McKelvey, 1984). Beginning at approximately the grade-three level (different children will be able to handle this activity at different ages), a group writing project is a learning experience that can involve several children working together to create a written product. Group writing projects are applicable to creative writing as well as to reports and essays. The optimal number of children in a group is four to six; an even number permits a dyadic subgroup formation later in the process that avoids groupings in which one child must work alone.

It should be emphasized that this activity, which does not require the use of computers, but can benefit substantially from them, can provide a natural link into programming activities because it contains many of the essential ingredients. These include planning, structuring ideas, peer review, sharing tasks, and modifying a product in order to improve it, most of the processes discussed in the earlier parts of this chapter. For a more complete description of this approach, see Ragsdale and McKelvey (1985).

Summary

Programming is often seen as an attractive activity for young students, since it appears to be a way of increasing cognitive skills, such as planning and problem solving, without teaching them. The actual experience has been more sobering. Not only do most students need to be taught these skills before they will (possibly) learn them, transfer to other contexts is also not automatic. Just as students in science classes seem unable to use the skills they mastered in mathematics, so students may solve problems in one context but not in another.

PERSONAL EFFECTS OF WORD PROCESSING

In addition to the links between programming and writing we must be concerned with the effects of electronic tools on our writing skills. Some very definite effects of electronic mail seem to be present, particularly in the users' choice of "flaming" language (Kiesler, Siegel, & McGuire, 1984), though it is possible that some effects are a function of familiarity (or lack of it) with the system and may be reduced over time. It is probable, however, as we become more dependent on the "writing helps" built into our word processors, these tools will have a very personal impact on our writing skills and styles.

In the past, when people have said, apologetically, "I only use the computer for word processing," my usual response has been, "You have already found out what it took me almost twenty years to learn, that computers are great for word processing." Recently, however, I have begun to reconsider the strength of my endorsement, based on my own use of writing with and without word processing. These observations are illustrative of some of the conclusions proposed earlier in this chapter. In order to make use of the functions of word processors, one has to know how to do the functions, such as planning, writing, and revising; and the effects of using word processing are likely to be very personal, dependent on the relative strengths and needs of the person using it.

The first draft of this book, a relatively short summary of about 25,000 words, was put together using a video display terminal which was linked to a large mini-computer system. Much of the material was gathered from previously written computer files and "pasted" together electronically to create a description of what the 11 proposed chapters might contain. Skills of electronic document construction had become well developed over more than a decade of computerized text processing, so this collecting and the writing of some new material went quite rapidly, being completed, on a part-time basis, in about two months.

The second draft was done under very different conditions. Agreement from the publishers came just before the beginning of a one-year study leave, during which full-time study and writing could be accomplished. The original intent was that this draft would be done on a microcomputer word processing system, while the author gazed contentedly at the Swiss Alps. The latter part of this intention was carried out, but the acquisition of the word processor did not, perhaps fortunately, take place. The logical reason for this serendipity was that the few months before the reaching of the Swiss writing location involved enough travel to make the carrying of even a microcomputer a potential "harmful effect," both for the carrier and the computer. As a result, perhaps as a benefit of uncareful planning, the second draft was written using a borrowed portable typewriter of the European variety, having the 'z' and 'y' keys reversed from their normal North American locations.

Advantages

This well-used little portable typewriter, not particularly "user friendly," proved to have unforseen advantages for me, but before these are described, it would be appropriate to review the positive aspects of computerized text processing. One of these features was amply demonstrated in the creation of the first draft, with a multitude of previously written paragraphs being retrieved from earlier documents and used again in this new context. This is, of course, not a new phenomenon for paragraphs to be reused. Even C. S. Lewis, known for creating a finished version in the first draft, is reported to have used paragraphs from his formal writing in the letters he composed. (A word processor could have saved the time of copying the text by hand.)

Text processing also greatly simplified the revisions which were done to the first draft, many of them being bridging material to link the previously written material, but some new sections were also written and revised. As a part of the revision process, the entire text was checked by a spelling program, and the flagged words were either verified as being correct (and added to my personal spelling dictionary for the program to use in the future) or corrected. The revision capabilities of the computer were also used on this and other occasions to improve some characteristics of style, such as locating all the uses of the word "there" in order to reduce the use of the passive verb form.

Finally, the computer system allowed the creation of a physically beautiful printed copy, with the laser printer and text formatting programs combining to create text with different size characters (for headings, etc.), different type fonts, including *italic* and **bold** characters, and visually perfect proportional spacing to create straight margins on both sides of the pages.

Disadvantages

However, numerous as these advantages were (and not all of them are listed), the creating of the second draft not only revealed some interesting advantages of not using word processing, but also seemed to indicate that what had appeared to be advantages of word processing in creating the first draft might have some negative consequences as well. For example, this was not the first time that my old documents had been used as a source of material for a new document. As a result, when several of these old documents were used in different places in the draft, some of the same passages of text popped up in more than one place, having already seen repeated service in previous writings. The electronic paste job also led to severe discontinuities of context, since the pieces used to make up a particular chapter might have come from earlier documents intended for very different audiences, based on very different assumptions, answering different questions, or a combination of these. Needless to say, the spelling program had also left some errors in place, such as 'from' being spelled 'form' and words like 'beyong' which were added after the last spelling check was made. It would be useful for spelling checkers to also indicate repetitions of words, but they rarely do, hence 'of of' also appeared in the first draft. Finally, the actual appearance of the draft has to be a confirmation of Grave's concern, "It comes out of the printer with such a nice layout that it may look better than its content really is" (Green, 1984b, p. 21).

All in all, the first draft left a great deal to be desired, in spite of the kind comments from the reviewers (who presumably made allowances for first drafts). The relevant question now has to do with the ways in which the use of a typewriter, not word processing, helped me in correcting these deficiencies in the first draft. Before getting into the answer, it should be emphasized that the following will not be a description of the benefits that everyone can expect to reap from *not* using word processing. It may not even be a list of consistent benefits for my own nonuse of word processing. It is, instead a list of what seemed to be my own personal benefits of not using word processing on this particular occasion.

Planning

The first benefit was in the form of better planning. As a computer enthusiast of long standing (or perhaps hunching), the lure of the keyboard and flashing cursor is still a strong attraction for me. Planning is usually limited to pausing a few moments, while the terminal warms up, with fingers on the keys, thinking about what it is that needs to be inflicted on unsuspecting readers. In other words, the use of computers is, in my personal case, a deterrent to the planning process. The typewriter which sat poised, waiting to begin the second draft, was not overtly hostile, but it was sufficiently unattractive that a full six months of study leave had elapsed before any part of the second draft was typed. During that period, time was spent on reading and underlining, outlining, discussing, giving a few talks, and a small amount of writing. The writing was of papers related to the topics of the book, but not actual content for the book. The payoff from this activity came when the first four weeks of January saw the production of more than 200 pages, or about 50,000 words of mainly new text, compared to the 25-page first draft of a paper, which had taken two weeks to produce in November.

Revision

Planning is to some extent a factor that can be traded off against revision, and one could argue that the revision capabilities of word processors more than compensate for shortcomings in the planning stage. This may be true for some people, it may even be true in general, but it is not true in my own personal experience. At least two aspects of word processing militate against my doing the depth of revision for which my first draft so plaintively cried. The first factor is similar to the conflict between the screen display and the printed copy, as described earlier in this chapter. Just as the programmer's listing is a true copy of the program only until changes are made, so the writer's copy quickly loses its resemblance to the version being modified in the computer. This change increases the memory load for the writer, since the printed memory aid is no longer reliable, and for me, tends to limit the length of my revision sessions. Of course, it is possible to print out a new copy when the memory strain becomes unbearable, but this means a significant delay for most microcomputer users, and when I am working at home on a video display terminal and the printer is at work, the delay is even more substantial.

Another alternative to the paper copy being updated is to scroll the text backward and forward on the screen, refreshing your memory as to what the text now says. Although some programs permit the user to view two or more different parts of the document being created, through the use of multiple "windows" in the display, it is rare that one can change the text in one window while viewing either a different part of the document or an outline of it in another window. A user is likely to want this capability if, for example, the conclusion of the article should parallel the construction of the introduction. This task is more easily accomplished if one can view them side by side while creating the second part, but most video screens are severely limited in what they can display from two pages, even if the programs have been designed to allow multiple views.

When using a typewriter, whatever its failings, the preceding is no problem at all. Whatever has come out of the typewriter is the "real" version, no other modified versions exist, and all the pages of that true version are available to be spread out on the table as needed. It may seem like an obvious and relatively small point, but it can be important in writing and revising, depending on the personal needs of the writer.

Important as the preceding points are for me, they still do not get to the most important feature in my revision process of proceeding from first draft to second. Again, this is a very personal effect, but given the presence of the first draft on a word processor, my response would have been to "work around" that draft, leaving as much of it as possible in its original form, doing most of the revision in the form of additions, with only minor changes made to the existing text. What this means is, though word processors offer extremely powerful tools for revision, they are effective only if you know how to use them to make revisions, and my own personal experience has been that they can inhibit the extent of my revisions. This inhibiting comes not only through the conflict between the paper copy and the screen display, as mentioned earlier, but through a desire to preserve the effort which went into creating the first draft. Thus, when faced with a defective sentence, my first and strongest response is to look for the smallest possible wording change to bring it back to health. The same is true for paragraphs or sections, a logical extension perhaps, of the notion that word processing can save effort through the avoidance of retyping.

It was tempting to preserve some of the pages from the first draft, inserting them in between pages of new material, since the existing paragraphs contained the desired ideas for that section of the text. It was important, however, in order to get the maximum revision benefit out of my style of revising, to adopt a procedure of reading each paragraph and considering possible revisions immediately before retyping, so that potential improvements, no matter how slight, would not be rejected as insufficient to justify retyping. Initially, most paragraphs were retyped with little change, but as the days wore on, the strategy began to pay off, with changes becoming more frequent and more extensive. From this, I might conclude that computers may be better at *helping* me to revise, but typewriters are better at *teaching* me to revise.

One could look at my experiences as an informal needs assessment, helping me to define my ideal word processing system (or as an evaluation of the writing instruction I received while in school). For example, while preparing to do the second draft, I created a one-page outline of each chapter. These detailed outlines were not only useful in helping to locate such things as repetitions in the text, but also provided an opportunity to compare the organization as seen by a reader with that seen by the writer. I have no illusions that AI research is going to provide an outlining system for general text, but a system which helped the reader to create outlines from text would be useful not only for feedback to writers, but also in applications such as creating personal filing systems.

Once again, it must be stressed that the preceding are not meant to be general conclusions about the use of word processors, but rather a personal view of my own experience. It would be unwise, on the basis of these results, to conclude that others should avoid the use of word processors, or even that I should avoid the use of word processors. However, it is reassuring to find some similarity in the experience of "A prize-winning nonfiction writer, for example, has found that he cannot use a word processor because the electronic recopying capacity takes over a step that he considers essential to his writing process. He identifies problems in a piece as he retypes it" (Daiute, 1985, p. 39). It may be that this experience has taught me enough about how I need to write that word processing will now be much more effective for me, but this remains to be seen.

It should also be pointed out that other users may see the relative advantages and disadvantages of word processing as being completely different from those listed above. One user told me that he saw word processing as interfering with his concentration, particularly when he created a first draft. Whenever he paused it was as though the cursor, blinking at the end of the previous sentence, was inviting him to "come back" and consider revisions to what had already been written. Another user, told of this problem, said that she found clearing the screen display to be helpful whenever she felt the urge to review was distracting. Schwartz (1985) suggests "invisible writing" as a means of encouraging the free flow of thought. To write invisibly, one can adjust the screen display to be too dim or distorted to read, then type ideas freely. The same technique can be used with typing or handwriting by using either a nonfunctioning pen, or "stencil typing" on a blank sheet backed with carbon paper and a second sheet.

More widely publicized in *Time* magazine are the personal reactions of William F. Buckley to the use of word processing. Since first being introduced to electronic writing in the winter of 1982, he has accumulated at least eight word processors for use in his various world locations (Murphy, 1985). His typing speed of 110 words per minute has helped him in producing a 7,500 word draft in only two hours, using a portable computer while on a yacht in the Pacific (an average of over 60 words per minute for completion of the draft). His speed of writing, including a book done in five weeks, makes his experience unlike that of most people who have read about his reactions. Although he feels that "it's a lot of twaddle that using a word processor affects the quality of writing for the worse" (p. 98), his personal effects of word processing are unlikely to be true for all the readers of *Time*.

This variety of effects arising out of the use of word processing, that one writer's tool is another's distractor, leads to some important questions. An early one has to do with the experience of children; do they have similarly personal and individual responses to the use of word processing? Until it has been shown that children respond uniformly to word processing, we will have to assume (and probably believe) that they react differently. If this is the case, what are the major implications for the use of word processing in classrooms? The most obvious first step is to inform teachers and students that word processing is not necessarily uniformly beneficial for all users in all writing contexts. At least one study has shown that the benefits of various features of an editing program depended on the characteristics of the student (Bryson, Lindsay, Joram, & Woodruff, 1986). A second step might be to collect and distribute evidence on the kinds of students who seem to benefit from word processing, or manual methods, in a variety of contexts. This would be in harmony with the suggestion that techniques which appear to help some student writers should not be applied automatically to all writers (Hayes & Flower, 1986). The third step, and the most important in maintaining a needs assessment orientation to the use of computers in education, is that teachers must constantly be monitoring their students for new instances of benefits or harmful effects derived from the use of word processing (for more information, see the section on the "teacher as researcher" in Chapter 10). In this way we can escape the "summative trap," restricting our options to a choice between typewriters and word processing, for example, and adapt a more useful formative stance, selecting the appropriate mix of handwriting, typing, word processing, etc., that is most effective in meeting the needs of each individual. Implementing word processing or programming, independent of the needs of students, is unlikely to lead to desirable long-term results.

7   *Student Role*

INTRODUCTION

The arguments for the use of computers in education are firmly rooted in explicit and implied benefits for students, but the role that students will play in actually acquiring these benefits is often less clear. One reason for this lack of clarity is that proponents of computer use in schools may agree on particular applications, but have very different reasons for doing so, based on very different perceptions of student strengths and needs. The problem is basically one of philosophy of education, not an unusual problem, but one that is more easily seen when the foundation of assumptions leads to obviously different methods. Because computers can take so many different forms through different applications, the disagreements among computer proponents often generate more heat than disagreements over whether computers should be used in schools at all.

Types of Students

Although any discussion of educational goals, methods, techniques, etc., must be linked to a philosophy of education, the purpose of this chapter (or this book) is not to delineate one or more educational philosophies. Government educational agencies, most school boards, and many schools have official statements of their educational philosophies, and most individuals have definite (though often incomplete) philosophies of their own. The purpose of this chapter is to consider some aspects of students, what they are, what they should or might become, and the ways in which they might move from one condition to another, and how these aspects of students affect, and are affected by, various types of computer applications. The consideration will obviously not be in terms of all possible types of students, but will focus on four different kinds of student needs to which computers might be applied.

One type is the "empty student," those who have need for certain skills, information, and knowledge, but have little idea about what they need to know and/or how it might be acquired. More directed in their efforts are the "searching students," who need an environment in which they can carry out their learning, but require less direction and/or motivation to guide this process. Another type is the "creative student," whose need is for the tools which facilitate creative work, not the foundational skills and knowledge which underlie that work. Finally, the "social students" need interaction with their peers and the world at large in order to solidify their learning, deepen their understanding, and further develop their creative abilities.

The preceding "types" are not meant to be exhaustive, identifying all ways in which students differ. Nor is it intended that they be categories which are mutually exclusive, with each student having the characteristics of only one type. On the contrary, it is expected that most students will possess attributes of all four types (and other, unmentioned types), and that the types are only four convenient ways of discussing the differences among students in their uses of computers. However, in these definitions we can see examples of computer applications in which students are assumed to be "empty," "searching," etc.

The domain of *computer literacy* is one in which a variety of possible applications of computers, plus the study of computers and their effects, are viewed in different ways by people who have different perceptions of student needs and strengths. As noted in Chapter 1, competing definitions have rendered the term "computer literacy" almost meaningless. Some proponents of computer literacy emphasize the need to provide students with a complete set of computer skills, information on how they are used, and knowledge of their effects. Others urge a less structured approach, allowing students to learn about computers through exploring their capabilities and limitations, often in the form of computer programming. Those who value the use of computers as tools would have students learn about them while using them to create materials of their own, through writing, drawing, or composing music. Finally, an emphasis on computers as communications media leads to the stressing of applications such as electronic mail, computer conferencing, or the ubiquitous "bulletin boards" which allow students to become familiar with computer functions while (or through) exchanging information with other students (and adults).

As stated in Chapter 1, the intent of this book does not include either defining computer literacy, nor providing a proposed program of computer literacy instruction. The reader is encouraged to create a personal definition or program of computer literacy, however, with this chapter providing some suggestions as to how the student's perspective might influence this creation.

EMPTY STUDENTS

O'Shea and Self (1983) begin their history of computers in education discussion with an excerpt from Paul Davies' *The Hydraulic Theory of Education*. The essence of the theory is that knowledge is a kind of liquid which is stored in large vessels (teachers) and teaching is the process of transferring this liquid from the large vessels to the smaller vessels (students) until they are filled. Davies describes the computer as a device which will inundate the students with a flood of knowledge, completely filling up all the crevices in their brains.

Several authors have used "model teachers" created by Charles Dickens. Osborne (1983) and Scheffler (1986) used Mr. Gradgrind, who not only valued facts, but seemed to value them even more if they were separated from reality. Osborne sees history teaching as often following this model as illustrated by an incident involving Sissy Jupe. Cecilia Jupe's father worked with horses, but his calling was much too menial for Mr. Gradgrind to allow it to be discussed. His rejection of the facts of Mr. Jupe's occupation led to Sissy Jupe being afraid to offer a definition of a horse. In Mr. Gradgrind's mind, Sissy Jupe passed from complete ignorance about horses to "knowing what a horse is" by virtue of hearing a boy reciting a number of descriptive (and detailed) facts about horses. However, quite the reverse was found by Nicholas Nickleby, through the preferences of Mr. Squeers, who believed that when a boy knew the definition of "clean" and "window," his education was best further advanced by going out and cleaning windows (Neatby, 1953).

Whether the emphasis is on theoretical, descriptive, or practical facts, it is true that the systematic delivery of instruction, of which Computer-Assisted Instruction (CAI) is one example, has often focussed on stuffing students full of facts. One reason for the attractiveness of facts is the concern with accountability, knowing to what extent the students are actually learning what is being taught. When the content is factual, assessing the degree of learning is much simplified. Little wonder, as noted in O'Shea and Self (1983), that the word education is alleged to be derived from *educare*, a Latin term meaning "to cram, or stuff full."

It should not be concluded from the preceding that the use of direct instruction, the delivery of content to the learner in a straightforward manner, is necessarily unproductive. In a number of contexts, particularly when the learner has made a commitment to mastering the material, this form of instruction is quite effective and efficient. This type of CAI is probably most useful for well-motivated learners who do not know enough about the subject matter to organize it themselves and want to be kept informed as to their progress and mastery of the material. Of course, implicit in this description is the assumption that the subject matter is well-defined.

Motivation

The question of motivation is often central to this variety of CAI, as it is to most forms of direct instruction, devoid of game formats, or other types of entertaining activities. Skinner (1984) has steadfastly maintained that success in learning is the most effective form of motivation; with it no other reward is needed, while without learning, any reward is misplaced. Morgan's (1984) review of intrinsic (contained as part of the task) motivation seems to lend support to this view, indicating that although the recipient's view of the reward is a crucial determinant, when a reward is seen as being given for merely participating in an activity, motivation to continue taking part in the activity declines. On the other hand, if the reward is seen as being given for high performance in some activity, then motivation to continue in the activity increases. Put in more practical terms, if students see themselves as being rewarded for spending a certain amount of time studying mathematics, perhaps through an interesting display of pictures on the computer screen, they are less likely to be motivated to study mathematics in the future. In the other direction, if they see their rewards as based on their achievement in mathematics, they will be more likely to be motivated to do more mathematics in the future. The key point is that the recipient's view of the reward (whether it is for participation or high achievement) is crucial, not the intent of the courseware designer or teacher. Thus it is possible that what appears as exactly the same form of reward to the teacher or courseware designer might be motivating in some circumstances and not in others. This kind of ambiguity is less likely to occur in the kinds of situations Skinner proposes, since he would limit the rewards to the act of informing students that they are correct in their answers. It also seems intuitively correct that being informed of the correctness of answers would be more of a motivating reward for those who have a strong commitment to learning the material.

Those who predict the widespread use of computers as effective teaching tools, based on the success of "empty student" CAI, are likely to be disappointed in the results that are actually achieved as computers, particularly computers used for CAI, become more numerous. That is, it may be that the current capability for computers to motivate students (or at least some students) is misleading us into believing that delivery of content via computer is an effective application of computers even when the content is poorly presented. It is more likely that the quality of content presentation will have to be improved to maintain motivation.

Information Retrieval

Unfortunately, the enthusiasm based on what may be the novelty effect of computers is not limited to CAI applications, but spills over into other applications as well. From this point of view, the most appropriate application for the empty student is computer access to "huge data banks of information." Stonier puts forward the view that

The high motivational state induced in children working with good educational software coupled with the emergence of a global network of databases which allow the child access to information with unprecedented ease, must have an impact on the understanding the children develop of the world they live in, and for that matter, on their understanding of themselves. (Stonier, 1984, p. 253)

In addition to his assumption about the high motivational state induced by good courseware, the key phrase in this statement is the "access to information with unprecedented ease."

The claims that the information revolution will drastically alter our very existence have been made so often that they are generally accepted as being true, with some notable exceptions (Roszak, 1986; Winner, 1986). What is usually not made clear is how an encyclopedia stored on a magnetic or optical disk becomes so much more useful than the same information in book form. Similarly, it remains to be shown that a library full of information is less useful than the same data accessed via computers. In fact, Alan Kay, in discussing information networks, has said that "You cannot rely on being able to find what you want. It's really more useful to go to a library" (Friedrich, 1983, p. 14).

A related question has to do with the demand for the information which this new access will make available. Most libraries are not so overcrowded as to prevent "information access," nor is it common for home encyclopedias to wear out from overuse. Boyd casts a dissenting vote on the general level of optimism in commenting on the features which he feels the library and data base have in common.

So much rubbish has to be waded through before anything valuable is found that most students are discouraged. These features have been carried over to most computerized information retrieval systems—which are really noise retrieval systems unless they query their users as to the value and timeliness of material in order to filter rubbish out of the data base. (Boyd, 1983, p. 52)

Unfortunately, the situation may be even worse than Boyd presents, for some evidence indicates the quality of the information stored in the data base, while important, is not sufficient to guarantee that the data base will be valuable to its users.

Blair and Maron (1985) evaluated the effectiveness of a "full-text" information retrieval system. A full-text system is one in which entire documents, not abstracts, summaries, or keywords, are stored and available to the user. In full-text retrieval, the user enters words, phrases, or word combinations and the computer system locates all documents meeting these specifications, that is, containing the words, phrases, or combinations. Full-text systems are appealing because the documents need no special preparation, no summarizing, abstracting, or indexing to make them ready for the data base. Not only is time saved, but the approximation of document content through abstracts or key words is avoided entirely. When key words or index terms are used, the reliability of indexers, even those with training and experience, can be insufficient, not to mention the fact that user judgements of appropriate index terms will often not coincide with that of the indexer.

Blair and Maron studied the use of a data base containing just under 40,000 documents, approximately 350,000 pages of text. The documents were related to the defense of a large corporate lawsuit and the users were two lawyers, principal defense attorneys in the case. Although the users were familiar with the contents of the data base and research results have generally shown full-text retrieval to be better than indexed retrieval, the results of this study are disappointing. The document collections resulting from the 51 information searches were generally high in precision, that is, the documents retrieved were relevant (79 out of 100, on the average), but quite low in recall. They represented only a small proportion of the relevant documents which might have been retrieved (20 out of 100). The second figure is the more disturbing because the lawyers not only felt that the system must retrieve at least 75 percent of the relevant documents to be useful, but they in fact *believed* that they were receiving the 75 percent that they needed.

Blair and Maron point out that previous studies had been done on much smaller, experimental data bases, while theirs was larger and operational, leading, they believe, to the contradiction between their results and earlier experiments. The larger collection of documents provides a more severe test for the assumption that users can foresee the exact words and phrases which will be used in the documents they desire to retrieve. In analyzing documents which were not successfully retrieved, they found, for example, that many of the documents relating to a specific accident never used the word "accident" in the text, particularly in the defense documents where the author did not even wish to acknowledge that an accident had occurred. The information retrieval system being used allowed the user to create a thesaurus of equivalent terms (among many other features of the system which were designed to help the user in locating documents), but the creativity of the document writers seemed to be greater than that of the searchers.

The size of the document collection is a crucial factor in lowering the recall rate (the percentage of relevant documents retrieved), according to Blair and Maron. On a small collection, one can use a single term which all relevant documents are almost sure to have, but in systems as large as the one they studied, some search terms, used by themselves, would result in over 10,000 documents being retrieved. Each time a new search term is added, in order to reduce the total number retrieved, some proportion of the relevant documents will also be excluded. The larger the data base, the more terms must be used to reduce the number of items retrieved, and the smaller the proportion of relevant documents located (recall). Because each document has many more words in its text than in its index terms (if such have been created), the problem of recall is more serious, and develops more rapidly as the number of documents increases, for full-text systems.

The study by Blair and Maron concentrates on the use of a specialized data base, so its results may not apply directly to the general use of data bases by students. However, one can generally conclude that as a data base gets larger, it becomes more difficult to obtain a high proportion of the documents relevant to the user's search request. On the other hand, small "subject-specific" data bases are not necessarily the solution. Not only is the selection of the appropriate data bases (from the hundreds commercially available) an increasing problem, but the difficulty of selecting relevant documents is even more pronounced in the case of specialized data bases. That is, when using a data base of newspaper articles, using the words "computer" and "education" might be adequate for selecting a high proportion of relevant articles, while the same words would be much too general when searching an educational research or computer science data base. In the latter cases, the addition of other terms to reduce the number of items retrieved would reduce the proportion of relevant documents selected.

Viewed in the light of the preceding results, and the general principles which seem to underlie them, "the emergence of a global network of databases which allow the child access to information with unprecedented ease" (Stonier, 1984, p. 253) cannot be accepted as a foregone conclusion. It will take more than access via computers to make the global collection of information "speak" to the empty students.

SEARCHING STUDENTS

Discovery Learning

Searching students are those for whom computerized discovery learning environments are designed, with the discussion in this chapter directed primarily at the discovery aspects of the LOGO environment (for other features of discovery learning see Chapters 5 and 6). Of course, it cannot be assumed that every use of LOGO involves discovery learning, nor that discovery learning is restricted to the LOGO environment, but the principal claims of Papert are based on the use of discovery learning. Papert begins his inspirational message on the use of LOGO by setting imposing goals for his book.

This book is about how computers can be carriers of powerful ideas and of the needs of cultural change, how they can help people form new relationships with knowledge that cut across the traditional lines separating humanities from sciences and knowledge of the self from both of these. It is about using computers to challenge current beliefs about who can understand what and at what age. It is about using computers to question standard assumptions in developmental psychology and in the psychology of aptitudes and attitudes. . . . But there is a world of difference between what computers can do and what society will choose to do with them. . . . Thus, this book is about facing choices that are ultimately political. (Papert, 1980b, pp. 4-5)

Sullivan notes the ambition of these goals, but comments that "texts of this kind become *oracular* rather than probing. Papert's optimism adds to this problem because his caveats are not as forcefully stated as is his advocacy of the computer" (Sullivan, 1985, p. 3). However, the problem is further complicated in that readers of Papert are not always accurate in their perceptions and rememberings of what he is trying to say. These misperceptions create a problem for anyone discussing Papert's work, for it is unfair to criticize ideas he has not written and useless to ignore the impact of his "perceived message" on the schools. One must note, however, that Papert is at least partly responsible for the misperceptions, through his emphasis on the positive aspects of computers without acknowledging their drawbacks. Therefore, it seems necessary to mention and comment on both types of messages from Papert, the stated and the perceived.

Papert begins with the assumptions that computers are inevitable and that they can provide intellectual stimulation for children in much the same way that gears stimulated him as a child. Although most readers might agree with these initial assumptions, other implicit assumptions precede his more specific conclusions, and these are usually not noticed, nor would they necessarily be accepted by all readers. The implicit assumptions include the requirement for extensive teacher training, the importance of teacher enthusiasm for the use of LOGO, and the relevant links (if any) between student work with LOGO and the rest of the curriculum.

Papert does specifically mention that it would be a mistake to provide every child with gears (on the basis of his experience) and that, similarly, it would be a mistake to consider the LOGO he describes as the ideal activity for all children. "It should be carefully remembered that LOGO is never conceived as a final product or offered as 'The definitive language'. Here I present it as a sample to show that something better is possible" (Papert, 1980b, p. 217). Unfortunately, these cautionary words are buried in the fine print of a footnote. Thus, although Papert proposes LOGO only as a sample and further states that present-day microcomputers are inadequate to even approximate his vision of computer use for children (this caution can be found in the "Afterword and Acknowledgement" section), his readers seem to remember him as saying that LOGO on current microcomputers is the answer to all educational problems.

One might paraphrase the central thesis of Papert's arguments as "Computers are useful for students to learn *by* discovery, *with* LOGO, *about* mathematics and other subjects." Ignoring the probable inaccuracy of the paraphrase, it is clear that educators are selective in remembering the parts of the statement. The most selective recall is to remember only LOGO and to put primary emphasis on learning LOGO (often by the discovery method) as if programming in LOGO is the most useful skill a child could acquire. This would seem to be a misreading of Papert, for he doesn't claim that his knowledge of gears was useful in itself, but only as a mechanism for his understanding of other concepts.

Other mis-rememberings of the Papert message focus on the study of mathematics or, more specifically, geometry, or, even more specifically, the creation of pictures. Now it is true that Papert makes use of student created drawings to show the power of LOGO, but they are examples of students creating prespecified (by the teacher or by the students) shapes. In classroom practice, the objective is often changed to the creation of "interesting" designs through the systematic, or random, varying of commands and parameters.

Computer Programming

Much of the work done with students using LOGO has focussed on computer programming and some of its appeal is based on the value of learning to program. As Papert puts it, rather than an environment in which "the computer is being used to program the child," as in CAI, with LOGO "the child programs the computer" (Papert, 1980b, p. 5). If learning to program is a positive feature of the LOGO approach, it must be evaluated in the light of current needs, not those of past decades. (Many of the arguments for and against the teaching of programming in schools are given in Chapter 6.)

Not surprisingly, voices are raised in opposition to the LOGO approach for young children. The strongest claim may come from Sardello who sees this form of computer education as producing a nation of psychopaths. He sees psychopathy as learning how to "debug life" and the psychopath as being able to imitate any form of behavior without being emotionally involved. Sardello's concern is for the abstract analytical emphasis in LOGO thinking, seeing it as turning "away from the world in order to program an imitation world" (Sardello, 1984, p. 637). His predictions may be overstated, but his concern has some basis in fact, as the results from Brooks (1978), discussed later in this section, indicate.

Davy (1984) expresses a similar fear, though in a more restrained form, writing on the experiential and perceptual impoverishment of funneling experience through a tiny screen. Douglas Noble raises this question in another form, questioning LOGO and other computer education in the context of the quest for computer literacy. He sees the drive for computer literacy as being mere manifestations of an ideology based on high technology. From this perspective, he views the programmer's control and mastery over computers as a "false sense of empowerment, 'a pseudocontrol'" (Noble, D., 1984, p. 610), which in reality is merely conforming to the constraints imposed by computers.

The factors of computer programming and discovery learning are intertwined at the core of the LOGO approach. Papert feels that the learning of programming techniques allows the student to discover the value of "thinking like a computer," a form of thinking which can be valuable in some contexts. Debugging of LOGO programs, finding the logical errors in them, is a critical part of this discovery process. Debugging is not only a part of discovering relationships, but is also a process of discovery itself in attempting to locate the errors. Lepper and Malone (1986) state that the intuitive appeal of discovery learning does not have strong research support. Nonetheless, Papert justifies his reliance on discovery learning on the basis that "Children seem to be innately gifted learners, acquiring long before they go to school a vast quantity of knowledge by a process I call 'Piagetian learning', or 'learning without being taught'" (Papert, 1980b, p. 7).

It is interesting to note that Papert does not always find it convenient to support the discovery approach, such as when he is justifying LOGO programming to teach children how they should think and learn analytically. He sees the choice as "*either* give the child the best ideas we can muster about cognitive processes *or* leave him at the mercy of the theories he invents or picks up in the gutter. The question is: who can do it better, the child or us?" (Papert, 1980a, p. 163). This seems to be somewhat less than a solid rock on which to base one's faith in discovery learning.

An emphasis on learning without being taught would seem to minimize the importance of the teacher in the LOGO process, but this point also remains ambiguous. Papert was displeased with the manner in which studies of LOGO learning were conducted by Pea and Kurland (Green, 1985). Teachers in the study were given strict guidelines to curtail their helping of children, and the results of the study indicated that the LOGO experience had not significantly increased the students' planning skills. Papert offers an alternative explanation, "We don't know whether it was well taught; in fact, we suspect it was very badly taught given the kinds of restraints teachers were placed under. In other places LOGO is better taught, differently taught, and maybe it has cognitive effects other than the particular one they chose to look at" (Green, 1985, p. 29). Later in the same article, in commenting on the results from Carmichael, et al., (1985) indicating a falling off of student competence with LOGO in the second year, he declared, "you shouldn't be surprised that we find we know much less about what to do in the second and third years than in the first year. I think we know how to make it work" (Green, 1985, p. 29).

Several observations can be made about the preceding quotes. First, it appears that "learning without being taught" is surprisingly dependent on the quality of teaching. Perhaps the phenomenon of learning without being taught is better described by Smith, in what he calls the "Can I have another donut?" theory of language learning. "Every child learns to say 'Can I have another donut?', not in order to learn how to make such a statement but to get another donut. In the process of trying to get the donut, the child incidentally learns how the request is uttered" (Smith, 1983, p. 7). From a beginning which is similar to Papert's, Smith does not move toward the computer as solution ("Computers will do for thought and language what the automobile has done for legs" [p. 121]), but emphasizes the role of the teacher in assisting students to find more donuts to ask for. In *Mindstorms*, Papert seems to be saying something similar to Schank's proclamation, "LOGO challenges the children . . . and compels them to think carefully about what is going on" (Schank, 1984, p. 206). Papert's later statements may indicate that he realizes that, as the results of Carmichael et al. and others have shown, without a proper teaching environment, LOGO does not compel students to do anything, merely inviting them to "fool around."

Papert's suggestion that LOGO may have "cognitive effects other than the particular one they chose to look at" is not only unconvincing, but reminiscent of the Minsky arguments for AI (discussed in Chapter 4). That is, it is consistent with suggesting the possibility of a great many vaguely defined benefits while resisting any attempts to determine if any specific benefits actually exist. It is also consistent with his suggesting that Carmichael et al. had access to information which he was unable to obtain, by virtue of the two-year span of their study. "It was almost inconceivable in those days to do a large-scale study where a lot of children had exposure to any sort of computers in a fairly free environment for a long time, say two or three years" (Green, 1985, p. 29). In focusing on the past, he avoids mentioning a continuing study of LOGO which began before the Carmichael et al. study. Turkle refers to it as the "Austen project," which began at least as early as 1981, and in which children (from preschool to grade four) have been given almost unlimited access to the use of LOGO. "I followed the Austen project from its inception. . . . The study of the Austen students was a collaborative effort with Seymour Papert" (Turkle, 1984, p. 98).

Papert's problem certainly cannot be a lack of access to data on the use of LOGO, for almost all teachers who use LOGO would delight in sharing their experiences with its creator. Rather, it must be that because he is (as he describes himself) in a "political" battle to extend the range of "what computers can do", it is only natural that his focus is not on the possible blemishes in his creation, but on the possible powerful benefits it might bring. Papert's optimism about LOGO matches his feelings about AI, where he says "that we can make machines that perform better functionally than people do. . . . If I were convinced that we could never have confidence in the powers that control our world, I would sacrifice my life to stop artificial intelligence. But I choose to believe we're able to change the world so we *can* have confidence" (Green, 1985, p. 59). It would seem that Papert *chooses* to believe in LOGO in much the same way, seeing his mission as one of converting others to believe, possibly at the expense of perfecting the techniques.

Microworlds

Dreyfus and Dreyfus (1984) have analyzed the implications of the discovery methods employed in the LOGO approach, as well as having looked at the foundations of CAI. They acknowledge the strengths of Papert's theory-based approach, the advantages of the microworld as a simplified environment in which important features are more easily recognized, and the possible benefits of having children view their own thinking in an analytical and algorithmic manner. Yet it is the strengths of microworlds and the thinking model which they believe become liabilities when children move into more advanced levels of achievement (their model of skill learning is more completely described in Chapter 5).

According to Dreyfus and Dreyfus, the microworld can actually get in the way of learning when the learner has mastered the knowledge of features and rules and is now ready to begin to recognize "aspects" and also begin accumulating a repertory of different "whole world" views of the problem. Their examples are a simplified model of chess, which must be left behind if the student is to learn the total game, and learning to drive in a parking lot, which helps the learner to concentrate on shifting and steering, but leaves out many important considerations which are a part of driving. Thus, unless the microworld has the ability to grow in complexity as the learner masters the simplified environment, it is useful only for a limited period of learning, during the student's initial exposure to the topic.

Mind as Computer

The searching student in the LOGO environment is also urged to view the mind as a computer. The value of a computer model for thinking is seen as having a failing similar to microworlds, being well suited for the early stages of learning but not for more complex later learning. That is, it is feasible to think of the learner programming a computer to deal with basic features of the problem environment, but when one is acquiring the recognition of aspects, or a repertory of maxims, programming this knowledge is likely to be impossible, particularly for nonprofessional programmers. However, the Dreyfus and Dreyfus criticism of the computer model for thinking is not limited to its use in programming. They see the analytical approach, attempting to determine the rules for accomplishing some procedure, as being a limitation on some types of learning. Language learning is their example, where, in agreement with Smith (1983), they see language learning as being much more than a collection of skills which can be mastered separately, but as an experientially-based process, with a variety of learning situations being crucial to true mastery. As with the microworld, thinking of oneself as a computer is most effective in the early stages of learning when rules and features are being learned, but actually retarding learning when the learner moves from the advanced-beginner stage to competence in the Dreyfus and Dreyfus model of skill acquisition.

Two examples are presented by Dreyfus and Dreyfus to supplement their model and buttress their arguments that the "mind as computer" model is not always useful. One has to do with Air Force pilot training and the fact that instructors who teach specific rules for instrument scanning appear to use no rules at all when they themselves scan instruments while flying. That is, the authors argue, experienced pilots learn to scan instruments in ways that are appropriate to the context and not based on rules.

The second example is from an experiment in nonanalytical concept formation, in which subjects who were told to be analytical were less successful in
learning the concepts than those who did not use analytical methods (Brooks,
1978). That is, subjects who tried to learn the rules used to generate two different sets of strings of letters (by analyzing the letter strings) were unable to do so,
which is probably not too surprising. What is more surprising is that the analytical subjects were actually less successful than those subjects who were not trying
to learn to distinguish between two sets of letter strings. The second group was
trying to learn the pairing of the letter strings with names of cities and animals,
and did not even realize that two grammars had been used, one for the letter
strings matched to city names and the other for those matched to animal names.
Yet when asked to distinguish between new letter strings from the two grammars
(in terms of whether they should be linked to cities or animals) and also a set of
letter strings from a third (new) grammar, the second group was superior to the
first group. One way of looking at this experiment is that the first (analytical)
group approached the task in much the same way as we learn a second language,
while the second (nonanalytical) group used an approach which is much more
like the manner in which we learn our first language.

This study illustrates the drawbacks to a strong emphasis on analytical thinking, or "thinking like a computer," in that one is led to conclude that either we
are less able to be analytical when we try to be analytical, or analytical thinking
is not appropriate for some important learning situations. This study also seems
to lend support, though in a different form, to the concerns expressed by
Sardello (1984).

Trial and Error

What may be another dimension to this discussion of "searching" students in
the LOGO environment is added by Salomon (1986), who uses the term "mindfulness" to describe learners' active participation in the learning process, their
nonautomatic and goal-directed activities. Although he uses analytical thinking
as an example of mindfulness, they are not equivalent concepts, for mindfulness
includes planning, generating hypotheses, comparing alternatives, and thought-
fully examining feedback in addition to analytical thinking. Also, it is the conscious, nonautomatic choosing to use any of the preceding skills that makes for
mindfulness, a choosing that should be based on the availability and appropriateness of the technique. Presumably, this means that true mindfulness would
include the selection of nonanalytical strategies when such are indicated.

Papert's hypothetical dialogue between students working with LOGO (see
Chapter 6) shows a high degree of mindfulness, but Leron (1985) reports that
most children he has observed use a "hacking" style of programming, characterized by a trial-and-error approach, rather than planning and reflection. Although
he points out that the hacking style should not automatically be condemned,
since it can offer an effective means for initial exploration, he feels it is inappro-

priate as a consistent and persistent method of exploration. Papert's major definition of the LOGO approach does not seem to have clearly illuminated the dangers of the trial-and-error technique. The entry "trial and error learning" in his index points to a section speaking against the practice some children adopt of not debugging, but beginning again from scratch when a procedure fails (Papert, 1980b). What appears not to be addressed is the practice of debugging through trial and error.

Schwartz (1984) provides evidence that not only is trial-and-error learning unproductive, but the trial-and-error experience can actually interfere with later learning. Two groups of college students were asked to attempt to determine the general rules which caused some sequences of computer key presses to be rewarded while others were not. One group (A) had no prior experience on the task, while the other group (B) had spent several hours on a similar task, being rewarded for each successful sequence. The important finding was that group B students (with experience) were much *less effective* in determining the rules than those in group A (no experience). That is, if this effect is true for the LOGO environment (and no direct evidence seems to exist on this point), children are better off to have no LOGO at all, than to use LOGO mindlessly. For it appears that mindless activity is a learned skill and the more you practice, the better you can do it.

The reports from Carmichael et al. (1985) show indications of trial and error, with students reporting the advantages of being able to try without having to think, and with students finding they could not determine the proper turtle commands to produce a given figure without the feedback from the screen to indicate if their guesses were correct. Perhaps the most interesting observation was the report that students who went through an involved search for a procedure to produce a square, then confided to the observer that they had gone through the same search the previous day, but had forgotten to save (either physically, electronically, or mentally) the result. It appears that at least some teachers were aware of this approach to learning, but did not seem to be concerned. One teacher reported, "They find out what works—then work backwards to find out why. I always tried to teach principles first and then their application, but if that's the way students think, I go along with it" (Carmichael et al., 1985, p. 276). Unfortunately, it appears that some students are just as likely to find out what works and not find out why.

In some ways, the reported results from Carmichael et al. are reminiscent of the phenomenon of "superstitious behavior," found by Skinner in pigeons some four decades ago. He found that pigeons who received grains of food regularly at random intervals, independent of what they were doing at the time, tended to develop stereotypes and frequent patterns of movement (Schwartz, 1984). That is, six of the eight pigeons appeared to develop "superstitions" about what was causing the grain to appear and were consistently engaged in some regular activity, such as turning counterclockwise, or swaying from side to side. Catania and Cutts (1963) found a similar result with human subjects who were given two buttons to press, one of which *never* produced a reward, while the other was occasionally rewarded on a random basis. Almost all the subjects continued to respond to the first button throughout the session, even though it *never* produced the desired result, often based on their own "theory" of how presses on the first button "caused" presses on the second button to be rewarded. Catania and Cutts also demonstrated that the effectiveness of a "changeover delay" (COD) also applied to humans. The COD is a procedure to guarantee that rewards to the second button will occur only when a certain time has elapsed since the first button was pressed. When the COD was used, the human subjects either reduced or completely eliminated pressing of the first button. The authors comment that the use of programmed instruction in teaching machines also requires a COD in the form of a forced delay between incorrect and correct answers in order to prevent superstitious behavior from developing.

Carmichael et al. were not looking for evidence of superstitious behavior, but their report indicates that many of the grade one students had a preference for particular numbers. These preferences, which sometimes interfered with their accomplishing what they had set out to do, might have been formed because they were numbers which happened to be used when something good, the reward, happened during their use of LOGO. As the authors report:

> [the preferences] became particularly evident when students in one grade one class were asked to walk the turtle along a path. Three students, for example, used RT 45 at all times, no matter what the question was. Others liked the number 12. One student used thirty-two 12's in combination of LT, RT, FD and BK. . . . One student who used twenty 12's FD, LT, or RT said "I use 12 all the time because it makes it go just a bit and I can see where it is going". . . .
>
> Several students made extensive use of the number 34. . . . Although students were developing a sense of bigger or smaller and playing with large numbers, some students did not connect numeric values with such relationships. For example, one student was able to move the turtle in one of the estimation questions exactly 40 units by small increments. She was told that all "these numbers" added up to 40 and then asked whether the next distance was bigger or smaller. She correctly replied "bigger" but then entered FD 9 and continued to proceed with small increments. . . . 40% of the junior-level students who had explored extensively with Logo for one year but with little direction from the teacher still were unable to give either the correct number of repeats or the correct size of the angle for making a square . . . even though these students had used triangles and squares. . . . (Carmichael et al., 1985, pp. 313, 316)

The preceding observations are not convincing evidence for superstitious behavior developing out of trial and error used in LOGO, being at best suggestive. However, until specific research is done on this question, the fact that a "changeover delay" was needed to prevent superstitious behavior in programmed instruction does provide credibility for a claim that trial and error could have this effect.

Most courseware packages could include a changeover delay and many of them do, in the form of messages explaining why the response was wrong, etc. But in the case of LOGO, and other forms of courseware such as simulations where it is not always (or never) possible to determine within the program that a response is, in fact, incorrect, the opportunity for this preventive measure is unavailable. As one teacher commented, "He works without hesitation—just keeps trying things until he gets it the way he wants it. He doesn't waste any time deliberating about whether or not his next move is right" (Carmichael et al., 1985, p. 276). From this, and the other suggestive evidence, one might conclude that the oft-cited advantage of the LOGO environment, immediate, nonjudgmental feedback, is at best a mixed blessing, leading to some instances of mindless trial and error, which results in the learning of irrelevant responses to problems.

Simulations

Simulation also offers an environment in which the searching student can explore. The major drawback, as discussed in Chapter 5, is that the simulation is not the actual environment one wishes to explore, but someone's description of the environment. More important, it is not just someone's description of that environment, but it is (necessarily) a limited description, unless the environment is trivial in scope. In creating a computer simulation, unless the event being described is itself well-defined and limited in complexity, critical choices must be made about the factors which will be included in the simulation and the way in which relationships between these factors will be defined.

Cuffaro (1984) comments on the shortcomings of computer experiences of this type by describing them as "reality twice removed." That is, "parking a car" through the use of concrete objects as models is already one step removed from reality, with the move to a two-dimensional screen making the task even more "unreal." In contrast, Licklider (1983) sees this as a benefit in problem solving, feeling that being "a little further from the real situation" can be a plus in solving a problem dealing with stacking bricks. However, just as the assumption that "there is no friction on ice" can be helpful in solving physics problems, but a definite drawback when curling, so the distance from simulation to reality is at best a mixed blessing.

Perhaps the best known example of simulation, one which does not require the use of computers (though it often does have computers), is the "theme park." Brian Greenleaf has remarked that people who live in North America are increasingly getting their "knowledge" about the rest of the world from theme parks. These parks typically offer a variety of simulated experiences, such as a cruise down the Congo river, a walk on a Paris street, a ride down the Matterhorn on a sled, or a voyage underwater via submarine. Although these simulations are created in great detail and at substantial expense, it is a mistake to believe that they give you the actual experience that is being simulated. That is, upon arriving in Paris, one finds that although some similarities are obvious, such as the presence of fast-food restaurants in both places, important differences can also be noted (it is left as an exercise for the reader to discover what the important differences are).

Simulations, whether in the form of theme parks or on computers, are often different from the real experience in systematic and predictable ways. The most usual bias in simulations comes from a stress on entertainment, with those aspects of the Paris street which are not entertaining, such as the cars, sleeping vagrants, garbage cans and other items, organic and inorganic, which obstruct the sidewalks usually omitted from a theme park simulation. This desire to entertain is a problem with all simulations created for public use, whether they are trips to foreign cities with famous people as simulated via television, or a student's visit with the early settlers in North America via a computer program. This is a danger not only because of the bias introduced in the selection of features to be presented, but also in the way that the student is treated. The searching student, using a simulation to discover more about a topic in which the student is already interested, not only does not need to be entertained, but the very presence of entertainment can give the student the message that this topic is not really interesting on its own. As a result, the searching student may be transformed into the "empty student," requiring additional motivation to stimulate learning.

Zajonc (1984) sees the use of a "computer reality" as a particular danger for children under the age of 12. He feels that the computer replacing the teacher is much less of a threat than the computer replacing the growing child. He notes that Waldorf nursery teachers have observed that children raised without TV in the home tend to have more imagination than those raised with TV. He fears that, just as television can replace the child's imagination, so computers have the potential to replace all of their mental functions.

A major advantage of simulation lies in their simplicity, the elimination of those features which are not essential to the event being simulated. As long as simulations are used to introduce students to complex events in a gradual manner, this advantage is maintained. It is when the simulation is used as a substitute for a more complex experience that the simplicity can turn into a disadvantage. One effective way of preventing students from being misled in this way is to have them involved in the creating of simulations, as described in the next section.

CREATIVE STUDENTS

The term "creative student" is meant to describe a change in the direction in which information is transmitted between student and computer. Instead of computers being seen as vast banks of information, the student is the source of the information, which is put into a computer for examination, restructuring, experimentation, etc. The most obvious of these applications is probably word processing, but most traditional educational applications of computers also can be seen as opportunities for creative students.

Word Processing

Word processing may be the most obvious application for creative computer use, but it does not allow total unrestrained creativity on the part of the user. As mentioned in Chapter 6, certain types of writing and revision are more greatly facilitated, or "encouraged" by word processing. In some instances, experienced writers have found it more difficult to write using a word processor when they tried to alter their style to take advantage of the procedures offered by the computer. In addition to the "natural" biases built into the word processor, the ability to shift blocks of text, substitute words, etc., one also finds increasing use of writing aids being built into word processors, particularly those designed for younger students. It is true that younger students are most in need of writing assistance, but built-in aids also have a shaping influence, as well as a tendency to limit the possibilities, or more accurately the probabilities open to young writers.

As an example of a technological innovation which is seen as being liberating, but also has (usually unseen) possibilities for limitations, consider the use of speech input to word processing, or typing devices. In considering the possible uses of speech input, the emphasis is almost always on the elimination of the need to learn typing skills and the greater relative speed for talking versus typing. What is generally ignored is the large difference between spoken and written discourse and the fact that our major difficulty is in knowing what and how to write (or speak), not in the physical process of getting our composed thoughts onto the paper. Dictation is a skill which most people have not yet learned, and a skill which will have to be learned by those who are going to make use of speech input. Not only must dictation be learned, but it must also be learned to a higher level of proficiency than for those who currently practice it, since dictating to an electronic device will require a higher level of precision than dictating to a human secretary. One only needs a short exposure to verbatim transcripts to discover that what is reasonably clear in spoken discourse can be almost completely unintelligible in a written form.

One should also keep in mind that although it is possible to acquire a speech input capability for your personal computer at a reasonable price (less than $500 for 500 words or more), these devices do not usually accept "normal" speech. That is, unless the speaker puts a distinct pause between all words, the speech input device will not function properly, since it cannot handle continuous speech. The effect of writers having to adopt an unusual speaking style would seem to be worth studying before planning to have widespread use of "listening" typewriters.

Music

Computers used in music creation, both in the composition and the perform-ance of music, have some similarities with the uses of word processing. The pos-sible drawbacks of these uses also seem to be similar, with a frequent concern being that the use of computers can lead to an emphasis on techniques which are easily handled via computer, such as transpositions, inversions, or other com-posing techniques, and the use of automated support systems for performers. By the latter is meant the use of electronic percussion or background harmony for a solo performer, for example, which creates the impression of a larger group, but at the same time prevents a creative interaction between the support and solo performers. This lack of spontaneity has been characterized as "antiseptic rather than aesthetic" musical performance. A similar description might be applied to a fascination with composing tricks which a music processor can accomplish, instead of the focus on communication which is the basis of musical creativity.

Music also has the equivalent of speech input, the ability of a computer pro-gram to translate an artist's performance into musical notation. When simple music is played on a keyboard, with the aid of a metronome, sheet music notat-tion can be created by a quite inexpensive device. However, when the number of voices and rhythmic complexity are increased, the problem of transcription be-comes much more difficult. "Near-perfect transcription without a metronome is still considered a deep, AI-level problem" (Roads, 1985, p. 164). The problem is similar to that of dictation, in that a performer is not providing an exact descrip-tion of the musical notation, but rather an interpretation of it, with the "value" of the performance being dependent, to a great extent, on the ways in which the interpretation differs from the notation. To set the goal of capturing the inter-pretation in musical notation is to try to eliminate this important difference between them, thus limiting the creativity of the performer.

The effect of trial and error can also be a factor in music processing, since a computer system can allow the composer to sample a great quantity of musical variations on a theme, without any "mindfulness" of which variations are most promising. One can argue that the trial-and-error approach is more likely to bring to light the unexpected or creative variation, but the use of trial and error also works against the composer, particularly the student composer, ever developing a sense of what works and why, a greater understanding of musical form. One can make a similar comment about text manipulating programs, such as poetry generators which randomly combine words according to certain rules. If these programs are used mindlessly, with repeated production of random variations in search of a creative gem, little value is obtained by the student, author, or poet. On the other hand, this kind of program can be very beneficial if the student is mindfully altering the rules and/or the selection of words in a purposeful ex-ploration of different strategies. Thus, as in many applications of computers to education, the difference lies in the user, as guided by the teacher.

Data bases

Data bases are another possible application for the creative student, an opportunity to reverse the direction of information flow between student and computer. A project from the Ontario Ministry of Education lessonware development activity provides an example. In its original form, Anne Delong's "Animals of Ontario" was a game for primary-age children, which asked them to guess the identity of an Ontario animal based on clues presented by the program. Six clues were stored for each of 20 animals, along with a picture to be displayed when the correct identification was made. Children could use the game individually, or compete with each other in attempting to identify the animals.

The original game was modified in an important way when the program was converted for use on a different (and larger) microcomputer. In addition to retaining the original format of 20 animals, along with their six descriptors and pictures, another version of the program was created. In this version, *Learning Game Generator*, provision was made for the teacher and/or students to enter new material into the program. The new material could be "flowers of Switzerland," "lakes of Minnesota," or "countries of the world," to name only a few possibilities. To create a new game, one must enter the names of up to 20 new items, the six descriptors for each item, and a picture of each item (created with the graphics editing program).

Although the use of this new program has not yet produced empirical results, it seems that it offers much greater learning opportunities than the original form. In the original, one might learn six facts about 20 animals, but in fact the best strategies for playing the game would not encourage the learning of all the descriptions. In the second version, a student or group of students would learn not only all the information entered into the program, but a great deal more, especially about the construction of a data base. In choosing the six categories of description and the one-sentence descriptions to fit each item-descriptor combination, they should learn a great deal about the often arbitrary nature of the contents of a data base. The selection of only six ways to describe countries of the world is certainly arbitrary, as well as the use of only one sentence to describe a country on a particular dimension. Thus, rather than learning that "I can run fast" can be used to describe both a fox and a mouse (in the original program), students should also learn that these statements are incomplete descriptions about how a fox and a mouse might move, and that the two types of animals are quite different in speed of movement, among other things. The results should be that a creative student can learn more about how to use a data base by first discovering something about data base strengths and limitations through the experience of building one or more of them.

It may be obvious that students can learn about data bases by building their own, but similar applications for videodiscs are less clear. Videodisc players are usually advertised for home entertainment uses, but many of the optical videodisc players have features such as single-frame display, slow motion, and reverse play, which makes them particularly attractive for educational use. Not only can any of more than 50,000 television frames be selected for display, but some players can be connected to microcomputers, creating a computer-based instructional system with great potential for both teacher and student use. Bernard Dubreuil of the INRP in Paris has been developing a videodisc application for creative students through creating programs which permit students to impose their own structure or organization of information on the contents of a videodisc. That is, students might classify information about British birds (the contents of a commercial videodisc) in terms of bird size, type of feet, colors, etc., using computer programs to locate the appropriate videodisc sequences corresponding to each of the selected features. The beauty of this approach is that it can be applied directly to commercially prepared videodiscs and doesn't require the expensive creation of special video materials, though they could also be used. This type of approach not only encourages students to comprehend the entire contents of the disc, but it can also challenge them to create their own structure for the information it contains. The latter is an excellent strategy for acquiring knowledge, often used by experienced readers who create their own index for a book as they read it. Perhaps the most important lesson for students is to make the distinction between using someone else's data base (the original format of the videodisc) and their own.

Data bases would also be more useful if they contained information about their users in addition to the original data on their subject matter. This addition can turn a data base into a "serendipity machine" (Thompson, 1979). If a data base were to contain information about its users and the types of information they had been seeking (subject, of course, to permission being obtained from the users to store and distribute such information), it would be far more useful. In using computerized information retrieval services, it is often more useful to find out that others have been searching for the same data than to obtain the data themselves. One usually finds that an exchange of information is beneficial to both users, since our approaches to the problem often differ, as well as our use of other information sources. It is also particularly valuable for young students to learn that other people interested in the same problem are often more useful than access to a huge amount of unevaluated data. Brown (1985) describes applications in a similar vein, pointing to the use of computer networks as environments for subcultures of users to form and to grow, not based on geography, but on the shared interests and/or beliefs of the participants.

It is crucial that students have an understanding of the limitations of data bases and are not led to use them indiscriminately. Current levels of motivation may be sufficient to encourage students to make liberal use of data bases, but as Thiessen points out, "What guarantee is there that the replacement of researching conventional reference sources (*a technique*) with the use of computerized data-bases (*a method*) will not still lead to a copying out of undigested and often irrelevant chunks of information by students?" (Thiessen, 1985, p. 319). Goodson provides an answer to this question in describing a student who was asked to do research on a topic and used an online data base, "asked it to print it out, didn't even read the paper, turned it in the next morning, and got two A's—one because the research was so complete and the other because it was typed" (Tech-Trends, 1985, p. 25). If a computerized data base is merely used as a variant of the copying machine, acceptable because the material has been retyped, not copied, the benefit for students will be minimal, if not nonexistent.

Courseware

Courseware is another application that can be a source of creative expression for students. By this is meant not the use of courseware to bring information to the students, but students creating courseware packages (appropriately limited in size and scope) in the same way that they create essays, not so much to edify others as to consolidate their own learning. Authoring systems, designed to permit teachers to create their own courseware, are often viewed with dismay by those who promote the rigor of the courseware design process, but they can provide an opportunity for students to demonstrate their knowledge in a novel manner. Not only does such an exercise allow an evaluation of student progress, but the students should also acquire a better understanding of the strengths and weaknesses of courseware in a way similar to that of the data base creation activity.

Perhaps the most useful type of courseware for students to create would be simulations. As indicated above, the designer of a simulation must not only choose which variables are the most important, but must also specify in detail the relationships between the selected variables. Just as in the data base activity, creating a simulation can give greater insight into the (necessarily) incomplete nature of simulations, both educational and commercial.

SOCIAL STUDENTS

It goes without saying that all students are social, in that all students have social needs, but their social needs vary over a wide range. The variation in social needs is not so much in terms of quantity, though this is a factor, but in terms of the types of social needs. In this context, the primary emphasis is on students working together and valuing each other as people to work with, though other types of social needs can be used to support this concept, as well as being important needs when considered on their own.

The social needs of students are served by many of the applications described earlier in this chapter, particularly those of the creative student, the applications which involve creating materials for others to read, sing, access, or study. In most cases, an aspect of peer review can be built into these activities, such as the peer review process used in programming and writing.

Group Work

The general principle involved in these applications is one of communications, both between the creator and the user of the materials and between the members of the team developing the materials. Group work is an activity which is often emphasized in schools, but computers may create new opportunities in which this can be done. Programming is an obvious example of an activity which not only encourages group work, but for projects of any substantial size, group effort is almost mandatory. Although a majority of students may not have a significant amount of programming activity as a part of their studies, the group programming which does take place may help to stimulate the group processes in other disciplines such as writing, which should be taking place even in the absence of computers.

Courseware development is even more demanding of group involvement than is programming, since programming is only one of the skills required in the process. If the amount of time required to create courseware is not too intimidating, this exercise could stimulate cooperative efforts in many areas, including writing, programming, and art. The important feature of this and other group efforts is that the probability of mindful deliberate involvement is greatly increased. The nonjudgmental nature of computer feedback is often praised, but it can also lead to apathetic trial-and-error responses. Humans are often inclined to be overly critical of the efforts of others, but the alternative should not be to reject human contact in favor of machines, but rather to develop the necessary social skills in students so that they can work together without causing injury through their critical comments.

Many writers have documented the importance of the peer group in the lives of students, with Goodlad's (1984) extensive study of the school environment being one of the largest and most recent. He sees the peer group as a powerful educational force, though its educational consequences are often not those which are desired by parents and teachers, themselves having been replaced as role models by the peer group. Since the peer group socialization process has become such a driving force for students, it is probably unreasonable to emphasize the *personal* computer, the *individualizing* of instruction, or the replacing of human interaction by computers in the school environment. Many students have already excluded most of the adult world from their active consideration, focussing instead on a small subset of their peers. Although some would argue that the possibility of computers hampering social development is extremely unlikely (Dickson, 1985), it is far too important an issue to be lightly dismissed. Our efforts with computers should be directed at widening their social contacts, not diminishing or eliminating them.

It must be repeated that the preceding examples are not meant to imply that efforts to improve and increase the socialization skills of students should be limited to their computer activities. Yet computers can be a part of the process. Composition skills, whether in writing, music, or art can be enhanced through the use of computer tools, allowing students to use these creative abilities as a means of establishing communication with a wider range of people. Similarly, the data base as meeting place, or "serendipity machine" can be used to bring together people of similar interests. This application offers new opportunities for establishing links between children and adults. One possibility is that a school could establish a data base of the senior citizens in its area, then students could use this data base as a starting point for creating others, using the interests and knowledge of the senior citizens as a resource in guiding their searches.

Finally, the creation of courseware as a group or class project could allow all of the preceding activities to come together. Writing, art, programming, and other composition skills could be used. Data bases could be used to locate information, but more importantly, other students and adults with interests and skills in the subject area. When these groups were brought together, those in the class with those from outside the class, the common focus of their discussions, beyond the topic of the courseware being created, would be the process of learning. In order to create effective courseware, one must be aware of the way in which the beginning learner progresses to the more advanced levels of competence or expertise (Case, 1978). Rather than spending their time in apprenticeship with computerized "expert systems," students could work with real experts, both inside and outside their classroom, "discovering" the ways in which the expertise had been acquired.

Peer Tutoring

Out of this discussion, one can see a possible solution to a puzzle mentioned in earlier chapters, particularly Chapter 5. The puzzle has to do with the nagging finding that peer tutoring, or cross-age tutoring, seems to be more effective (and more cost-effective) in raising student achievement. The specific puzzle is "Why do we put so much emphasis on using computers to teach (CAI) when such a plentiful classroom resource, namely peers, seems to do a better job?" For example, consider the two studies reported by Anderson, Boyle, and Reiser (1985). In the first study they found that computer-tutored students took significantly less time to complete a course than those working alone (15 hours versus 26.5), but that human-tutored students took even less time (11.4 hours), though this difference was not statistically significant. Given that these results show what seems to be a clear superiority for computer tutoring over working alone, but not over human tutoring, one might ask why their second study omitted the human-tutored group and repeated the comparison between computer tutoring and working alone?

The answer to this direct question is probably in terms of our fascination with technology and our valuing of technology beyond academic achievement or other human beings. However, the solution may be possible without having to correct our strange love for technology and CAI. One approach is to combine CAI with group work, emphasizing cooperation among students who are using the same courseware, a technique which has been shown to result in higher achievement than competitive or individualistic use of CAI (Johnson, Johnson, & Stanne, 1986). Another possibility is using the classroom development of courseware as a technique to stimulate the peer and cross-age tutoring relationships which are so valuable. The increasing disillusionment with CAI among teachers can be seen as a positive step, enabling them to consider their students as CAI developers, which may, in the long run, be the solution to the courseware quality problem. That is, when children grow up considering the problems of learning via CAI, while becoming expert computer users themselves, when they reach adulthood they may learn to develop courseware materials that are far more effective than what we have been able to provide for them. However, whether the development of quality CAI material ever comes to pass, the focus on human interactions, particularly between generations, will have produced more than adequate rewards for our culture.

COMPUTER LITERACY UPDATE

Having reviewed what computers in education could or should mean to students, one could view this review as a definition of computer literacy, though a very general and tentative definition. The definition must be tentative, since the solution of problems can be done by working from the problem to the solution, working from the solution to the problem, or working from both directions toward the middle. Since this consideration has emphasized the problem area of elementary and secondary schools rather than the solution area of university or adult life, it is necessarily incomplete.

University Projects

Project Athena, introduced at MIT in 1983, may give us some idea of where the computer literacy movement should be heading if it is intended to prepare students for the university of the future. Heavily supported by major computer manufacturers and other corporations through grants of hardware, software, equipment maintenance, and some technical staff, the project also has an internal MIT budget of some $20 million for software, operations, and staff (Balkovich, Lerman, & Parmelee, 1985). The purpose of the project is to explore the potential uses of advanced computer technology in the university curriculum and its results should have implications for the types of skills that entering university students will need.

Although Project Athena is being carried out in a technologically advanced environment, the level of computer literacy among students and staff is high, and the goals of the project include the investigation of curriculum applications which are not currently practical in the context of current technology, it is doubtful that any investigation based on 1980s thoughts and skills can adequately describe the kinds of skills which students presently in elementary school will need when they reach university age. However, even though these results, and those at other universities (such as Carnegie-Mellon) engaged in similar research, are almost certain to be significantly incomplete, they do offer a different view of the computer literacy problem, if not its solution.

Without getting too deeply involved in the possible futures for educational computing and associated research, it is possible to speculate briefly on the likely outcomes of the MIT project and others like it. One strength of the MIT and Carnegie-Mellon projects is that they are centers of technological progress and in a better position than most universities to anticipate the future advances in electronics and other technology, sharpening their insights into emerging applications in education. Adding to this strength is the associated characteristic that many of their students are enrolled in technically-based programs, those which are more likely to see immediate benefits from technology applied to the curriculum. In addition, both MIT and Carnegie-Mellon have strong departments in nontechnical areas, not only in the social sciences, but also in the arts. This should enable them not only to evaluate the impact of technology over a wider range of subject matter, but also permit the evaluation to be based on a variety of points of view.

The early results from Project Athena indicate an interesting range of activities, with about 60 different educational development activities in progress (Balkovich, Lerman, & Parmelee, 1985). Although these activities cover most of MIT's academic departments and promise a wealth of ideas, little is currently available from these efforts. Balkovich et al. do present paradigms for the use of computers in the curriculum, sprinkling them with anecdotes of MIT applications, then develop a model of computation to support these paradigms, and discuss how the use of the model might affect the university. Unfortunately, the question of how students should be prepared for this university of the future is not addressed. It is not surprising that in universities, as in other levels of education, the need to bring computer literacy to their own staff and students is clearer than what will be done when computer literacy for all has been achieved.

Business Examples

The business world also has problems in knowing where it is going on computing, or even where it is now. Christoff (1985) examines some of the popular uses of personal computers in business and questions the value of many of them. In most cases he believes that the vision of an "ideal" application has been used to sell a computing concept, such as data bases, while the actual implementation is usually far from the ideal, leading to widespread dissatisfaction. The ideal concept of data bases is that of nonredundant data bases, which is one data base to be shared among various applications, rather than one data base for each application, while in real applications the software packages come from different vendors, with separate data bases, and redundancies abound. Even more obvious (in hindsight) is his observation about the proliferation of personal computers in business settings. He laments that although we would think it silly to suggest that those people who have flown 200,000 miles as passengers can fly a jumbo jet, it somehow seems plausible that those who have used a large number of computer programs can, with only a few days training, suddenly create their own programs and use them on their own computers. After a number of similar analyses, Christoff's conclusions are the familiar story that applications must be based on evaluated needs and the environment in which the work is to be done.

Attewell and Rule (1984) reviewed the research results relating to the use of computers in organizations and found an abundance of contradictions. Their most definite conclusion is that those who believe they know the future effects of computers on organizations are wrong. They found evidence to support the belief that computers result in "deskilling" jobs, decreasing the human skills needed to do the job, and also found evidence that computers tend to "upgrade" jobs, removing drudgery and increasing the intellectual aspects. They also found that workers' perceptions of computers were generally positive, but caution that these results are mainly from public bureaucracies, do not distinguish between levels of computer use, and may be a function of the novelty effect. Similar contradictory findings are reported in the areas of unemployment and management effects.

Turning to more specific studies, Turner (1984) reports on an on-line computer system used in some U.S. Social Security offices which not only had a definite negative effect on the work environment for those using it, but also seemed to result in more client claims being rejected than was the case in offices where other systems were being used. Gochenouer (Strehlo, 1986; Gochenouer, 1985) also reports an intriguing finding, that management personnel who made extensive use of computers received smaller salary increases than those who made little or no use of computers.

The problem in defining computer literacy for elementary and secondary schools is little helped by the experience from business. Should the training be based on where business is now in its use of computing, on a projection based on where it is now, or on an evaluation of how business *should* be using computing? All of these choices have the possibility of being seriously in error if a continued misapplication of computers leads to a rejection of widespread computing, so that workers in the future may need to know less about computers than they do now. The last comment is only partly facetious, given the results reported by Gochenouer, which illustrate the potential for unpredictable effects. If one accepts that the rejection of programmed instruction was caused by overenthusiastic adoption of poorly prepared material, rather than a flaw in the concept, it is not difficult to see the same process happening with respect to *some* computer applications (probably not computers in general, but some applications).

If the future use of computers in university and business settings is unclear, then elementary and secondary schools will have little external guidance in providing computer skills for their students. In such a context, their best course of action is to provide students with skills that can help them in attaining the currently identified educational goals. Defining some ways in which this might be done has been the main goal of this chapter.

8   Teacher Role

INTRODUCTION

The expectations about teachers, traditionally held at an unrealistically high level, have gone even higher in the past decades. As Goodlad (1984) points out, the schools of North America were being condemned for doing a poor job of educating students more than 50 years ago, but now they have added burdens thrust upon them through the steady weakening of the home and the church. With more than 50 percent of mothers of school-age children working, more than 25 percent of mothers of children aged seven and under working, and almost half of today's infants facing the prospect of living with only one parent before they reach the age of 18, the home is losing its impact on the development of children. The church is similarly declining in influence, both through a general decline in church attendance and through the increasing legal barriers to its participation in education in the United States.

Faced with the decline of these traditionally stable institutions, many have looked to the school to not only hold its own in difficult circumstances, but to pick up the slack, particularly in areas of moral development. Since adolescents typically spend only five minutes a day alone with their fathers (half of that spent watching television together), 40 minutes alone with their mothers, an hour a day with both parents together, and about 15 minutes with other adults, teachers are the most important adult contact through which they can learn about the culture in which they live (Csikszentmihalyi & McCormack, 1986). The roughly three hours per day that teenagers spend with teachers is still small when compared with the four hours spent with friends and the two hours spent with television and other media. It becomes even smaller when the factors of student-teacher ratio and general student apathy toward school involvement are added. Yet it is possible for teachers to have a marked influence on some, if not all of their students, particularly if they can convey an enthusiasm for their discipline and a concern for their students.

Stacked against this growing importance of the teacher's influence on students is the structure of the educational system, which often works against a teacher's efforts to be effective (McLaughlin, Pfeifer, Swanson-Owens, & Yee, 1986). Teachers are frequently discouraged by large heterogeneous classes, lack of proper materials, increasing demands and expectations, administrative interference, isolation, and a lack of recognition. In many ways it appears to be a vicious cycle of dissatisfaction with the educational system leading to decreased support, further dissatisfaction, etc. Solutions are proposed from all corners, with Goodlad (1984), perhaps the most prestigious of the recent analysts suggesting that teachers should teach fewer hours, with smaller classes, in order that they might, among other things, be able to spend more time preparing and put more energy into their teaching, leading, he asserts, to an overall greater effectiveness of teaching.

This chapter cannot possibly provide a complete analysis of the teacher's role, either in general or with respect to computers in education. Instead, the intent is to consider some of the ways in which teachers have been, or might be influenced by their use of computers, or by their students' use of computers. In order to organize this consideration, the various aspects of teachers and teaching will be treated under five rather general and overlapping headings. The first of these is the *theoretical teacher*, the ideal job description which contains some of our unrealistic expectations, some of the implications of this ideal, and some contrasts with the actual. The second is the *dispensing teacher*, the source of knowledge who fills each student with the required educational content. The third and fourth are quite similar, being the *guiding teacher* who directs students in their quest for knowledge and the *collaborating teacher* who actually follows the same path in learning along with the students. Finally, overlapping all the other categories is the *professional teacher*, taking responsibility for their professional needs, destiny, and their relationships with their students.

Deeply imbedded in these descriptions are the values of teachers, students, and society, the needs of these groups which might be met through computer applications, and trade-offs which occur as computer applications are implemented, and the impact on teacher workload from innovation, particularly technological innovation.

THE THEORETICAL TEACHER

The theoretical teacher is a product of philosophies of education and the values, or world views, which underlie these philosophies. The most widely held views about education often seem to be in terms of what education is not. That is, we often hear that education is not multiple-choice testing, workbooks, huge lecture halls, memorizing facts, or numerous other features that many people seem to agree with. Adding to the puzzle is the seeming agreement on a number of features which *are* a part of education, namely learning to solve problems, thinking clearly, generalizing, constructing a reasoned argument, and the like. If substantial agreement can be found among the features that define what education is and isn't, why should so much disagreement continue to exist? The answer seems to hinge on the selection of means rather than ends. That is, in attempting to evaluate the learning which has taken place we often find it more convenient to use means such as multiple-choice tests that emphasize facts rather than attempting to measure the more desirable, but harder to identify higher-level goals such as problem solving. Or, it may be that the goal is individualized instruction for every student, but the means is a room with 35 students and one teacher, again leading to a clash between means and ends.

The definition of the theoretical teacher, like the philosophies of education, probably finds more areas of agreement in the goals than in the means to achieve them. In some cases it could be claimed that no means exist for achieving some highly desirable goals, particularly those goals which have been carried over from the times when only a select portion of the population continued their education beyond elementary school levels. It is in these areas, where attainment of desirable goals is seemingly impossible, that the vision of computers as the solution to all educational ills is the strongest. Often, however, the vision fails to progress to a more material form.

Expectations about Teachers

Teachers of today are still expected to give their students discipline, instruction in the basic skills, and moral standards while inspiring their creativity, developing their higher cognitive skills, and providing them with individualized learning experiences. However, taking discipline as an example, not only has the teacher been given a greater problem, but the parental support of 50 to 100 years ago has been turned into opposition. A report in Britain remarks on five-year-olds who are aggressive, disobedient, use foul language, have poor concentration, and no toilet training (Stott, 1985). Yet it is too simple to paint this as a struggle between teacher and parents. If television is presenting the message that violence works, society in general has thrown out traditional rules of behavior, and the questioning of all authority is now the accepted norm, it is unfair to limit the blame to either parents or teachers (Stott, 1985).

The outstanding characteristics of the ideal teacher, at least in the minds of students who remember being strongly influenced (in a positive way) by a teacher, are enthusiasm for their discipline and learning in general, plus a concern for and involvement with their students (Csikszentmihalyi & McCormack, 1986). Similarly, adults tend to remember and feel influenced by school activities in which they became interested and deeply involved. The theoretical teacher, then, would not only have great interest and enthusiasm for the material being taught, but would also be able to pass this level of interest along to students. This has important implications for teacher workload as well as job satisfaction.

Most teachers say that they have entered the teaching profession in order to help children to learn, and creating an enthusiasm for learning in their students is likely to be intensely satisfying. Unfortunately, this usually means that failure to achieve this highly prized goal is also strongly felt, in terms of disappointment and frustration, which often turn to apathy and withdrawal. The possibilities of failure or at least perceived failure are strong, not only in terms of the initial challenge, but also in terms of the implications for workload. Few teachers are capable of maintaining their level of enthusiasm, concern, and involvement at a high level throughout all the approximately 1,000 hours in their teaching year. In fact, we probably don't expect them to maintain this level at all times, but, unfortunately, students are always learning *something* even when they aren't being taught, often learning something other than what they are being taught. Thus, in the relatively short period of time that a teacher might not show enthusiasm, interest, etc., the students might quickly "learn" that the teacher's apparent enthusiasm is not real, negating some of the effects of many more hours of expert teaching performance. For example, a large-scale survey of secondary schools in Ontario found that over 80 percent of the teachers felt they were concerned about the students' personal problems, but less than 20 percent of the students felt that their teachers were concerned about their personal problems (King & Warren, 1987).

If only a small slip on the part of the teacher can undo the effects of long-term interest, concern, and enthusiasm, leading to drops in student interest and performance, it is not unexpected that many teachers are quickly disillusioned and likely to say, "I can't give what it takes to be an elementary teacher for 20 years" (McLaughlin et al., 1986, p. 420). However, it is in exactly this area, consistency of performance, that many people see the strongest advantages of computers in education. That is, whatever good qualities computers have in the educational environment, they can repeat this performance day after day and year after year.

But if consistency is a strong point of the educational computer, it is also its downfall. For consistency in the ideal teacher means being able to attain the same goals in spite of changes in students, society, etc. Unfortunately, for most educational applications, consistency for computers means always using the same approach, whether it works or not. For example, one special education teacher reported that his students became extremely frustrated when the computer, with its "infinite patience," continued to repeat a question that they were unable to answer. Real teachers continue to learn as they teach, modifying their techniques to the benefit of their students, as long as they have support in their efforts to improve.

Goodlad (1984) has studied schools in detail, culminating in his recent study that involved over 27,000 people, students, teachers, and parents. He observes that although some teachers are capable of effective teaching, they often do not use these practices regularly in the classroom, perhaps being inhibited by the forces working against effective teaching. Moreover, mathematics teachers consistently expressed a desire for their students to "learn how to learn," to be logical thinkers, to solve problems effectively, and to think for themselves, but were observed not to go beyond rote learning and dependency on textbooks, in themselves unlikely to bring about the hoped for behavior. The problem seems to be similar to one described in Chapter 6, where the features of word processing and the goals of writing do not lead to student success unless the students actually learn how to use the features to reach the goals. Teachers seem to have access to the features of good teaching and aspire to the goals, but may not know how to use the features to reach the goals.

For example, Goodlad's observational team reported that in only 5 to 10 percent of the classes observed did they find any evidence of intense student involvement with learning, indicating on the one hand that this is a possibility, but on the other hand that it is often not reached. They also found that teachers tended to outtalk the entire class by a ratio of about three to one, that only about 5 percent of instructional time was designed to encourage students to respond, and that student responses, when they did occur, were rarely responded to with a supportive, corrective, or other type of meaningful acknowledgement. Most important, the relationship between teachers and classes was almost completely lacking in any form of shared emotional involvement, such as shared laughter, angry outbursts, or overt enthusiasm. In total, less than 3 percent of classroom time was devoted to praise, criticism, joy, humor, or other similar outbursts.

Again, an area of possible computer strength emerges. Educational courseware usually provides feedback to students in the form of praise or corrective suggestions and, of course, does so consistently. The crucial question remains as to whether one uses this fact to replace teachers with computers or encourages teachers to make more effective use of their own ability to provide feedback to their students. That is, the issue should not be one of summative evaluation, "which form of instruction do you choose?", but rather one of formative evaluation, "How can all forms of instruction be improved?" For example, Pogrow (1987) has found that teacher-student dialogues are more likely to produce learning than is successful use of software, but he cautions that teachers must learn not to "over-teach" or "over-help" students using computers.

Much more could be said about the characteristics of the ideal teacher, but the essential characteristic, with all of its strengths and weaknesses is that of humanness. It is this human quality that enables teachers to be genuinely caring, enthusiastic, and involved (not simulated), but the human quality also means that the strains of the educational system, their personal struggles, and the often uphill battle to reach their goals will probably be reflected in a decreasing ability to perform in the teaching role. However, while the weaknesses of humans are an inconvenience and an impediment to attaining the goals of the educational system, their strengths are an absolute essential to the maintenance of any desirable form of society. With other forms of direct human influence on children's development, such as the home, decreasing in their effect, it becomes imperative that the human aspects of the school at least be maintained, if not strengthened.

THE DISPENSING TEACHER

The dispensing teacher, or that part of any teacher which is the dispensing part is currently the most easily replaced, not only by computers, but also by movies, video and audio recordings, or books. The most classic examples of these are probably the introductory level university courses in psychology or similar subjects, where from 300 to more than 1,000 students may be playing the part of the audience for a lecturer who receives only a slight amount of feedback from the crowd, and then only from the first few rows. When sitting in the back rows of such a throng, it is not unusual to wonder why the first few rows of people are not brought into some comfortable studio where they can provide feedback to the lecturer while the rest watch via television on which they could at least see the expression on the lecturer's face as an added cue to the words.

Programmed Instruction

The answer, of course, is in the student, not the lecturer or the room. That is, when the student is in the lecture hall, even though it is easy for the mind to be elsewhere, the social norms enforce more attention to the lecturer's words than one feels forced to give to a televised face, which is one of the reasons why the special university campuses designed for television have not been used for such. And it was a response to this need to enforce attention, among other things, which led to the creation of programmed instruction (PI) as a form of automatic information dispensing. In its ideal form, PI requires the student to pay close attention to the text in order to answer the frequent questions that are interspersed. The same technique is used in effective teaching, maintaining class interest and attention through the use of frequent and relevant questions, or probing. Although this is an effective technique in either setting, talking about it is easier than doing it effectively. The trick to effective programmed instruction, in addition to obvious features such as readability, accuracy, sequence, etc., is to make the answers to the questions totally dependent upon reading the text carefully. Ideally, the question should be impossible to answer without having read the text and simple to answer after having read it. PI failed in the classroom because of an overabundance of poor material, which did not meet this necessary condition. With poor material, it can be either very difficult to answer the questions after having read the entire text, or more likely, too easy to answer the questions without having read all of the text. A frequent student strategy is to try and answer the question at the bottom of the page without reading *any* of the text, then read the text only if the question cannot be answered successfully. If some or all of the text is important to learning the material, but irrelevant to answering the question, the student loses the advantages programmed instruction is supposed to give. Conversely, if the student is by nature a careful reader of text material, poor questions will only be an irritant which slows down the reading.

Studies of PI materials, done mainly in the 1960s, showed that in many cases between 50 and 90 percent of the text material could be deleted without interfering with the student's ability to answer the question *for that particular block of text.* This fact is of more than historical interest, since much of what was first put onto computers as CAI (see Chapter 5) was just PI material which had been repackaged. The threat to the dispensing teacher had been averted in both cases because of a focus on the form of delivering instruction, rather than on the effectiveness of the content.

Again, what is often raised as a summative question, "Is CAI (or PI) more effective than the teacher in delivering instruction?", should be looked at as a formative question, "How can the delivery of instruction (in general) be improved?" The important factor is that of maintaining attention and interest while information is being presented. For teachers, CAI, or PI the important point is to ask *questions that require understanding* of the material in order to be answered.

As mentioned earlier, Goodlad (1984) and his colleagues found a strong emphasis on teachers *telling* their students for about 70 percent of the instructional time, little emphasis on students being expected or required to respond, and little information in the feedback to students when they did respond. In many ways, what these observers describe might seem to be an answer to the question, "How should you teach if you want to be replaced by a computer, television set, tape recorder, programmed text, book, or stone tablet?" In a few words, the answer is "talk, don't ask, don't answer."

CAI and Teacher Workload

Some have suggested that the use of computers (or equivalent devices) to present instructional material may be a good way either to weed out those teachers who only dispense material, or to change these teachers by eliminating that part of their repertoire. Skinner (1984) sees PI as a way of not only changing the teacher's workload, but also reducing it. Similarly, a recent advertisement by a major computer manufacturer asserts that one of the most important things they have learned in schools is that "computers give teachers time to teach." If this is the case, why not have computers (or PI) take over most of the straightforward instruction and just let teachers handle the remaining tasks, thereby reducing the teacher's workload. Megarry (1983) reasons along these lines in suggesting that class sizes might be increased to pay for computers, while Papert (1980b), though not proposing the use of CAI, nevertheless sees increased class size as the answer to some of the funding problems associated with introducing computers into schools.

Evidence about the effect of computer use on teacher workload is not abundant, but what is available indicates that one might argue just as convincingly for a reduced class size with CAI as for an increased class size (Mathinos & Woodward, 1987). When all the members of a class are working at their own pace via CAI, it is possible that most if not all of the students in the class will be on different topics at any one time. Attempting to deal with student questions on 35 different topics is not a reduction in workload (or stress) from having to deal with questions on one topic. Even though CAI might be more effective in reducing the number of questions that students ask on a single topic, say from ten per student to one per student, the ten questions per student on a given topic would be highly overlapping and might boil down to only 20 to 30 different questions, all on the same topic, while the CAI questions in one day could well be on 35 different topics.

Another effect of the individualized approach is that it creates a repetition in the questions that arise. That is, if study of a certain topic prompts students to ask a particular question, having each student working at a different rate and reaching the topic on a different day means that the same question might be raised 35 different times on 35 different days.

Of course, what has been described as the problems of individualization is part of the motivation for those working on Intelligent CAI (ICAI). Although successful development of ICAI might alleviate some of the teacher's problems, ICAI (discussed further in Chapter 4) is not sufficiently advanced to be a solution to the individualization problem in the near future.

It should be stressed that the preceding is not to be seen as an argument against an individualized approach to instruction, but rather as questioning the assumption that the use of CAI (or equivalent self-paced instruction) results in a reduction of the teacher's workload. If one fails to question the assumption, and it is indeed false, then the result is likely to be that teachers will either try to avoid an implementation of individualized systems because of the extra work involved, or not realizing the amount of extra work involved, will feel angry and misled after the individualized systems are implemented. In either case, the response of teachers is likely to be against the individualized systems.

Evidence of the effect of this extra workload was seen in a small survey of science teachers done by Doug Hayhoe, a graduate student at OISE, in which those teachers who felt that computers had affected their workload were split almost evenly between those who saw it as being reduced and those who saw it as being increased. However, those who saw their workload as being increased were primarily using computers with their students (CAI and other applications), while those who saw their workload as being reduced were using it for their own work (word processing, student records, and the like). Some of the teachers who were using computers for their own work reported that they had begun by using them with their students and had then changed their applications on the basis of their experience. Carmichael et al., (1985) comment several times on the extra work taken on by their teachers as a consequence of their participation in this two-year study. In one instance, they remark that one of the teachers didn't "have time to deal with" the factors that caused the boys to have more access to computers than did the girls. Swinton, Amarel, and Morgan (1978) also describe a case study of a teacher who felt the computer system provided her with information which could have been useful for her students, but she did not have time to make use of the information provided on all the students' individual progress.

The dispensing teacher seems to exist not so much because teachers see this as a most effective technique for teaching students, but given their conditions for teaching, particularly in terms of class size, it is probably the most safe approach to take, since a truly individualized approach for each student is clearly impossible. Once it is seen (or *if* it is seen) that the use of computers to individualize instruction does not lead to an increased class size, but may necessitate a reduced class, the more formative form of the question may be considered. That is, the answer to the question of how instruction might be individualized may then be seen in terms of reduced class sizes with or without the use of computers, rather than beginning with the computer as an assumed essential.

THE GUIDING TEACHER

Computer Managed Instruction

Just as the dispensing teacher has a computer counterpart in CAI, the guiding teacher is imitated by Computer Managed Instruction (CMI). CMI is defined as "the use of computers to assist in the management of classwork or class grading and record keeping" (New Webster's, 1984, p. 56). It can include the presentation of instruction as in CAI, but the emphasis is on monitoring the progress of students and prescribing new material or activities for their continued learning.

Merrill et al. (1986) use a broad definition of CMI, including any tool applications of computers that can be used by teachers and administrators in managing the instructional process. Their list of CMI tools includes the computer grade book, test scoring, and test generation in addition to functions which can be a part of using "terminal-based CMI," such as collecting data on student progress and creating reports. By any definition, CMI might be thought of as more versatile than CAI, since the instruction can be carried out in a variety of forms, including CAI, so long as the record of that instruction and its results are entered into the CMI system.

One dimension on which CMI systems can vary is the degree to which they complement or supplement the teacher. That is, a CMI system can be programmed to suggest new learning activities for students on the basis of their previous learning or, more frequently, the system provides a summary for the teacher to use in making these curriculum decisions. The latter approach fills a need for most teachers, since it is virtually impossible to monitor the progress of all students in a large class with any amount of precision. Access to data on student progress, provided that teachers have sufficient time to use them, allows teachers to exercise greater control over not only student learning, but also over their own professional lives.

Swinton, Amarel, and Morgan, in evaluating a large scale implementation of CAI used in elementary schools, comment that "elementary teachers demand, and perform more effectively when given, control over curriculum" (Swinton, Amarel, & Morgan, 1978, p. 25). In the cases they studied, the issue of control created a problem for teachers. During part of the evaluation the control options were not available to teachers, yet when teachers were given data on which to base such decisions, the necessary time was not always available for them to use them. Moreover, Swinton et al. state that some appropriate data, particularly factors such as identification of when students are "goofing off" rather than doing serious work, cannot be collected automatically, and even if they were collected, algorithms for making curriculum decisions based on these data do not exist.

Classroom Control

The problem seems to be similar to one found frequently in business settings. With the use of computerized data management systems, managers may be given voluminous reports at regular intervals, but be unable to assimilate the data in time to use them, nor are algorithms available to "boil down" the data to the relevant items. A backlash in the business setting may take the form of relying on "management by walking around," rather than depending on copious amounts of quantitative data. This choice, similar to using naturalistic rather than experimental methods, may provide the manager with fewer data that seem to have more validity.

Using computers in classrooms seems to encourage the guiding teacher, often by replacing, or perhaps more accurately displacing the dispensing teacher. That is, teachers who have had a "teacher centred" classroom in which the teacher is working with the total class for most of the school day find that introducing computers tends to discourage this arrangement. Instead of all students being available for the teacher to talk at them, with a computer in the room some students are usually separated from the class, working with the computer. As a result, many teachers have found that the presence of computers has caused them to move from the teacher centred style to an "activity centred" or "student centred" approach. In the latter approach, most commonly found in lower elementary grades, students move from activity to activity throughout the day, with many different activities going on in the room at any one time.

For most teachers, moving from the "front of the room" starring role to a more serving, circulating around the room style is a significant change, both to their practice and to their self-image. As Goodlad (1984) observes, teachers feel the need to be in control of "classroom circumstances," something which is more difficult to do when a variety of activities are in progress. However, most teachers report that continued exposure to the activity centered classroom makes them feel more at ease and pleased with the outcomes.

The classroom computer may also be altering the teacher's control in a way that most teachers are not aware of, namely in changing the priorities of classroom activities. Teachers who have activity centered classrooms often stress that the activities are of equal importance, particularly those teachers who have been using this approach prior to using computers. For the latter group, it is usually emphasized that the computer is just another activity, not any more important than any of the others. Yet the behavior of these teachers often contradicts their stated beliefs, something the students will very quickly learn. For example, if a student at the computer runs into difficulty, the teacher often arrives quickly to put things right, abandoning whatever else was being done previously. Similarly, students may be given a free choice of activities to take part in throughout the day, but they can't help but notice that when their time comes to use the computer they better move there quickly or the teacher will be upset (Rose, 1986).

Curriculum Control

In establishing its higher priority, not only is the computer seen as more important, but the process tends to steal time away from other activities, particularly the curriculum which has been officially defined. Thus, if the teacher is working with one or more students on important reading skills when the student at the computer has a problem, the time for learning reading skills is lost. Carmichael et al. (1985) report that one intermediate level teacher was disappointed that some of his students were not taking time away from their other subjects (taught by other teachers) in order to spend more time with computer activities, which were not a part of the official curriculum. In another setting, a mother stated that her son's teacher gave assignments in all required curriculum areas at the beginning of the week, worked only with the students using the computers, allowed students to spend all of their time with the computers after their regular work was finished, and never provided feedback on regular curriculum work. Needless to say, these sorts of behaviors speak volumes to students about the value of the traditional curriculum, the subjects for which they are supposed to be acquiring an enthusiasm.

Computer activities can also create problems for teachers as they try to discover the source of students' problems in working with the learning materials. When students are using worksheets, or working on paper solving problems from a text, the teacher can usually "work back" along the student's written work to discover the source of the problem, or work back through the text to see where the student went wrong. With computer displays, however, the student's previous work and the previous text from the program are not only hidden from view, but may be extremely difficult to recover. As a result, much of the time that CAI (or a similar application) has saved is once again lost as the steps must be retraced, and the teacher's perception of computers as time-saving slaves may be lost forever.

If the major issue for the dispensing teacher is one of time, the central issue for the guiding teacher is probably the slightly more general one of control. This would include control of the teacher's time as well as the activities of the students and control of the curriculum. In all of these aspects the effect of computer use seems to be contradictory as "the computer giveth and the computer taketh away." On the positive side, computers allow students to work on their own while records are automatically kept, activities are available in a wide range of areas, and the regular curriculum can be supplemented. On the negative side, the records of student work done on the computer are seldom used due to their volume and/or inappropriateness, a given classroom may have little selection of computer activities or students may choose unproductive activities, and the regular curriculum may be reduced, both in time and in importance, because of the computer's priority.

One suspects that many of these problems of control and/or time are related to the novelty of computers in classrooms and might disappear as computers become more numerous. Yet, the time before computers become common may be lengthy and the attitudes and habits developed during that period may have serious consequences for future as well as present computer uses. Therefore, it seems necessary to treat these problems as important, though possibly transient. More will be said about these issues in the section on the "Professional Teacher."

THE COLLABORATING TEACHER

Intelligent CAI

The collaborating teacher, learning the same subject matter as the students, has suddenly become commonplace as computers make their debut in more classrooms. If a counterpart to the collaborating teacher is a part of computer applications, it must be in the form of artificial intelligence, particularly Intelligent CAI (ICAI). In ICAI, the program is not actually learning with the student, but a model of the student's learning is often a feature of ICAI, so that in some sense the student is learning along with a computer model learning the same material. Although the intent of ICAI is to capitalize on this parallel learning, Bruner (1985) asserts that many models are required to account for the learning of any one student, and the experience for the collaborating teacher is much more personal and emotional than that which is possible through a computer program.

Joint Learning Experiences

Cuffaro, in discussing the uncertainty with which many educators approach computers, says, "The vulnerability of not knowing, of being a novice (a position not particularly comfortable for many educators), has become a shared experience" (Cuffaro, 1984, p. 565). Most teachers find it strange and possibly difficult to share this experience with fellow teachers and other adults, but many are sharing it with their students.

The strength of the joint learning experience is that it allows and encourages the teacher to convey to students an enthusiasm for learning in a totally natural, honest, and believable way. In some ways it is like the approach which can often be used in graduate education, where professors are able to offer courses in areas about which they would like to learn in order to have their students help them. However, in practice, the collaborating teacher is usually found in elementary schools learning computer programming with LOGO, or perhaps BASIC, along with the students. (At least one secondary teacher has reported a similar experience when asked to teach a new, for him, computer programming language at short notice.)

Providing students with an honest feeling of enthusiasm for what they are learning is a crucial benefit, but the teachers are often more ecstatic over their own personal experience. Eaton and Olson (1985) report on a group of elementary teachers who were "doing computers" along with their students (see also Olson, 1985; Olson, 1986; Olson & Eaton, 1986). In many ways the experience should have been disappointing, in view of the "nonofficial" status of the subject matter, their inability to reach their desired goals in increasing problem-solving skills, etc., and their perception that computers posed a threat to classroom control. Yet these teachers were determined to continue to "do computers" because it made their classroom more interesting and enjoyable, it improved their relationships with students, and most of all, it makes a statement about the kind of person they want to be.

Desirable as the experience of collaborative learning might be, one has to question whether it can be continued at least with the same topic, year after year. The previously mentioned secondary school teacher reported that he was unable to recreate the shared learning environment after the first time he taught the previously unknown programming language. Carmichael et al. (1985) report that in the second year of their study teachers were generally less involved in their students' work with LOGO and that student achievement also declined. One has to suspect that the teachers studied by Eaton and Olson, despite their intentions, would not be able to preserve the experience of learning with their students for this next attempt.

Peer Tutoring

Although the primary effect on teachers of collaborative learning is in terms of increased enthusiasm, particularly their own, the effect of new teaching strategies is also important for both them and their students. Olson (1985) reports that the collaborative teachers, presumably because of their lack of expertise, but also because of time constraints, made extensive use of the "teach yourself" strategy. By this he meant that the teachers did a minimal amount of whole class teaching on the computer topics, relying heavily on peer tutoring and student use of written materials, primarily manuals, to facilitate learning by the entire class. In order to further save time while supporting what was not part of the official curriculum, the teachers also made use of students to preview software, chose software and activities which required minimal teacher support (for this reason they chose to use BASIC rather than LOGO), and made computer access part of the classroom reward structure.

Although the teach yourself approach seemed to offer the necessary time saving for the teachers, a number of factors prevented these savings from materializing. As a result, teachers found themselves trying to do "two things at once" much more than they had anticipated, mainly because computer programming seemed to require more support than they had expected. In addition, they found that the alternative support systems did not function as well as they had hoped, with peer tutors finding errors, but not tutoring, while manuals and display screens proved difficult to read and use. Although teachers may have been surprised to find that students found the computer work boring rather than compelling, the most alarming factor was that student difficulties, usually easily remedied in other "teach yourself" contexts, were often quite intractable. That is, the teachers' previous experience with self learning contexts were not upheld in the computer programming environment, resulting in a much greater time requirement than they had anticipated.

Note that Olson (1985) and Eaton and Olson (1985) are referring to the same teachers, but from slightly different points of view. This highlights the finding that these teachers who had had a substantially negative experience, in terms of their plans and expectations, were nonetheless pleased with the results and determined to continue.

It is interesting that the teachers made use of peer tutoring, for the teachers themselves were being put in the position of peers to some extent. That peer tutoring was not satisfactory might be a result of improper training for the tutors, a possible false saving of time. For with peer tutoring, as with learner control of CAI or word processing in creative writing, the availability of a feature to the students is only useful when the students know how to apply the feature to what they want to do. That is, students given control over their learning process have to know how to exercise that control effectively, students trained to use a word processor have to know how to write in order to use a word processor in writing, and students given the opportunity to learn from each other via peer tutoring have to know how to accomplish the peer tutoring process effectively.

An answer may lie in a more explicit linking between the teacher's first year of collaborative learning and the process of peer tutoring. During this first year, teachers are likely to find themselves in the role of both tutor and tutee, getting a fresh view of what it means both to teach and to learn the material they are working with. In this setting, their most effective investment of time might be in developing techniques of peer tutoring, both in terms of the general tutoring process (which might be applicable to other subjects) and specific techniques for dealing with particular parts of the study of computers and programming.

The major issues for the collaborating teachers also seem to be control and time, with perhaps more emphasis on the latter. Collaborative learning is in itself an attempt to save time, the time needed to learn the subject well enough to teach it. The "teach yourself" approach as part of the shared learning experience was also an attempt to minimize the teacher time spent on instruction. Finally, Carmichael et al. (1985) noted that the teachers in the second year of their study were less inclined to spend the extra amounts of time they had given in the first year, citing this as a factor in the students' decreased achievement in the second year.

THE PROFESSIONAL TEACHER

The professional teacher is an important part of every teacher, independent of classification within the previously defined categories. Professionalism is also a major issue among teachers, as evidenced in the report to the Quebec Minister of Education (The Conditions of Teaching, 1984). Although many more topics could be considered under this heading, only three organizing concepts will be used. The first of these is control, primarily control of their own destiny, not only in terms of time, but also with reference to accountability, values, and curriculum issues. The second concept is that of needs, including teachers' definitions of their needs for new skills, support, and changes in the classroom, school, and educational system. The final issue is that of teachers' relationships with their students, with a particular focus on the relative position of the computer within the triangle of teacher-student-computer, along with the general question of the effects that class size has on these relationships.

Teacher Value Changes

Teachers' values seem to be central to the issue of controlling their own destiny. Hoyle sees these values as a major impediment to the extensive use of computers in schools, the obstacle on which "have foundered so many educational innovations: programmed learning, team teaching, resource-based learning and so forth" (Hoyle, 1983, p. 60). He sees this arising from the fact that many teachers are "restricted" rather than "extended" professionals, relying more on personal experience, intuition, and interaction with students than on the knowledge available in the professional literature. He refers to a study by Carlson (1965) in which teachers were found to have taken a number of actions which had the effect of reducing the range of achievement in a class using programmed instruction as a form of individualized instruction. That is, teachers prevented the more able students from getting too far ahead of the less able by allowing only the slowest students to take their work home and by requiring the fastest students to spend more time with enrichment materials, among other ploys. It might be concluded that these teachers had acted in a logical manner, placing a higher value on maintaining control in the classroom (and of their time) than on opportunities for some students to move ahead more rapidly. However, Hoyle only speculates briefly as to the specific values involved, placing more emphasis on the power of teacher values, whatever they may be, to modify the impact of innovations in the classroom.

Hoyle's observations seem to be accurate, but they only convey half of the process of interaction between technological innovation and teachers' values. In the two-year study reported by Carmichael et al. (1985), one can see evidence of a two-way process, with teachers' values being altered by their use of computers, as Ellul (1964) and others have observed, as well as their values affecting their use of computers and their students' perceptions of computers.

In the case of a primary teacher, her values seemed to shift between the computer environment and that of the normal classroom. In using LOGO, she emphasized that students should feel free to explore, making errors and taking risks in order to discover new things about LOGO, geometry, etc. She found that the better students in the traditional environment had considerable difficulty in adjusting to this discovery environment, while those who were lower achievers and behavior problems in the normal classroom "took off" with LOGO. A plausible explanation for this effect seems to be that this teacher, as with most teachers, highly valued error-free performance in her regular classroom activities and her encouraging of errors in the LOGO environment was particularly difficult for those who had been most successful at eliminating mistakes in the normal setting. Those who normally made mistakes in any environment had no adjustment to make, hence they could "take off" in LOGO faster than the high achievers. (Some researchers are motivated to study the use of LOGO by even younger children for this very reason, because these children are less likely to have learned that making mistakes is "bad.")

For one intermediate level teacher, the computer seemed to function as a medium through which he could convey his valuing of competition. This is not to say that this teacher, or any other teacher, needs to use computers to create a competitive classroom environment, nor that the use of computers necessarily creates competition among students. Rather, this classroom seems to be an example of how students might come to view computers as an environment for competition because of the value orientation of their teacher. In this case, the teacher had weekly challenges in which the *first* student to solve the challenge was rewarded, and both the teacher and observers noted that sharing of information about computers among students was declining over the course of the study. Students also commented that they felt correct solutions, if they were not the first correct answer, were not valued.

Thus, teachers might be seen to exercise control over their lives through actions derived from their values, while at the same time, the intrusion of technology, usually not entirely under their control, does seem to alter the very values on which their actions are based. It is interesting to note that a similar interaction among control, values, and technology seems to occur in the area of accountability.

School Principals

The school principal is usually seen as being accountable for the instruction carried out by the teachers and this may lead to disagreements between the principal and teachers on the issue of technological innovation. For example, Olson (1986) notes that in the case of the four teachers "doing computers" (see previous section on the "collaborating teacher"), all of the school principals expressed concern about the educational value of the teachers' use of computers. The teachers were aware of these concerns, but had no doubts of their own, carrying out the task with enthusiasm and being pleased with the results, even though they did not achieve their intended goals.

On the other hand, in a number of schools where the principal has committed the entire school to an innovation much like "doing computers," the behavior of some teachers indicates a feeling that the principal, having made the commitment, is now totally accountable for the results. For example, some teachers who run a very disciplined, goal-oriented classroom, seem almost totally indifferent to student misbehavior in the computer laboratory, a possible indication that they don't feel accountable for what happens in the computer environment (Rose, 1986). This may seem like an obvious consequence, but it often seems to be ignored when plans are being made for all teachers to use computers, based on the experience of those teachers who have chosen to use computers.

Eggers and Wedman present a scenario describing the steering effect of a hypothetical school principal who begins by organizing fund raising so that microcomputers will not be limited to the math department. The principal finds that the use of the individual computers by teachers in their classrooms leaves much to be desired and arranges to move them all into a supervised computer laboratory. The story line is based on the authors' perception that "Computers are not nearly as threatening to teachers as teachers are to computers" (Eggers & Wedman, 1984, p. 29). Principals who subscribe to this point of view are likely to put considerable pressure on their teachers to use computers in the "right" way.

Perhaps the most intimidating computer of all, in terms of its effect on teacher behavior and competition for control in the classroom, is the "temporary computer." If a teacher has a computer in the classroom on a permanent basis, it is somehow much easier for the teacher to ignore the computer than if it is present on a temporary basis, for a certain number of weeks per year, or days per month. Permanent computers are frequently observed to be unused, either because children do not choose to use them at all times, or because the teacher has unplugged it and put it in the corner. However, the "limited time offer" has a similar impact in the classroom to that in advertising. It seems very difficult for teachers to maintain their normal routine in the face of a computer on loan, or for them to allow their students the choice of activities that is normally permitted. This can be seen as a good finding, in that it indicates that teachers will feel more freedom to exercise control over the curriculum when permanent computers are more commonplace. On the other hand, this could be bad news if it means that our observations of teacher use of temporary computers are misleading us into expecting patterns of use which are merely transitory.

The Innovation Process

The preceding is all part of the innovation process as it affects teachers, a process much more thoroughly described by Fullan (1982). It does, however, serve to illustrate his points that it is unrealistic to expect all teachers to be interested in change, but that a large number of teachers do choose to adopt innovations. Bourque and Ramage (1984) describe what they call the "hidden" costs of computer innovation" in the context of a pilot project using word processors in the Writing Center of Montana State University. They describe their project as being successful on the whole, but enumerate several of the many unexpected factors which were significant drains on their time and energy. In fact, they explicitly state that the cost to them was not only large, but "the drain on our time and energy exceeded our worst nightmares" (p. 36). Yet, similar to the teachers who were "doing computers," they found the overall experience rewarding.

A nightmarish experience when one has chosen to participate and the overall results are satisfactory is one thing. But as Fullan notes in summarizing Lortie's findings, teachers typically operate in an environment where they are uncertain that their teaching is having any positive effect, and where they never have enough time to accomplish what seems to be needed. If a nightmarish experience with computers is imposed on teachers, rather than being of their own choice, one can hardly blame them for resisting the innovation.

Of course, one expects, or at least hopes, that the initial experience with computers does not have to be a nightmare. Malone (1985) points out that as computer hardware declines in price, optimizing the use of the computer should become less important and other resources, particularly those of people's time and effort, should become more important. Unfortunately, at least two factors retard the adoption of this enlightened attitude. The first is that even when computers have declined in price to a level much less than it is today, their costs to schools will still appear to be large, since school budgets typically have little cash once the costs of buildings and staff have been taken care of. The second factor is that a concern for staff time and energy often does not proceed beyond the level of lip service. The general issue of teacher support will be discussed later, but an illustration from business may serve to illustrate the point. In an article describing what appeared to be some superficial applications of computers, the manager for cosmetics of a U.S. department store chain explained why computerized makeup systems are limited to two weeks in one store. The rationale was that after two weeks, "the novelty wears off, and the people who have to run the machine get exhausted" (Elmer-DeWitt, 1986), but this rationale is logically inconsistent, if not self-serving. If one were primarily concerned about staff being overworked, the removal of the machines after two weeks does nothing for their overwork, since the overwork should cease when the novelty wears off.

Turner (1984) offers another disquieting example from business, more accurately from government, in describing how workers in a U.S. Social Security office found their work environment substantially degraded when they were given access to an improved computer system. One specific result may raise concerns about teacher-student relationships, since workers using the new computer system were more likely to reject client claims than those workers using the old system. Attewell and Rule (1984) review the general effects of computers on organizations and conclude that none exist. That is, the range of effects is so wide and varied that they feel any prediction of future effects in organizations is almost total speculation.

An anecdote from a large Canadian corporation provides an excellent example of the contrast between the perfection of intended results and the blemishes of negative side effects. A new electronic mail system had recently been installed in a division with 1,800 employees. Use of the system had been encouraged and most business communication took place via the system. After a time, however, the managers began to complain that not only were their assistant vice-presidents requesting their end-of-month reports earlier, but the value of the report seemed to be totally dependent on how early it was submitted. The reason for the situation seemed to be a side effect of the electronic mail system. The assistant vice-presidents were sending their reports, previously delivered in batches by the internal mail system, to the vice-president by electronic mail and a competition had developed over who would be first, since all messages on the mail system were dated (to 1/100 of a second). It is interesting to speculate on how this competition affected the efficient administration of the division and also to ponder the similarity between this environment and the classroom where competition was stressed.

The issue of teachers' needs, especially their definition of needs for new skills and support, is also a central part of the innovation process. Becker (1985) reports that the results of his national (U.S.) survey indicate that teachers see their three most important needs as insufficient resources, insufficient time for their computer work, and insufficient interest on the part of their colleagues.

Teacher Workload

Attempting to acquire new skills can lead to time expenditures far beyond what one could reasonably expect. One teacher found that the course on LOGO was not meeting her needs, took a university offered in-service course to supplement, then found that trips to computer stores were still necessary to locate useable software for her students. This teacher wound up spending two nights per week in courses, plus spare time in computer stores, in preparation for a class which only occupied 40 minutes of her teaching week (Rose, 1986). Her problem not only illustrates the lengths to which teachers will go in order to help their students, but also indicates that a teacher's perception of adequate support is often not the same as that of the agency providing the courses and other support, be it local school board or university.

Some school boards offer training sessions to the entire staff of a school (usually elementary schools), so that not only do the teachers learn in their own school, but also with all their colleagues, providing a wider base of expertise for their collective further work with computers. Unfortunately, even though this training is usually presented on a volunteer basis, teachers are well aware of pressure to attend the courses. The pressure comes from other teachers, board officials, parents, students, and, of course, the principal who is often instrumental in having these teacher development sessions scheduled. Of these pressure groups, the students are perhaps the most effective, particularly if the school rule is that classes may not use the computer laboratory unless the teacher has taken part in the courses.

Experiences with the use of computers may often lead to teachers seeing their most important needs as being a reduction in class size, particularly if the school has a computer laboratory. The first few visits to the computer laboratory can be the most painful, since almost all of the students will require individual attention during these initial sessions and class size will become a more apparent problem. Other school and board factors likely to make themselves felt are those of additional staff for assisting teachers in the computer laboratory, or support to allow splitting the class for laboratory work, and the provision of extra time for preparing to use the computer with their students, cleaning up after student use, and practicing computer skills.

Since most teachers place a strong emphasis on their personal helping relationships with students, the impact of the computer on this relationship takes on a considerable importance. In particular, will computers intrude between teacher and student, or will the computers be alternatives to teachers, turning students away from the usual relationship? Out of this concern can be seen the reason for some teachers and students meeting at the computers to work together. Obviously, class size is a factor in the relative roles of these three classroom actors. As the number of students increases, and the number of computers does the same, the possibility for teacher and student to work together at the computer becomes less likely.

Student data

Gray (1983) reports that one use of a centralized computer-based curriculum management system led to a reduction in the amount of teacher-student, learning-oriented interaction, a change seen as reducing the teacher's role toward that of a technician rather than a professional. This would seem to find some agreement with the results reported by Swinton, Amarel, and Morgan (1978) that teachers were unable to find the time to use the data generated by the computerized management system. Presumably, to find the time to process these data they would have to reduce their time for other activities, including their interaction with students. This would also seem to agree with the findings that computer use tends to steal time away from other classroom activities (Carmichael et al., 1985; Olson, 1986), and that along with its associated overhead activities, leads to a reduction in the time teachers can spend with students' learning problems.

The problem does not seem to lie in the feedback to teachers of student progress being irrelevant, for Bloom (1984) lists improved teacher feedback on student learning as one of the four most important factors in making significant progress in improving instruction. The problem seems to be that the feedback that Bloom sees as important, information on teachers' differential treatment of students, is not the information which computerized systems typically provide. Thus we have the frustrating situation for teachers of realizing that they need feedback on their students' progress, being presented with unreasonably large amounts of data from computer systems and, if they manage to sacrifice the extra hours of time needed to absorb the data, probably finding that it doesn't help them improve their teaching.

Not only do the computers' data not give them the needed information on differential treatment of students, the use of computers can also lead to further unwanted differentiation through its altering and distorting of values. For example, a teacher who feels that time on the computer is very important may tend to tell children who finish their assigned task before the majority of the class to "do it again," a "busyness" type of attitude which actually undermines the perceived importance of the activity. That is, if using computers were really so important, we wouldn't be asking students to mindlessly repeat what they had just finished doing. In another example, one finds a teacher who emphasizes group work and cooperation in her classroom, to be actually prohibiting students from working together in the computer laboratory, or using the sharing of a computer as punishment (Rose, 1986). This teacher seems to be intimidated by the fact that shared computer use might result in some (expensive) computers standing idle, but the message may be confusing for those students who were learning that sharing is a good thing. The message is similarly mixed when students from a noncompetitive classroom find that only the best computer drawing will be printed out on the printer because it's too expensive to print one for everyone.

With Goodlad (1984) building a strong case for a reduced class size, and McLaughlin et al. (1986) presenting a strong case for class size being a major source of teacher frustration, and the increasing evidence from Olson (1986), Bourque and Ramage (1984), and others that the use of computers in the classroom increases teacher workload rather than reducing it, one might expect that reduced class size would be seen as a requirement for the introduction of computers in classrooms. Yet Papert (1980b) takes the opposite approach, one echoed by Megarry (1983), that the use of computers will allow teachers to handle larger classes, thereby solving the problem of paying for the additional computers. But this is not the only area in which educators seem to fail to grasp the magnitude of the implementation problems. It has been reported that one of the United

States is considering a proposal that teachers take *nine hours* of computer training before they teach a computer course (*Education Week*, 1984). This suggestion brings to mind the reaction of a principal who took a full-day course on "You and your MS-DOS" and realized that "I do indeed now know how to turn the machine on and off, but what else can it do?" (Cameron, 1985, pp. 4-5). The problem is not just one of course length, or even limited to North America, as a number of Swiss teachers complained that their 200-hour course was too theoretical and had little to do with what one might be able to do in a classroom (Des maîtres mécontents dénoncent, 1986).

Malone's (1985) assessment that human time and effort must become more important than optimal utilization of hardware is accurate, but the educational climate militates against it. Johnson (1987b) documents the additional resource materials and enormous expenditures of teacher time needed to implement effective use of data base systems in studying social history in grades seven and eight. Lee (1987) notes that computer labs seem to be used much less frequently than teachers report, with Mathinos and Woodward (1987) finding the same result and attributing it to teachers being "overwhelmed." When the emphasis is placed on computers, and in quantity, without recognition that their use *requires* substantial expenditures not only for software, but also for user education, operating expenses, and perhaps even reduced class sizes, the stage is set for disaster. When the error is compounded further by financing computer acquisitions through the reduction of other essentials, such as instructional materials, support staff, and professional development for teachers, the overture to the disaster has begun. If the next step is to relegate the teacher to a role of assisting computers to do their classroom role, then the curtain will surely rise on a disaster in full progress.

9 *Parent Role*

Computers add another confusing factor to parents' concerns about their role in their children's development, with respect to the roles played by the school and other parts of society in general. With regard to the school, as Goodlad (1984) notes, the relationship between parents and schools has substantially deteriorated from the almost unquestioned support which was given in earlier times. He believes that the result has not only been a weakening of the collaborative effort of working toward common goals, but also a moving of the school toward more emphasis on the "safer" seatwork-based instruction, in order to avoid the lawsuits which might come from field trips, or other more risky activities.

The role of parents is complex and changing. All members of society find they have less and less time and parents are no exception. It is tempting to suggest technology as a path to increased parental involvement in schools (one of our graduate students proposed computer bulletin boards), but technology (and learning to use it) seems to cost time, not save it. Even if they had the time, can we assume that parents want to be involved? However, rather than focus on parents alone, the crucial questions have to do with student needs and the way in which parents can meet them. In particular, student needs in the areas of values, educational attainment, and family relationships will be examined.

In this chapter, the role of parents will be considered in four parts. The first deals with the function of parents as "transmitters of values" as they attempt to influence their children and schools, while competing with other value sources in society. The second section is more limited in focus, being concerned with the specific connection between parents and classroom activities. The third component moves in a new area, the questions about the possible benefits and drawbacks of having computers in the home, with respect to children in particular, but also as they affect family relationships. The last section is intended to tie the first three together in considering possible ways in which parents, students, teachers, and computers might all be brought together in useful combinations.

PARENTS AS A VALUES SOURCE

Each generation passes a mixed collection of "inheritance" along to the succeeding generations. Our first reaction is probably that the bulk of this transference is in the form of vast amounts of knowledge which this and preceding generations have created for the enlightenment of those who follow. Others, however, present views that give a contradictory, or at least wider view of the process. In discussing the issue of responsibility for technology, Jonas (1973) points out that only *present* values can be heard when decisions about the use of technology are made, that future inhabitants of our world have no lobby or power in the decision-making process. Lewis (1978) makes the case even more strongly, asserting that not only does "man's power over nature" usually translate into some men's power over other men, but that all long-term exercises of power mean the power of earlier generations over later ones. That is, each generation, through its decisions and actions, places limits on what future generations are able to do through eliminating certain alternatives, though we tend to see the result only in terms of the alternatives which have been extended, not those which have been closed off.

In considering the transfer of knowledge in the electronic age, Brod (1984) uses the forms of culture transmission defined by Margaret Mead. In her analysis, the *postfigurative* culture is one in which change is almost imperceptible, where the past of the adult is the future of the child. In the *cofigurative* culture, it is natural for the behavior of each new generation to differ from the preceding, but the elders still have the effect of placing limits on the amount of change. In today's technological society, which can be seen as *prefigurative*, the experience of adults is not only poor preparation for their children's world, it is actually limiting in its effects. That is, as Margaret Mead foresaw, we are now in an age where it is not uncommon for adults to learn from the intelligent young. Merging these observations with those of Jonas and Lewis, one can see that present and future generations of parents may not only see that their decisions can have a limiting effect on their children, but also may be acutely aware that their children have a more adequate knowledge base for such decisions than they do as parents.

The preceding point is deliberately overstated, since in the perception of many parents it is likely to be this strong or stronger, even if it is not true! A concern that parents may be immobilized by a fear of technological inadequacy prompts this remark, for parents' most important contributions to their children are not to be found in the form of technological know-how, but as a value base on which the use of technology can be built. As seen in the preceding discussions of equity in computer use, artificial intelligence, and the application of computers to courseware, writing, and programming (see Chapters 3 to 6), consider-

ations of how to use computers that are not based on an explicit value foundation inevitably seem to lead to the materialistic conclusion that "more is better."

Changes in Families

Children do inherit values from their parents, but the values are not limited to
those that parents (or children) want to be passed on. Child abuse is a striking
example, with most abusers having been abused themselves and often vowing
that they would never treat their children in the same way. This tendency of
humans to perpetuate the behavior by which others have hurt them (or, as in
Romans 2:1, to "do what you condemn in others") is not widely understood,
but has frightening implications for our continuing high rates of child abuse and
broken families, compounded by the number of teen-aged mothers who are
raising their own children before they have matured emotionally.

Values based on neglect and abuse don't require that parents and children spend large amounts of time together, in fact, quite the opposite, but the
transmission of desirable values from parent to child is hampered by the small
amount of time that parents typically spend with their adolescent children.
Csikszentmihalyi and McCormack (1986) report these times as five minutes
alone with the father, 40 minutes alone with their mothers, and an hour with
both parents in the average day. These figures lead the authors to propose that
the time teenagers spend with their teachers is the single most important opportunity for them to learn about their culture from adults.

Of course this limitation on the time that parents and their children spend
together is not limited to families with teen-aged children. As Menzies (1981)
has reported, the percentage of married women working outside the home (in
Canada) has risen from 10 percent in 1951 to 44 percent in 1976, while the
percentage of single women working remained stable at 56 to 57 percent. Goodlad (1984) quotes similar figures, supplementing them with the fact that approx-
mately 25 percent of the mothers with children under the age of seven are also
working outside the home in the United States. Although in many cases it is a
necessity rather than an option for the mothers to work, in some "two-career"
families, the choice to provide more material benefits for children can lead to a
reduction in the more important nonmaterial benefits.

Stott (1985) reports that in Britain not only are children becoming more
aggressive and disruptive, but that the onset of this behavior occurs as much as
five years younger than was the case only five years before. Although increases
in the number of single-parent families is seen as imposing tremendous stress on
children, and other family factors also seem to be important, considerable feeling exists that the effect of television viewing must also be given substantial
weight in the changes which have been seen. With the television set being an almost constant companion for many children, even when their parents are at
home, the persistent message that "it pays to be violent," that violence works in
getting what you want, is simple enough for most children five years old, and

even younger, to understand. Added to a questioning of authority which, though it might be argued has been needed, has in many cases been overdone, both parents and classroom teachers find that the task of providing guidance to young children has become significantly more difficult to accomplish.

The attempted solution which Stott describes in a British setting involves a deliberate joint effort by parents and the school, a restoring of the alliance whose demise was noted by Goodlad. The school she describes in detail has gone from having to physically restrain very young children when it opened only 15 years ago, to having completely eliminated that level of disruption. Her argument seems to imply that it is necessary for home and school to join forces if the values promoted by television (often those promoted by society as a whole) are to be successfully challenged.

The role of parents as value sources seems to be threatened in three ways. One is a function of decreased contact with their children, often in an effort to bring a better life to the children. The second is a feeling of irrelevance, brought on by the rapidity of technological change, leaving parents feeling that they have no basis for communicating with their children. The third is competition from the other value sources in society, principally television, but also including allied media of music, movies, newspapers, magazines, and books, plus the peer society influenced by the same media.

PARENTS AND CLASSROOMS

Parents and classrooms are not often seen as a natural combination. As Fullan comments, "parents are at a very great disadvantage if the school wants to keep them at a distance, as most do" (Fullan, 1982, p. 209). Yet, home environment (and the peer group) is seen by Bloom (1984) as one of the four areas in which substantial gains might be made in the effectiveness of instruction and a U.S. survey found teachers recommending greater parental involvement as the first step to improved education (Bennett, 1987). The critical distinction seems to be that while most educators want to see the parents supporting the school from their homes, relatively few want the parents to have any direct or continuing contact with the classroom. The use of computers might be used to bring about either form of parent involvement. At this point the emphasis will be on home support, with more direct involvement considered later, in the last section of this chapter.

Home Environment

Bloom lists five home environment factors that seem to have a high relationship with school achievement. They include work habits of the family, academic help and encouragement, stimulation and opportunity to explore ideas, language development, and academic expectations. He describes a study in which groups of parents met with a parent educator for about two hours twice a month for six months. Although this method seems to lead to large gains in achievement, the costs of implementation are also high. A more economical form of increasing parental support of children's learning has not yet been found. Although one could speculate about interesting ways in which computers might play a role in this process, concrete proposals have not yet been developed. However, the level of parent interest in computers still seems to be high, with a recent survey of 5,000 Quebec parents' interest in "micro-informatique" obtaining responses from an amazing 88 percent (Farine & Hopper, 1987).

The two-year study conducted by Carmichael et al. (1985) makes relatively minor mention of parent involvement, but does seem to indicate three ways in which the effect of parental interest might be felt. In addition to their direct support of computer activities in the school (and at home), parents also seemed to have an effect on achievement through communicating their "awe" of technology to their children and through differential expectations about computer use by boys and girls.

Much of the direct influence by parents was positive, though three parents (in a study involving more than 400 students) did express concern over the use of computers, one on the basis of health hazards and the other two on the basis of them being distractions from the students' regular work. Generally, parents' concerns were in the opposite direction, looking for increased use of computers, often culminating in fund-raising activities to purchase computers for the school.

Parents also demonstrated their support for computer use in the form of purchasing computers for the home. In one rural school, 26 percent of the grade three students had a computer in their home by the end of the study. Over all grades, the level of home computers increased steadily, from 7 percent at the start to 37 percent at the end of the second year. (The use of computers in homes will be discussed in the next section.)

It is impossible to do more than guess at the source of the parents' motivation in buying computers for their children. It could have been a belief in the beneficial effects of computers, or perhaps more likely, a fear that their children would be disadvantaged and left behind without access to computers. As Lyon puts it, "Not the goal of the race, but fear of the anticipated consequences of failing to join it, seems to be the key motivator" (Lyon, 1985, p. 13).

Parents and other adults also contributed to the success of computer use through their expression of awe and admiration for the students using the computers. One student claimed to feel better about himself because his parents said he was a computer whiz. Students also commented on how much they liked to have visitors in their classrooms, a more frequent occurrence when computers are present, because it gave them a chance to show off, or it made them feel that their class was important.

Sex Differences

Unfortunately, the amount of support given to boys was often substantially greater than that given to girls, although this difference did seem to narrow as the study progressed. In one class, at the beginning of the study over 80 percent of the boys reported parental encouragement in using computers compared with only 26 percent of the girls. At the end of the two years, at the same site, all the boys and 80 percent of the girls reported encouragement (note that a ceiling effect, the boys could not receive more than 100 percent encouragement, may make it appear that the difference in encouragement has decreased more than was actually the case). The observers also reported that boys would occasionally bring magazines or LOGO problems given to them by their fathers, but that girls never did. Similarly, teachers reported that parents were encouraging most of the boys in their computer use based on a perceived need in the future, while few of the girls received such encouragement. On the other hand, the fact that in one class all the boys and some of the girls had games at home but all the girls had word processing indicates that in some cases it may not be a disadvantage to be slightly deprived in terms of software selection.

Generally, the picture emerges that computer use, at least for the present, is one way of getting parents to express encouragement to their children about their school activities. The major drawbacks which also emerge are that parents are often not very discriminating in terms of what are beneficial and constructive computer applications, and many of them maintain the impression that the use of computers is more appropriate for boys than it is for girls. The trick seems to be to try to maintain the general support for computer use while shaping it into a more discerning view of how computers can be helpful to their children and their learning.

COMPUTERS AT HOME

Assumptions versus Benefits

The assumption that computers in the home can be beneficial and constructive seems to come in at least two parts, based not only on the learning needs of children but also on the contributions computers can make to the lives of adults in general. The former is our primary concern here, but it is perhaps worthwhile to consider the validity of a general computer need for adults.

Early in 1985, when IBM was seen as withdrawing from the home market because of a lack of sufficient sales of their smallest computer, some analysts claimed that "the home market doesn't exist," even though the number of computers in homes was rising rapidly. This analysis of the home market was extended to mean that the home market would not exist until computers were available for less than $600 (Canadian), conveniently ignoring the fact that a number of computers were selling (and in large numbers) for less than $600. What the analysts seemed to be saying was that the home market would not exist until IBM was selling home computers in large numbers, just as the micro-computer market only obtained legitimacy when IBM entered it. Similarly, they seemed to mean that the home market would exist when IBM began selling com-puters for less than $600 (Canadian).

Although the legitimizing influence of IBM is an interesting part of the com-puter scene, it is not the main point of this story. The amazing part of the analy-sis being offered was that no mention was made of the computing needs which exist in homes and how these might be met. In fact, one could easily get the im-pression that $600 was the upper limit of what families are willing to pay for something they don't need. Is it not possible to define the existence of a true home market for computers in terms of the needs which will have to be met?

Unfortunately, the image of the home computer has not become much clearer since the "kitchen computer" was the featured item in a large department store's catalog over 20 years ago. Whether one looks at projected uses in North America (Hunt, 1985), or Europe (Thomson, 1984), the list is unlikely to go beyond games, education, word processing, data processing, controlling devices, and accessing data banks. This is certainly a fine list of novel activities, but the need for them in most homes is either not clear, or it is not clear that a home com-puter is needed to fill the need. For example, a long-standing application of the home computer has been maintaining the checkbook balance, yet the appear-ance of small checkbook calculators, though not currently offering all necessary functions, probably foreshadows a more convenient form of electronic assistance. That is, if one can enter the necessary information into a device built into the checkbook, it is likely to be much more convenient (and more likely to be used) than if one has to enter the information into the computer upon arriving home.

However, we must not underestimate the attractiveness of doing things on a computer, even when it is more inconvenient or takes longer. Bywater (1985) describes his experience with a program designed to keep track of appointments, names and addresses, and telephone numbers. He spent some eight to ten hours putting the necessary information into the program, but later observed that find-ing a phone number or address while in the middle of doing word processing could involve "about two or three minutes of waiting around doing nothing, when I could have looked it up in 15 seconds at the outside in my Filofax—an efficiency drop of 800 per cent" (p. 37). What is even more interesting is his admission that it took him several weeks to realize this deficiency, during which time he felt much more efficient and dynamic. Perhaps this application will also be moved to a special purpose computer.

The trend from general computers to special purpose computers can also be seen in the control of devices, such as those for home heating and cooling. As this is being written, the indoor temperature is under the control of a small special-purpose computer built into the furnace in the basement of this Swiss chalet. It can be programmed, using a calculator-like keyboard, for up to 15 changes in central heating or hot water supply throughout the week. Also, the amount of heat supplied is regulated by a temperature sensor *outside* the chalet, allowing the furnace to begin heating water in anticipation of falling indoor temperatures when the outside temperature drops. Lest this be made to sound like the ideal heating system, be assured it is not, for sensors for sunshine and wind would be natural and useful additions to improve the regulation of indoor heating. The important point is not the sophistication of this device, but that a manufacturer of heating systems is probably more likely to provide this type of control system, at least for the next several years, than to attempt to create a heating system which can be connected to the wide variety of home computers, or which would require the purchase of a home computer in order to make the heating system fully operational. Even without a controller built into the furnace, complex programmable thermostats are available for less than $100. As Adam Osborne put it, "The future lies in designing and selling computers that people don't realize are computers at all" (Friedrich, 1983, p. 16).

Tinnell (1985) studied 12 families who owned personal computers and found that they typically reported that the computer had saved them neither time nor money. She divided the computer users into "addict," "dabbler," and "applicationist" categories and found a general lack of job satisfaction among the addict and dabbler husbands. Whether their love for computers caused the lack of job satisfaction, or the reverse is not explained by Tinnell's results. We do know, however, that at least one study has found that an increase in time spent working with the computer seems to lead to a decrease in job performance (Strehlo, 1986; Gochenouer, 1985).

Interpersonal Relationships

Brod has also studied the effects of microcomputers in the home, with a major emphasis on the effects on interpersonal relationships. He feels that greater amounts of time spent with computers, dealing with the problems of using computers, is likely to reduce one's ability to relate to other human beings. He attributes this to a decreased ability to empathize with others or to identify what others are feeling, presumably from their increasing experience with situations in which feelings have no bearing on a successful solution.

Survey results have found that families with children form the population in which the most rapid growth in home computer sales is occurring, this being attributed to their expectations that their children's education will be advanced by such a purchase (MCSR, 1983). The focus is usually on computer programming, but some feel that computers can make home-based learning a practical alternative to schools (Merrill et al., 1986). However, a similar clash can occur between expectations and results in terms of the assumptions about home computers being used for the education of children. Brod also detects problems in relationships between child and adult as a result of the addition of a computer to the home life. He notes that children may become more intolerant of adult behavior ("they talk too much"), exhaust themselves mentally, be depressed after unsuccessful debugging, or be prone to seeking isolation after intense computer work. One mother bought her 11-year-old son a computer, hoping he would watch TV less, but found that he spent so much time with the computer that he was even more isolated from other children and she was sorry she had ever bought it. In some ways these results parallel findings regarding television watching, that people were more likely to watch TV when they were "down" and less tolerant in social settings after "heavy viewing" (Kubey, 1986).

In some families, particularly single-parent or dual-career families, a computer may be purchased for a child in order to make up for the lack of real attention. One father, a single parent, bought a computer to diminish his older son's demands for his attention, leading to a typical evening of the father doing work from his office and the younger son watching TV while the older son used the computer. The father now complains that his older son resents being interrupted by his father and he misses his former contact with his sons.

Although the strength of video game appeal has waned significantly, their effects may offer insight into possible results from other similar computer uses, either now or in the future. Mitchell (1985) studied 20 families who were new owners of video games and found the effects were generally not as bad as folk wisdom might lead us to expect. She found significant sex differences in interest, skill, and enthusiasm, but also found that families spent more time together and were generally enthusiastic about the change in family life. Brod, however, over a longer period of time has found a number of traits in video-game-playing children, which he feels are the negative consequences of extensive playing. Among these are a decrease in patience (other games are too slow) and an increase in impulsive behavior. Although they often have a reduced interest in television, they are also likely to feel that teachers talk too slowly and use too many words (which may, of course, be true). Perhaps his most interesting observation is that video game play is "all rehearsal," that the player is always practicing and refining techniques, rarely exploring and creating.

Perhaps the largest investigation of home computers studied 282 users of home computers by means of response to an extensive questionnaire (Vitalari, Venkatesh, & Gronhaug, 1985). It was found that the subjects, selected through computer clubs, tended to be technical professionals, well-educated, and with above average incomes. The most significant changes in home life seemed to be in the area of time allocations, with most families reporting *less* time spent watching television, sleeping, or in leisure activities with the family and *more* time spent alone. Most of the respondents used business or word processing applications, conforming to an observed shift away from recreational or pleasure-oriented activities and toward task-oriented activities. The authors feel that since many of their subjects had previous experience with computers, the impact on future new users may be even more pronounced than the effects they found. That is, they expect that future users may have to allocate even more time to learning to use their computers, further shifting their time allocations.

Parent-School Cooperation

If the use of computers in the home offers so many traps for the unwary parent, what assistance do parents need, and how can schools and teachers help to provide that assistance? One example of such a program is in operation in Houston, Texas (Sturdivant, 1984; Chion-Kenney, 1984). Their involvement in computers and assistance to parents operates on several levels, beginning with an increase in school computers from 280 in early 1982, to around 5,000 by the end of 1984. Because of a perception that middle- and upper-middle-class children were likely to be advantaged because of their greater access to computers at home, the school district has instituted a plan whereby lower-income parents may borrow computers for up to three weeks at a time, along with educational software. In order to make sure that the computers can be used effectively in their temporary homes, each family must take 12 hours of training before they are eligible to borrow the computers and software. (Approximately 45,000 parents per year were being trained by 1984.) Parents with higher incomes, who buy computers through the district's reduced-price purchase plan, can also have the 12 hours of training, a free one-year membership in the software lending library, and a free copy of a district-developed word processing program. The normal yearly fee for the software lending library, open to the public, is $60.

Parents in the Houston Plan report that their children are spending less time watching television, but since the software used is that selected by the school as being beneficial, the extra time extracted from television viewing is a supplement to their classroom study and homework. Houston is a city where the tax base allows the school district to be more innovative in its use of technology and the long-term impact of such a plan may be considerably less impressive than first results, but the basis for the plan has some good features. The most important of these is the coordination between schools and parents, and the steering effect available to the schools through their arranging bulk purchases of computers and software, enabling them to pass these savings along to the parents when the parents buy products recommended by the school.

Possible Health Hazards

Although only one of the parents of the over 400 students in the two-year study reported by Carmichael, et al. (1985) expressed a concern about the possible health hazards of computer use, it is still an issue which raises disturbing questions. Also, it appears that scientists may be rethinking some of the health factors in which it was previously felt that little or no health dangers existed (Kleiner, 1985). The possible health risks considered by Kleiner in his review include nonionizing radiation, glare, X-rays, static electricity, noise, and posture. Most of the questions are still unanswered, but it may be getting clearer as to which questions should be asked.

Of the most disturbing sets of findings are those concerning nonionizing radiation, radiation which does not alter the atomic or molecular structure of substances through which it passes. In the past, most scientists have argued that nonionizing radiation could not affect humans unless it was intense enough to produce heat or electric shock. More recently, however, it has been found that very weak, low frequencies (less than 3,000 Hertz) are capable of affecting the development of chick embryos. As a result, the low frequency output of computers, particularly from video display terminals (VDTs), must be reexamined. One doctor reported that fatigue and pregnancy problems at one hospital were more frequent at some types of VDTs, those which were relatively high in low frequency emissions.

The effects of static electricity are also probably unfamiliar to most computer users, but the buildup of static charge, primarily from electrons striking the face of the VDT screen, can cause skin rashes or other discomfort from the particles being deposited on the operator's body and face. The positively charged environment around a VDT also changes the proportions of positive and negative ions in the air, leading to high positive ion concentrations which seem to affect the body through changing blood levels of serotonin, a powerful hormone.

The physical effects of computer use, like the mental effects, are not clearly defined and are still a matter of continuing dispute. The problem is not clarified through stout denial that such effects are possible, but through cautious and thorough research. Adults need to pay close attention to their own and their children's use of computers and effects which seem to arise, particularly until the health issues have received more clarification.

PARENTS, STUDENTS, TEACHERS, AND COMPUTERS

Computers in education offer a new opportunity for parents to be involved in their children's education, though the preceding discussion should have shown that this involvement is not without peril. The same might be said about the school's opportunity to use computers as a bridge for closer cooperation with parents. In this section we consider the ways in which such a relationship might be begun and continued, some of the possible benefits of such a relationship, and also some of the hazards which might be encountered.

Government Plans

In some corners of the world, governments have set up or proposed plans to provide their citizens with training in the use of technology. France has considered the establishment of up to 50,000 computer centers for this purpose, though the initial stages of their "Informatique pour tous" is aimed primarily at providing computer facilities for schools.

The Province of Ontario has also initiated a plan, in addition to those computer efforts directed specifically at education, which is aimed at bringing computer skills and knowledge to the general population. The essence of the plan is that a nonprofit community organization can obtain microcomputers free of charge (usually from five to ten) if they agree to provide open access to the community for some part of the day over a period of three years. Certain portions of the day are set aside as being for access by children and other times are for adults. Over 300 of these centers have been set up throughout the province, in community centers, churches, and schools. Some schools have used this opportunity to increase their computer inventory without any capital cost, in effect paying for the computers through the provision of community access for the three-year period.

Although no overall evaluation of the project's effects has been done, attributable in part to its rapid growth, some anecdotal reports indicate a mixture of success and disappointment. As with most projects of this nature, the major stumbling blocks are those of training staff, availability of adequate software, and operating procedures and costs. However, beyond these problems, which seem to persist in new projects in spite of their being widely discussed, other patterns may be beginning to emerge. For example, it appears that schools in urban areas, which made use of this chance to acquire some additional computers, were not as likely to be successful in creating community involvement as some of the other settings. This result is probably due partly to their priorities, with community involvement being secondary, or perhaps being seen as imposed on them. However, the urban society may also have an effect, with the prevalent isolation of urban subcultures leading to barriers in getting the community and school subcultures into a common effort. This seems to be borne out in the achievements of centers in more rural schools. These schools also may have been motivated by the chance to acquire equipment, but the greater degree of communication within the rural culture may have led to a higher degree of participation. Whatever the cause, some of the more rural settings provide excellent examples of cooperative learning between children and adults.

Although this summary of the Ontario experience is based on data which are entirely inadequate for drawing solid conclusions, one factor, observed in other settings, does seem to be supported. As Carmichael et al. (1985) found in their two-year study of elementary school use of computers, a finding also strongly stated by Swinton, Amarel, and Morgan (1978), people (in these cases, teachers) make an enormous difference, often overshadowing the differences due to computer use. That is, although centers in urban environments may succeed through the strong efforts of the people involved, the normal differences between the people of rural and urban cultures seems to make the task more difficult in the urban setting.

Increasing Parent Involvement

Bloom (1984), as mentioned above, defined five home environment processes which seem to have an effect on school achievement. He also stated that methods of changing these factors of home environment are expensive, though the payoff might be sufficient to warrant the expense. Nevertheless, the generally high level of interest that parents currently seem to have for computers, or their children's involvement with computers, opens up new and possibly less expensive avenues for increasing the communication and, one hopes, the operations between home and school (of course, when the novelty of computers wears off, and it may not take long, the opportunity may be gone). The possibility exists that an exchange initially based on the use of computers in home and school could gradually become based on all of the processes defined by Bloom as being important to student achievement. In order to begin and develop this cooperative relationship in an effective way, a clear understanding of the need for parents to be informed about educational computing and the process by which this might be achieved is a necessary foundation.

One avenue for increased parent involvement might be based on the prediction that schools as we know them will cease to exist in the future, with children being educated more and more via computers, and with a significant portion of this computer learning occurring at home. (Of course, the preceding rests on a number of assumptions, among them that most children will have an appropriate home environment in which to learn, a possibly shaky assumption.) One way of testing the implications of such a development and possibly setting up mechanisms for its achievement is through a greater involvement of parents in the life of the school. Although some schools have already made extensive use of parent volunteers in both their recreational and instructional programs, particularly at the elementary level, the link between parents and computers has generally been limited to the use of computer literate parents in a few special programs. If the new definition of the school is to result in a stronger structure than presently exists, a cooperative approach to computer use, involving both schools and parents, would seem to be a necessity. Such an approach should be designed to bring the parents into closer contact with the educational planning being done by the school, resulting in a stronger school, rather than a disappearing one.

Courses for Parents

As mentioned in the description of the Houston program, some school boards or schools have started to offer computer education courses for parents. In-service education for teachers is a largely unresolved problem for most boards, so one might question why they would spend their limited resources on courses for parents. At least two reasons might be offered to justify the school's providing computer skills for parents.

The first reason is that commercially developed educational courseware will be, and already is being, developed with parents as the primary audience, not for teachers and schools. Expenditures by parents on software began to exceed those of schools during the 1984-85 school year, after having been approximately equal during the previous year, according to one set of estimates (Chion-Kenney, 1984). Another source had home spending on educational software being more than five times that of schools by the 1983-84 school year (Hassett, 1984). Whatever the figures, since the average school budget for instructional materials is usually on the order of fifteen to twenty dollars per student, it is not surprising that parents who have computers, a number that is steadily increasing, will spend considerably more, per child, on courseware. As a result, the advertising of courseware had already been directed at parents for the past few years. This means that if schools want to exercise leverage in encouraging software developers to raise the quality of their products, it is important that they help parents to become more informed consumers, able to select the best courseware packages from among the many being made available.

It is not necessary that the parents make their purchases directly. The lending library approach, used in the Houston school district, allows the library to make the purchasing decisions, using the subscription fees from parents to supplement their purchasing power.

A second reason for educating parents, and the public at large, about the applications of computers in schools is to prepare for the forthcoming or perhaps already existing call for evaluation of computer uses in schools. At the moment, in the eyes of many people, it is sufficient that schools have computers for students to use and relatively unimportant what is actually being done with them. When this situation changes, and with large amounts of money from restricted budgets being used for computers (often at the expense of other worthy projects), it is likely to be soon, it is critical that the public have some notion of what it would mean to use computers effectively in a school setting.

Some would argue, and with considerable justification, that it is too soon for an evaluation of computer uses in education, that students have had insufficient exposure to computers for significant effects to be observed. Yet it is probably unrealistic to expect the public's assessment of educational computing to follow the educator's timetable. The experience of my own institution may provide an illuminating example. In the first two or three years after its creation in 1965, the Ontario Institute for Studies in Education (OISE) was often the subject of newspaper articles praising the Ontario government for being so wise in establishing this combination research center and graduate school. However, in only a few more years the consistent charge was that the OISE had not brought about major positive changes in the schools. This statement was probably true, but the time interval was much too short to allow the planning and implementation of major research programs, their completion, and the dissemination of their results to schools, much less to have the schools and their students show any effects of the recommended changes. It should not be surprising if the public reaction to the use of computers in schools soon changes in the same way, demanding hard evidence that the money now being spent has brought results.

It would be incomplete to prepare parents to recognize the features of sound educational computing if teachers were not able to make the same judgments. It is possible that the development of parents' evaluative skills might have a steering effect on teachers, particularly those who are reluctant to use computers on the basis of nonpedagogical reasons. Already it has been observed that schools and teachers come under pressure from both students and their parents if it is perceived that adequate numbers of computers are not being made available. If the parents' reasons for wanting computers were educationally sound, it might be more difficult for teachers to resist their suggestions, or put more positively, it might be easier for teachers to see the wisdom of using computers in their class-rooms.

The contents of an educational program for parents might include material on the evaluation of courseware, how courseware can be used, the use of tool programs such as word processing, and consideration of the ethical questions related to computer use, including software copyright. It is unlikely that parents would become skilled evaluators of courseware as a result of taking such a course, but it should be possible to arrange laboratory exercises which would convince them of the difficulty of making quick and accurate evaluations of a courseware package's strengths and weaknesses.

A course for parents might also stress the notion that computers and their software carry their own cultural content and their own ideology, one of the main reasons for the Quebec and French governments' decisions to insist on French-designed microcomputers for their respective school systems. However, regardless of the content of the course for parents, a major concern has to do with the provision of staff and facilities to carry out the program. Because of the already extensive demands on the time of those teachers knowledgeable about computers, and the unfilled computer education needs of the current teaching force, it is difficult to see any easy answer to this problem.

Not only should evaluation be a major part of the course for parents, the increased involvement of parents in the school should also be evaluated. An important aspect of such an evaluation would be the detection of side effects, but these may be even more difficult than ever to determine, since little experience with these types of working arrangements is available to draw on. Another possible problem in assessing the results is that the effects may be felt more strongly in the home than in the more easily observed and measured environment of the school. Even when the detection of effects is relatively complete, the weighting of the overall value will probably involve delicate comparisons between the positive and negative effects for teachers, students, and parents, with changes in their current relationships having both subtle and obvious components for all three groups.

A specific example of a generalized program for parent support is provided by the Educational Products Information Exchange (EPIE), which has established a clearing house for information and exchange of ideas on home-school cooperation (*Schooltech News*, 1984). Ken Komoski, EPIE executive director, has been quoted as saying that schools "could double the amount of learning they now achieve in both quantity and quality" by helping parents to use educational computing at home. School districts that have been working with EPIE to implement such programs include Houston (mentioned earlier), districts around San Francisco, and the Bronx-Westchester area.

EPIE has a number of recommendations for schools wishing to assist their parents with their educational computing. They begin with provision of computer education which will enable the family to use the computer effectively for home learning. They also suggest that parents be given a list of software evaluated and selected for their children's use in school, including information on what each is designed to teach, along with a list of other evaluated software to meet the district's requirements. This type of information might be obtained by the school from the publications of a joint effort set up by EPIE and Consumers' Union, the publishers of *Consumers Reports.*

EPIE has also recommended that schools not only coordinate educational computing activities at home with those at the school, but also negotiate with computer vendors to extend the district's price, warranty, and repair agreements to all parents, teachers, and others who have taken the computer courses offered by the district. The recommended arrangements with vendors also would encourage them to donate one computer to the district's lending pool for every so many machines purchased. These donated machines would then become available as a result of increased sales, through the district, to parents and be made available for loan to low-income families.

Finally, EPIE suggests that schools inform parents of the criteria used to purchase school computers and work with Parent-Teacher Associations, public libraries, and appropriate community organizations to establish communitywide software exchanges to increase the variety of school-recommended, curriculum-compatible software available for home use.

One of the major objectives of the EPIE effort is to reduce the 1,000 or more hours that students spend watching commercial television each year by converting their activities to the use of educational software. The district that most closely approximates the EPIE ideal is that of Houston, where a mother reports that this has in fact happened. Her children would normally finish their homework by 3:30, then watch television until at least 5:30. With the computers, they first do math and reading programs on the computers, then their homework, leaving no time for television (Chion-Kenney, 1984).

It is not necessary for parents to have a fully structured EPIE-based program, though it would be a benefit for many parents. The important factor for them to remember is that the effect of computers, like that of television, is dependent on the content. Children's unsupervised and unplanned use of computers or television is an abdication of responsibility by their parents. It is not sufficient for parents to distract their children from television by means of computing unless the content of their computing is more suited to their needs than the content of their television viewing. More effective communication with a school whose teachers make use of computers in an educationally sound way can help parents to make this evaluation.

10   *Teacher Development and Research*

INTRODUCTION

Importance of Teachers

"Teaching effects are real, large, and idiosyncratic" (Swinton, Amarel, & Morgan, 1978, p. 25) is the first conclusion derived from a five-year evaluation of the use of the PLATO computer-assisted instruction system in elementary schools. By this is meant that the difference one finds between teachers, in terms of their effects on students' learning, is so large that it makes the effects of computer use in normal classrooms difficult to detect. In addition, the authors emphasize that computer-assisted instruction, although appearing to be the same thing in all settings, actually interacts strongly with its environment, an environment in which the teacher plays a major role. Although some computer proponents talk of "teacher-proof" programs and instructional methods, in practice the impact of the teacher on students' learning is considerable.

Carmichael et al. (1985), in discussing the results of their two-year study of microcomputer uses (primarily LOGO) in elementary classrooms, also place a great deal of emphasis on the role which teachers played in helping to produce the results they observed. The influence of two specific teachers is described in Chapter 8, but the theme of the teacher as an important classroom force appears throughout their report. In their concluding findings, they also begin with the factor of good teaching and follow through with the importance of the teaching/ learning environment.

Although evaluation of computers used in education often pays homage to the teacher's influence on learning, the path by which teachers may be mobilized to join the computer campaign is less clear. Consideration of the teacher's role in the use of computers in schools usually concludes with a statement such as "To breed the confidence in handling computers which is essential if they are to use them inventively and to encourage children to experiment, a large scale campaign of in-service education is essential" (Megarry, 1983, p. 25). This concern is expressed on a number of fronts, including teachers (a British teachers' union leader called, in 1982, for a year's crash course of in-service for primary teachers), educators (the Association for Computing Machinery education board, with two other ACM groups, published a report on the topic of teacher training in 1983), governments (the Ontario government has established a series of three courses on the topic of "computers in the classroom"), etc. Such concerns are not confined to education, with recent reports indicating that most computer users in business are self-taught (Nelson & Cheney, 1987). However, along with this expression of a common concern, important differences also develop, particularly in the area of who is to be educated, by what means this is to happen, and most important, to what ends.

In response to a first draft of this material, Gary Boyd impressed upon me the importance of progressing beyond the notion of "teacher training," focussing instead on teacher education and/or teacher development. Weizenbaum (1984) makes a similar point, inspired by his reading of Smith (1975), that to think of himself as merely providing training in computer science would be to diminish himself as well as his profession. More important, he saw such a focus as separating himself from the intellectual and moral life of the university. We must be aware that an emphasis on training in computer use, at any level of education, invites the acquisition of computer skills without the necessary moral and intellectual foundations.

The purpose of this concluding chapter is to consider some of the implications for teacher development arising out of the ideas discussed in the previous chapters. Since much of what teachers must learn is still unknown, the topic of research, particularly in terms of the goals of research and the teacher's role in research, is also considered. The sequence for the chapter is to consider first of all a number of sources that contribute to the problem associated with teacher development, then consider four frequently proposed solutions: pre-service education, in-service education, graduate instruction, and research. After reviewing the notion of computers as communications media, and the importance of needs assessment, a plan for determining teacher development requirements is proposed. Following this plan, based on identifying values, assessing needs, determining objectives, and implementation, some of the implications for teacher development and research are explored. In this final section, a number of published views on the future of computing in education and the preferred goals for educational computing research are also reviewed, along with some elaboration on the teacher's role in the research process.

PROBLEMS OF TEACHER DEVELOPMENT

Computer Literacy

Often the question of teacher needs is answered in terms of "computer literacy" requirements. That is, based on the frequent assertion that students need to have computer literacy, one is led to the claim that teachers will also need computer literacy, if only to be able to teach it. These claims might be examined, assessed, and acted upon if the term "computer literacy" had an agreed upon definition. Unfortunately, as mentioned in earlier chapters, agreement seems to be limited to stating that students might find computer skills and knowledge useful in their current studies, their future studies, and their lives after the end of formal schooling. What is subject to considerable disagreement are the specific components which make up the three broad areas, the relative weighting of the areas, and the years and/or subject areas in which the study would fit. Consequently, very few specifics can be concluded about teacher development needs if one begins with needs as vaguely defined as those of computer literacy.

The approach of this book has been to ignore the growing literature on the definition and implementation of computer literacy and to attempt to deal with some of the basic issues underlying the effective use of computers in education. In so doing, an implicit definition of computer literacy may have emerged, but it should be pointed out that it is a definition which would vary according to student (or teacher) need, not a comprehensive definition for all people. (One could also comment that the current definitional status of computer literacy makes it part of the problem, not part of the solution.)

Teacher Motivation

Another issue clouding the teacher development process is that of teacher motivation. The past years of computer in-service have provided instruction for the more enthusiastic teachers, those who were most eager to learn about and use computers. Because computers have frequently entered the classroom at the invitation of the teacher involved, this has led to biased expectations about what other teachers are willing or able to do. Teachers who began to use computers because of their own personal interest were willing to invest huge amounts of time, money, and energy (both physical and mental) to implement computer activities in their classrooms. In the coming years, a growing proportion of teachers may be much less enthusiastic, possibly using computers and seeking the relevant courses out of a sense of duty, fear, or both. If we base our expectations on the achievements of those who "love" the use of computers, the development process becomes more difficult. Approaches that worked with groups of teachers in the past may not be as successful with future groups.

Eggers and Wedman (1984) acknowledge the importance of teacher perceptions as they describe teachers as a bigger threat to computers than computers
are to teachers. A possible source of diminished enthusiasm for computers could
be that many teachers see the suggested applications of computers, and the associated educational demands, as quite unrealistic and with little payoff for them.
For these teachers, it would seem important that it be clearly demonstrated that
computers can be useful tools for them and for their students. Such a course
should probably begin, as many already do, with the teachers being introduced
to useful programs, programs which do something that the teachers want done.
It is also important that the teachers actually be able to use the application programs, rather than hear promises of programs which are said to exist or might
soon be created.

Lack of Formal Training

Associated with the self-selection of computer using teachers is a lack of
formal training, which can have some serious consequences. The most serious of
these is likely to arise not so much from a lack of formal computer training, as
from a lack of pedagogical, or evaluation skills. As a result, teachers newly involved with the use of computers are likely to be enthralled with the prospect of
creating their own programs for instructional uses. However, though we might be
quite impressed if teachers could teach their dogs to speak, we wouldn't necessarily assume that they had something important to say to students. Teachers
who create their own computer applications are often so caught up in the thrill
of accomplishing a difficult task that they lose their critical evaluation skills. It is
not surprising that noncomputer-using teachers often react to these informal
products much as nonparents react to the accomplishments of other people's
children. Thus the lack of formal training helps to reinforce the impressions
among the nonusers that educational applications of computers, and by implication the associated training, are quite unrealistic and have little payoff for
teachers.

Multiple Roles of Computers in Education

Although computers are continuing to expand into a variety of roles both in
education and in society in general, the tendency remains to talk about "the
computer" as though only one application existed. One reason for the persistence
of this phenomenon is the continued existence of subgroups for which only one
application of computers does exist, or only one is seen as important. That is,
some people focus entirely on the computer (and computer programming) as an
object of study, others feel that the delivery of instruction (Computer-Assisted
Instruction, or CAI) is the most important application, an increasing number see
the use of computers as tools in all discipline areas as most important, etc. Although the preceding chapters should have shown that current educational uses

of computers cover a wide range of activities, as long as these more narrow views are vigorously proposed, teachers will continue to be confused about their development needs.

The Values Factor

Rising above all the preceding problem areas is that of value considerations. That is, the particular computer applications we choose are a function of our values, but this is not the whole story. It is also true that the use of computers can change aspects of our values, just as use of television and automobiles have had this effect. For example, just as the automobile has altered the value of "the neighborhood" or the "nuclear family," so it appears that the use of computers can affect the type of business communication which is valued. When computers are used as word processors they seem to lead to increased time being spent on composing and polishing memos, while their use as electronic mail centers seems to lead to more informality in language, sometimes called "flaming language" (Kiesler, Siegel, & McGuire, 1984).

One goal of this book has been to give more explicit mention to the values component, since it is often an important determiner of why people support or reject the use of computers in general, in education, or for other specific applications. The role of values will be further explored in the first step of the plan for determining teacher development requirements.

Other factors also enter into the definition of teacher development as a problem area, among them the number of teachers requiring additional education. The rate at which computers are moving into the schools, the average age of the teaching force, and the lack of computer courses in many faculties of education all lead to the conclusion that most teachers will need some additional education in computer use over the next five to ten years, more likely the former.

Many teachers also feel pressured and are experiencing some anxiety because of uncertainty about the specific skills they require. The unnecessary fear that they will need to learn how to be a computer programmer continues to haunt some teachers. Even if teachers are sure about the skills they need, they often have a problem because the required courses or experiences are not available.

Because of the large number of teachers requiring additional skills and the scarcity of resources available to provide the needed instruction, this is a problem which may well continue over a number of years. In the next section, frequently proposed solutions to this important problem are reviewed.

POSSIBLE SOLUTIONS

Pre-service Education

The pre-service setting, usually a university program for educating student teachers, seems to offer a number of obvious advantages for teacher development in the area of computer use, but it also has some offsetting problems. The major advantages are the clear definition of those to be educated, their relative homogeneity, and their availability for this purpose alone, for a defined period of time. Further, one could argue that pre-service is a preventative approach to the problem and preferable to remedial approaches such as in-service. Having quickly pointed out the advantages, it is important to look at the problems in more detail, those factors which must be overcome if this setting is to be an effective site for teacher development of computer skills.

Collis and Muir (1986) state that 43 (out of 49) Canadian faculties of education were providing a total of 260 undergraduate courses as of February 1985. However, they also found that a considerable amount of diversity in both content and sequence was prevalent, but also found a general lack of consistency (between institutions) in the requirements for computer-related experiences prior to certification. Moreover, sequences of courses appropriate to the needs of computer-using educators are also rarely found, nor do many institutions offer specific courses in methodology and content pertinent to secondary computer science.

Some of the problems take on slightly different forms, depending on the country involved, particularly between the United States and Canada. For example, because of the greater emphasis on one-year bachelor of education programs in Canada, the task of finding time for new material in a curriculum which is already full takes on greater importance. Similarly, the greater demand for new teachers in the United States could give less emphasis to the problem that the teachers educated through pre-service are not likely to form a large part of the teaching population for some time. Yet even this consideration is far too general, with large regional differences existing in Canada, and the increased demand in the United States being primarily for mathematics and science teachers, leaving other teaching areas with relatively stable populations.

Even if time can be found, the implementation of the necessary courses still poses problems in locating resources, particularly equipment and staff. Equipment may be the lesser of these worries, since one continually reads of the declining cost of computing equipment. This could be a misleading judgment, since the cost of computer software can easily offset the savings which might be made from hardware costs reductions. In addition, since budgets are already strained, it is unwise to casually dismiss the added costs.

Even if the money were freely available, which is unlikely to occur, the problem of staffing for the courses would still remain. The easiest and most direct approach to the problem is through the creation and staffing of new courses dealing with educational applications of computers. Unfortunately, this approach, in terms of courses, is much less satisfactory than the integration of computer techniques and applications into the existing curriculum of the school of education. Thus, the problem of pre-service education becomes a problem of in-service education, since the existing faculty of the school of education must acquire the new computer skills before they can integrate them into their courses.

One final problem for this discussion of the pre-service setting, one which can't be resolved by money or staffing, is the lack of teaching experience for those who are acquiring the computer skills. This point relates back to the earlier claim that many of the proposed educational applications of computers have been uncritically accepted and teachers need to balance the thrill of being able to control the new technology against their knowledge of individual student needs. The pre-service population has little basis for such judgments and may easily fall prey to the enthusiasm of recent converts to computerism, particularly if it appears to them that computer skills are a highly emphasized part of the pre-service curriculum.

One possible solution to this particular problem can be found among the many recommendations in a recent report to the Ontario government (Fullan & Connelly, 1987). The authors suggest that teacher education, normally one year beyond the undergraduate degree in Ontario, be extended through the first four years of teaching experience. They refer to this as a "period of induction" (two years) and an apprenticeship (two years). During the induction, the teaching load would be reduced (to 60 percent the first year and 80 percent the second), while the apprenticeship involves working alongside innovative teachers, usually outside the home school, for 10 percent of the normal teaching days. This extended period of education would allow teachers to acquire computer skills, knowledge, and experience more thoroughly and in a more natural setting.

In-service Education

In some ways the problem of in-service courses are the reverse of those for pre-service education. That is, the teachers are less homogeneous and have less available time, but they do have teaching experience and are likely to continue teaching for some considerable period of time. In addition, of course, some of the pre-service problems are common to in-service education and at least one new difficulty appears.

Equipment problems continue to plague in-service education, even though increasing numbers of school boards have set aside special facilities for developing teachers' computer skills. In most cases, school computer equipment is in high demand, not only throughout the day, but often for night and weekend classes as well. This not only makes the offering of in-service courses difficult, but also diminishes the effectiveness of what is being offered. Teachers will usually have difficulty in obtaining access to computers outside their in-service course hours, but more important, may have no access to them at all once the course has ended.

Staffing problems take on a similar form. Although instructors can usually be found, problems in locating instructors who are not male, mathematics or science teachers, and uncritical computer enthusiasts still remain. However, even when the appropriate staff can be found (and this, fortunately, is happening more often), because of their special abilities, they are often already overworked and consequently not available for consultation outside the class hours or, and most important, not available after the course has finished.

Motivation of teachers, or their desire to take in-service courses is a relatively minor problem at present, but it may take on another form and become more important in the future. Currently, the effect of motivation has been that more teachers have been requesting in-service courses than can be accommodated. Although this is a problem which concerns those responsible for providing the courses, it is in one sense, a "good problem." However, this current state of demand may be drawing attention away from those teachers who not only don't want in-service courses at the present time, they aren't likely to want them in the future. This could foreshadow a major problem in the future, but it is also possible that this will in some ways be a "good problem."

Teacher rejection of computer in-service courses can indeed be a major problem if the courses are seen as being imposed on them and result in a hardening of their attitudes, reinforcement of "computer phobias," and computers being used according to rule, rather than by need. However, the resistance to this kind of use of computers in education and the associated in-service courses can be a benefit if those reluctant teachers have their views and needs considered fairly and honestly. My personal view is that teachers who demand to see the benefits of computers for their students rather than being caught up in the desire to possess computers (whether they will be used meaningfully or not), are an important, but possibly dwindling, natural resource. It is unfortunate that they don't seem to have a sufficient impact on current in-service offerings, but we can hope that their input will be given more attention in the near future.

Graduate Instruction

Graduate programs are not really an alternative to pre-service or in-service courses, but some problems have arisen because they are sometimes seen to be alternatives. Collis and Muir (1986) found that 20 Canadian institutions offered a total of 85 graduate courses on computers in education as of February, 1985. However, this report can be somewhat overoptimistic, since some institutions give, or have given, graduate credit to teachers for learning "how to" program in BASIC, or more likely LOGO, a subject which is also being pursued, often with more success, by students in elementary schools. (This is not to say that elementary school students actually become programmers, but rather that they often come closer to this goal than do teachers taking graduate-level courses in computer education.)

The role of graduate programs should not be to focus on the "how to" questions of educational computer applications, but rather to delve more deeply into the "why," "when," and other related questions. The hope is that potential in-service teachers will acquire a perspective on the latter issues through graduate courses, a perspective which they can pass along to their fellow teachers. It is assumed that these graduate students (and many of our students are on sabbatical leave precisely for such experience) will have already acquired the "how-to" skills, or will do so in noncredit courses.

Research Directions

The vagueness in the definition of teacher development requirements points up the need for the answers to research questions. Research should be providing a major input into the courses for pre-service and in-service education, but has so far failed to do so. The problem does not seem to be one of a lack of agenda items, for many have written about what this agenda should be and all have stressed the urgency of the need (specific recommendations will be reviewed in a later section). Yet even among those items for which high agreement exists, little of the agenda has been accomplished.

A possible solution to this lack of information is greater emphasis on the teacher in the role of researcher. This suggestion is based on the exploratory nature of the research required. That is, the need for hypothesis generating is greater than the need for hypothesis testing. This topic has already been examined in Chapter 2, but put into simpler terms, it means that we must know what the questions are before we can succeed in answering them. Gottfredson (1984) describes similar benefits for what he calls a program development evaluation approach, emphasizing strong collaboration between the researcher and the implementer of the new program. The teacher is usually the implementer of new computer education techniques, but is rarely an active participant in the research process.

Teachers are in an ideal position to identify the side effects of computer use (unintended outcomes, either positive or negative), but are not always prepared to look for them. With a greater sensitivity to the importance of side effects, a sensitivity obtained either through pre-service, in-service, or graduate courses, teachers can help to identify the questions which can be answered through more systematic research efforts. Moreover, this sensitivity to side effects could also provide teachers with direct answers to some of the questions they have, while the creation of systematic information exchanges between teachers could serve to decrease the need for training courses. That is, if teachers saw themselves and other teachers as sources of research knowledge, and began to share that knowledge, many of their questions about the effective use of computers in their classrooms could be answered during this exchange. (The topic of teachers as researchers will be considered in more detail later in this chapter.)

COMMUNICATIONS MEDIA AND NEEDS

The detection of side effects by teachers is of crucial importance because the important effects of communications media, of which the computer is one, are so difficult to predict. As described in Chapter 1, Lias (1982) reviews the historical effects of new media, such as the telephone, television, the automobile, etc.,

pointing out that in each case important consequences of their adoption were
not seen when the media were initially introduced, or even considerably after
their introduction. For example, television has been in common use for about
four decades, yet its effects on human behavior are still being discovered.

If we assume that because computers are communications media, not only are
their most important effects hidden from us, but even the applications themselves are not clear, structuring the appropriate development courses for teachers
poses definite problems. Specifically, how can we possibly expect to prepare
teachers to deal with the unknown effects of unspecified applications? One part
of the answer is that we should not expect to build our courses entirely on the
hopes of computer enthusiasts, those who see computers providing the answer
to all the current problems of education without producing any negative side
effects. In fact, we have to go further than that, questioning seriously the assumption that computers in general or any computer application in particular
must, by definition, have positive effects that outweigh the negative effects. One
step in developing this necessary critical orientation is to focus on specific needs
of both students and teachers.

Needs assessment often seems to have been limited to determining the needs
of educational technology, rather than the needs of students and teachers. That
is, the concern is often for "showing what computers can do" rather than defining the kinds of assistance students require. Although Salisbury (1984) gives
a compact description of how needs assessment techniques might be used in considering CAI applications, it would be misleading to give the impression that
needs assessment in general is a clear-cut uncomplicated process. Not only is the
definition of "need" itself in dispute, but the determination of needs is usually
subjective, and the entire process of assessing and meeting needs is heavily influenced by values.

As a result, in the following sections the concept of needs assessment will be
handled in a manner similar to that of side effects. That is, it is very difficult to
define how one can determine either side effects or needs, but it is important
that one sees the necessity of evaluating for side effects and assessing needs. In
fact, it is the very perception of this necessity that is a prerequisite to the successful identification of most side effects and, one could argue, to a similarly
successful assessment of needs. Thus, what is being proposed in the following
section might be more accurately described as a needs assessment "position"
rather than a technique or strategy. The importance of needs assessment will
be stressed, along with some indications as to how this might be accomplished,
but specific procedures will not be defined.

A PLAN FOR TEACHER DEVELOPMENT

The focus of this plan is not so much on the teacher development process itself as it is on the method for determining the requirements (of teachers) which
such a development process must meet. The procedure is essentially that pro-

posed for needs assessment in Chapter 2, but with a greater emphasis on teacher development needs.

Determining Educational Goals

This step is more in the form of an assumption about what will precede the consideration of educational computer applications, rather than a step in determining the specific uses of computers. Specifically, it is assumed that the question, "What kind of students should the educational system be producing?" has already been answered, at least in terms of establishing curriculum goals for individual schools or districts. It is to be hoped that the process of answering this question began with the underlying values of the population, using these to develop an educational philosophy which incorporates the "absolutes" of the educational system. Such a process provides a solid foundation for the steps which follow. If inconsistencies exist, such as the values demanding adherence to a moral code while the philosophy would have students develop their own moral code, the remainder of the process is likely to be mainly speculation.

It might be observed that the foundation for this process should be outside of the schools, although involving educators. It should also be noted that this process of setting educational goals does have some direct impact on the use of computers in schools, but it is primarily in the form of computers as objects of study, such as computer science courses (one of the possible components of computer literacy). This use of computers would be most strongly influenced by answers to the question, "What computer skills do graduates need in order to succeed in the business or university world?" Since a number of universities have begun to require that their students own a computer, the answer to the question may be getting clearer. On the other hand, it should be noted that the mandatory purchase and use of a computer does not imply the same length of preparation as would the mandatory purchase and use of a piano.

Of course, the preceding is an idealization of how important educational goals are determined. In practice, particularly where large purchases of computer equipment are involved, certain political realities begin to intrude. For example, the French plan, "Informatique pour Tous," has resulted in almost all of the first 120,000 microcomputers for the schools coming from French firms, while the general market for microcomputers (including business applications) in France is dominated by U.S. and British companies (Etheridge, 1985). It is evidently more important that the French government plan for the schools also support French industry than for the computers in the schools to be the same as those used in industry. This is not to say that the wrong values are influencing computer purchase decisions, but merely to point out that the underlying values are not confined to the domain of education. One can find similar effects in Ontario, where a government fund for industrial development has financed a large part of the software and hardware acquisitions for Ontario schools, emphasizing Ontario and other Canadian products. A slight variation occurs in Switzerland, where the teachers in the canton of Vaud expressed some displeasure with their government's efforts to use computers from both the United States and Switzerland, through provision of a means of using the same programs on both computers (Des maîtres mécontents dénoncent, 1986). A further elaboration of the impact of cultural values on planning can be found in Rust and Dalin's (1985) description of the Norwegian plan for computer education. Special emphasis is given to the development of software that is compatible with the local culture and language.

As a result of the goal-determining process, curriculum objectives will be defined. The definition of these objectives might be looked at as a problem-solving task, in which the problem is to transform the original state of the student (entering the school system at age six, etc.) into the desired solution, or forwards from the problem, in practice it is often a combination of the two. However, to look at curriculum definition only in this way is to focus on the external demands and possibly to underestimate the internal demands. That is, the introduction of a new element into the curriculum, such as computer literacy, may be seen as an isolated change, but the consequences of such a change can reverberate throughout the rest of the curriculum. This has been demonstrated repeatedly as students who have had access to computers for computer literacy instruction in grade n, put considerable pressure on the teacher in grade $n + 1$, and beyond.

Assessing the Needs

This is the first part of the planning sequence which is not assumed to have already happened. That is, it is assumed that our current state is that of having defined goals and objectives, but not having determined how computers are to help in meeting the objectives, nor what skills the teachers will need, nor how they are to acquire them. In order to give some organization to the discussion of needs and their assessment, it would be helpful to begin with a definition of the ways in which computers will be used in the schools, preferably specified in terms of grade-level and subject matter area. Unfortunately, partly because of the communications media effect (the phenomenon that the dominant uses of media seem difficult if not impossible to predict), a consensus set of specifications does not exist, particularly in terms of grade and subject matter combinations. Thus, the following discussion will be more general, based on a set of three broad categories of computer uses in education. The three areas are those of teaching *about* computers, teaching *through* computers, and teaching *with* computers (Ragsdale, 1982).

Teaching about computers

Teaching *about* computers is increasingly expanding into the elementary school curriculum. Current trends indicate that in the very near future, instruction about computers in elementary schools will cover a wider range, in terms of level of instruction, than in either secondary or postsecondary institutions. It will probably range from the earliest introduction of computer concepts to the preparation of sophisticated programs and can be subdivided into three parts: precomputer instruction, developing skills for computer users, and programming.

Precomputer instruction includes a number of activities dealing with systematic planning and problem solving, the study of the impact of computers on people, the identification of computer uses, and so forth. These activities at the primary level will precede computer use and at higher grades will supplement the activities which require the use of computers.

Developing skills for computer users is extremely dependent on the context. In those schools where students in the second grade are using word processors, for example, they must be educated in using the computer for this specific task. As other applications become available for student use, and their relevance is verified, the appropriate instruction must be supplied.

Programming skills will be acquired at early grade levels as well, if present trends continue, though not always as an objective of the school. Evidence seems to indicate that, depending on the language being used, instructing grade three or four students in some programming skills involves little difficulty. Since some students will begin to program at this age level regardless of school activities, and girls may find it easier to begin programming before they are fully molded in their sex-role stereotypes, strong arguments might be advanced for programming instruction to begin (with simple programming) at a low grade level. The important point is that at whichever level programming begins, it should be based on the important conceptual aspects of programming, assuming that such aspects exist, not as a casual or entirely student directed activity.

One factor which may decrease the load for individual elementary teachers, in terms of their having to teach new material, is the possibility that although computers may be introduced early, the instruction may be spread over a number of elementary school years. Another possible ameliorating factor is that peer tutoring may accomplish much of the instruction about computers. In fact, peer tutoring probably will be an important factor even if it is not planned, which means that its positive influence on cooperative behavior is also likely to be felt. Bitter and Camuse (1984) describe a plan that allocates computer activities to grades from K-12, also including an emphasis on student cooperative work and peer tutoring.

Teaching through computers

Teaching *through* computers is the use of computers to present instructional material, along with associated diagnostic testing, often called Computer-Assisted Instruction (CAI). Examples of CAI exist across all grade levels and in most subject matter areas, though mathematics instruction has received the most heavy emphasis. When CAI materials are properly developed, the teacher need have little knowledge about computers. Unfortunately, little CAI is properly developed, particularly for microcomputers. As a result, teachers who attempt to use CAI are likely to feel the need to modify the programs, which requires moderate programming skills, or even write their own programs because of their dissatisfaction.

Teachers who do set out to create their own CAI materials find that the development of CAI programs requires not only a great deal of time, but also multiple skills not often found in one person. These skills include those of instructional designer, subject matter specialist, master teacher, computer programmer, graphics designer, etc. Teachers who attempt to create their own CAI frequently become frustrated by the size and complexity of the task.

Teaching with computers

Teaching *with* computers refers to the use of computers as tools, particularly as aids to students in their work with the subject matter they are studying. Example applications include word processing, information retrieval, and music composing programs. In each of these applications, students are not only able to complete tasks (writing, locating information, composing) more rapidly, but are often able to do things (transpose a melody) they might not have attempted without computer assistance. Many tool applications are independent of subject matter and can be used across subject as well as grade levels.

When students are using computers as tools, the teacher must be aware of the skills that the tools provide, but need not be an expert user of the particular tool program the students are using. This may be a fine distinction, but it is intended to separate the concept of how the tool works from the details of using a particular program. Some of the tool applications, such as word processing, have developed out of business applications and are designed to be easy to learn and use. Peer tutoring can also be effective in acquiring skills for tool use. The greatest challenge to the teacher will be to use effectively the new skills which students will acquire.

Having quickly reviewed three broad categories of educational computer use, we can now consider the task of determining, within the defined curriculum, the areas of greatest student and teacher need. That is, what computer assistance might students and teachers benefit from in attempting to satisfy the requirements of the curriculum? Weick (1984) provides a conceptual framework for such an approach in proposing the strategy of "small wins." By this he means that the solution of small specific problems as a demonstration of the effectiveness of an innovation is likely to be more acceptable and convincing than a large-scale implementation which applies the innovation in all possible areas. One of his examples is that of Alcoholics Anonymous, which tells members to stay sober for a day, rather than a lifetime, even though the latter is the true goal of the program.

Thus, in the domain of education, one might ask, "What is the greatest obstacle to students becoming creative writers?" or "What is the most important factor impairing the physical fitness of high school graduates?" or "What is the most important factor in preventing eight-year olds from gaining a proper grasp of elementary mathematics concepts?" The most important element of this step is that the focus must be on human needs rather than machine needs. That is, we are not asking "How can the computer help, . . ." but rather "What do students and teachers need in order to achieve what the curriculum has defined for them?" Unfortunately, the computers in education literature often contain questions of the former type, such as "how to maximize the potentials inherent in learning to use a computer" (Norton, 1985, p. 40).

A second important feature of this step is that it must be iterative so that we can identify the new needs which arise as a result of satisfying earlier needs. For example, if I were given a typewriter on the basis of an earlier needs assessment, the use of it might bring to light a serious need for spelling skills, previously hidden through my judicious use of ambiguous scrawling. Another way of stating this might be to view the discovery of a new need as a side effect of the previous need being satisfied. Not that the new need did not always exist, but that it only surfaced when another need was met.

Another important aspect of this step is that it is meant to include *all* teachers in the process, or at least to include all teachers in the population from which the participants are selected. The goal of the process is to identify the problems of those teachers who do not use computers, as well as those of teachers who do use computers. In particular the problems are not to be restricted to those encountered by teachers as a result of using computers.

Changing Curriculum Objectives

One possible outcome of the previous step is that curriculum objectives would be changed, though this is not the primary intention of that step. For example, the failure of eight-year-olds to achieve their mathematics objectives might lead to a change of objectives for eight-year-olds, or for seven-year-olds, or indeed, for every year in the curriculum. A more likely change is that of adding to the curriculum (presumably with a compensating subtraction at some other point), in the form of new content or new processes that are designed to facilitate the learning which is not occurring. An example of this might be the use of LOGO as a programming language by which young students might learn about mathematics concepts, particularly geometry. (In practice, most teachers report their use of computers in the classroom as being outside the normal curriculum, so the usual effect of computers seems to be explicitly additive and only implicitly subtractive.)

It is important to bear in mind that changes in process for one part of the curriculum can mean changes in content for other parts of the curriculum. An obvious example is a decision to use the process of word processing for creative writing, with such a decision implying that somehow students will learn the content of "how to use word processing," either as a prerequisite or as a co-requisite. It is tempting, but dangerous to ignore the content changes, or equally crucial attitudinal changes that must accompany the successful implementation of a new process, either for students or teachers. Inclusion of "changes to curriculum objectives" as a specific step is intended to make it less likely that these required changes will be ignored.

It should be pointed out that the use of word processing as an example in the previous paragraph should not be taken as an indication that specific processes, as solutions to assessed needs, are selected at this point. Instead, the consideration of solutions should remain deliberately general, such as "What alterations to the curriculum (content, process, or other) will meet the needs defined in the previous step?" Thus, a proposed solution might be of the form "Students need to be able to produce and revise text with less expenditure of time and effort" rather than "Students need word processing."

Implementation Strategies

Once the student and teacher needs have been put into the form of general curriculum solutions, the consideration of specific solutions can begin. In order to follow through on the examples used earlier in "assessing the needs," let us assume that more physical activity outside the school is seen as the solution to the physical fitness question, an increase in review and practice is the solution for the mathematics question, and an increase in the amount of student writing is seen as the solution to the creative writing problem. (These are not proposed as ideal solutions, but merely as examples of activities which are sometimes seen as having value in these contexts.)

To the computer enthusiast, champing at the bit, the question is, and always was, "How can we use computers to achieve our aims?", but that is (obviously) not the appropriate next step. Instead, we must develop, as creatively and exhaustively as possible, a list of "critical competitors" for the role of possible solution. These are alternatives that must be compared with the program or product being evaluated, a concept which is discussed in more detail in Chapter 2. In considering our three examples we will use a limited list of critical competitors, namely technology (including computers), parent involvement, and peer tutoring. Obviously, a much wider range of alternatives should be considered, but in practice it is often difficult successfully to encourage the consideration of any alternatives to the use of computers, even the use of other technology.

One example of computers being favored over other technology might be seen in a primary level reading/writing curriculum developed with support from a major computer and typewriter manufacturer. Field trials of a version of the curriculum which used only typewriters, tape recorders, and workbooks produced impressive gains in student achievement. However, the version of the product which is now being aggressively marketed requires the use of microcomputers in addition to the typewriters, tape recorders, and workbooks. No direct comparison between the two versions seems to have been made, although the noncomputer version would seem to be a logical critical competitor. Unfortunately, given the prevalent attitude in our society, it is probably easier to sell the computer version at its higher cost, even if it turns out not to have any curriculum advantages over the noncomputer version. And indeed, a recent evaluation reports that "once word-processing was introduced, the children 'would not go back to the typewriters' and 'the typewriters were totally forgotten'" (Collis, Ollila, & Muir, 1987, p. 6).

Mathematics

In pursuing our examples of needs, we should attempt to answer the question, "What is the best way of teaching the curriculum we have defined?" using the (necessarily abbreviated) list of needs and critical competitors. One of the first uses of computers in education was in the teaching of mathematics skills to primary level children, so more than 20 years' experience relates to its effectiveness. Fortunately, studies of at least one critical competitor, peer tutoring, having also been done, with the results of a meta-analysis showing a clear advantage of peer tutoring over CAI in increasing the mathematics skills of young children (Levin, Glass, & Meister, 1984). When the relative costs are considered, the differences are even more impressive in favor of peer tutoring.

One of the advantages of CAI in mathematics, or other subjects, is explained in terms of the greater motivation, leading to more time spent on mathematics. One must question, however, how long computers will continue to be motivating, considering our past experience with video games, for example. It is relevant that those who have achieved highly in mathematics or other academic areas often mention the support of their parents and their valuing of academic achievement as being important in supporting their success. Certainly the factor of parental support has a long-term potency that is more than equal to that of computer novelty.

Creative writing

Consideration of the creative writing need leads to similar observations. One of the consistent claims of the word processing proponents is that students write *more* with word processing. Further investigation has usually revealed that students are spending more time writing, hence, are writing more. However, one also finds that students (and adults) will often spend even more time with electronic mail systems than they will with word processing. What is the difference between the two systems? A well-defined audience seems to be one of the critical differences, leading naturally to a consideration of the effect of peers and parents on writing. Peer tutoring is often a part of the writing program (usually in the form of peer review) and parent approval is often given as a source of motivation, based on displays of products and techniques on Parents' night.

Physical fitness

Computer programs have been developed to help individuals in achieving physical fitness, though more to justify the use of computers than to show dramatic gains in fitness. Nevertheless, the motivating effects of computers will still be proposed for this application and critical competitors must be considered. Those who have studied school society carefully sometimes suggest that one of the reasons students tolerate the requirements of the school system is that it offers them a chance to socialize with their friends at the same time (Goodlad, 1984). This seems to suggest that peer involvement might be important in physical fitness, not so much in directly answering the question, but in at least reducing the target group to that of the most popular students. That is, if one can get the most popular students to participate in the desired fitness activities, most of the others are likely to join in. Similarly, one can observe that parents who use their automobiles to minimize their activity outside the home and use other technology, from television to electric toothbrushes to minimize their activity inside the home, can also create a substantial barrier to participation in physical activity by their children. Any instructional goal becomes substantially more difficult to achieve if it runs counter to the underlyilng values of the surrounding culture.

It might appear that the preceding description has taken an unnecessarily large number of words to provide an example of what has already been stated in Chapter 2, that the use of computers in education should be based on some systematic and logical analysis of the needs of the educational system and its components. This may be true, but the needs analysis is crucial to the successful implementation of a teacher development plan. Only if the use of computers is directed toward real needs can we (or should we) expect teachers to acquire the associated and required skills.

Loucks-Horsley, French, Rubin, and Starr (1985) have looked at the problem of implementing technological innovations in terms of teacher incentives and rewards. Although their study emphasizes the process of implementing technology, not the process of deciding if technology is appropriate, some aspects of their findings seem applicable. Their focus is on the role of incentives and disincentives within the system, rather than within teachers themselves. That is, they feel that teachers' personal incentives should not be relied on to sustain innovation, but rather that active efforts must be made to eliminate disincentives from the system, such as competing school goals, or lack of equipment, etc. In this same vein, one could look at a careful analysis of teachers' and students' needs as providing a strong foundation for building incentives and eliminating disincentives.

Perkins (1985) has also taken a critical look at the implementation of computers in educational settings. He feels that much of the effort has been based on an assumption that "opportunities get taken." That is, if teachers and students are given opportunities to be more effective in their teaching and learning through the use of computers, they will choose to use computers in such a way that these benefits will be realized. Perkins questions the assumption that this will occur, citing LOGO, word processing, and data bases as applications where the expected benefits have not been fully realized. He believes that the opportunities are really there to be taken, but that the potential "takers" may not recognize them or may not be sufficiently motivated to take them. He suggests that a major part of the problem may be that expectations of transfer learning from these tasks may be based on "high road" transfer, while the desired transfer is unlikely to take place except by means of "low road" transfer. By high road transfer he means an analytical approach, mindfully abstracting principles and applying them to new contexts, while low road transfer results from varied practice over a long period of time. This conclusion is similar to Pea and Kurland's (1984) analysis of the effects of learning to program, as well as Salomon and Perkins' (1986) analysis of the same topic.

The preceding observations that the availability of opportunities does not guarantee that they will be taken and that system incentives must be structured to support teachers in following the innovation path they have begun are in some ways reminiscent of a comment made by Bob Davis at the 1983 AERA meetings in Montreal. Davis spoke of "Nullification through partial assimilation" as a method whereby teachers and schools can avoid the effects of innovations. By that he meant that a school or teacher can adopt the most trivial aspects of the new technology, such as the architectural aspects of the "open plan" without the more important organizational or pedagogical changes. Papert (1980a) sees "school math" as a similar phenomenon, those areas of mathematics which have outlived their usefulness, but which live on as a tradition. Keller puts the problem in colorful terms, saying that although "reform has been defined as taking a bone away from a dog. It is more like dragging a wounded moose from a pack of starving wolves" (Chance, 1984, p. 44). Consequently, in implementing computers in the classroom, particularly when such implementation is seen as being forced, teachers may be looking for the most nonthreatening and innocuous ways of introducing computers rather than uses which have important impacts on teaching and learning, and hence require substantial changes on the part of the school, teacher, or curriculum. An innovation process based on a strong needs assessment foundation can result in an implementation phase in which teachers see the proposed changes as being in the best interests of everyone, including themselves.

IMPLICATIONS FOR TEACHER DEVELOPMENT AND RESEARCH

The plan just proposed has implications, not only for the teacher development problems presented at the beginning of this chapter, but also for research questions, both the methods for determining and answering the questions. First of all, based on this plan and the preceding discussions in this book, a definition of computer literacy has emerged, namely that students should be required to acquire those computer skills which will assist them in mastering the remainder of the curriculum. In addition, of course, computer skills which are important to success in business or university might also be included.

Second, the problem of teacher motivation can be honestly dealt with only when the development process leads to skills that the teachers themselves have determined to be important. This effect is closely related to the factor, "lack of formal training', since the emphasis is on teachers making decisions in their own discipline areas and including input from teachers who do not use computers. Though some teachers will still be influenced by their informal experiences with computers, the participation of other teachers, both those with formal training and those with no experience at all, should provide a stabilizing effect.

Third, this process should help to clarify the multiple roles of computers in education by tying the applications more directly into the curriculum demands of specific disciplines. At present, the differentiation is usually at the level of distinguishing between computer studies teachers and "others." A discipline-oriented analysis allows a more specific definition of the development requirements than an approach which focuses on the technology.

Finally, and most important, this process incorporates a value component, not only from the general population through the process of determining educational goals, but also the values of teachers. It is unreasonable to expect teachers to increase their workload in order to incorporate computers into their teaching, without making sure that the computer applications are in congruence with their values. Jacques Ellul (Vanderburg, 1981) has described the problem well, in explaining a contradiction of technological advancement, namely, that as technology increases we are required to be more disciplined in our behavior in order to use the technology, but at the same time the need for discipline is further and further removed from underlying values, as society in general loses its values. The result is a tendency to challenge and/or reject all discipline, while at the same time increased use of technology is making the demands of discipline more. If the demands that computers used in education place upon the teacher are seen (correctly, in my view) as a tightening of discipline for the teacher, the need for a value foundation should be evident.

The issue of future research will be considered in three parts: possible views of the future of computers in education, goals proposed for educational computing research, and the role teachers might play in the research effort.

Possible Views of the Future

Suppes' (1966) prediction that CAI would soon create tutors equivalent to Aristotle is one example of the risks involved in predicting the future. Even though Suppes seems to have been off the mark, the replacement of teachers by machines is not a new theme, having been presented more than 40 years before by Virginia Church in a poem from her book, *Teachers are People.*

Antiquated

Mr. Edison says
That the radio will supplant the teacher.
Already one may learn languages by means of Victrola records.
The moving picture will visualize
What the radio fails to get across.

Teachers will be relegated to the backwoods,
With fire horses,
And long-haired women;
Or, perhaps, shown in museums.
Education will become a matter
Of pressing the button.
Perhaps I can get a position at the switch-board. (Church, 1926, p. 59)

Bork provides a more recent illustration of the dangers of futurology in his chapter on "Computers and the Future of Education," which contains the comment that "better machines such as the Coleco Adam and the IBM PC jr. are beginning to appear" (Bork, 1985, p. 169). By the time this book appeared, these two computers no longer did.

On a more substantive level, Bork believes that computers will be the dominant delivery system for all levels of education, with teachers, books, and films often linked with computers in new learning materials. He also sees the home as possibly becoming a major center of education, while the teacher's role will become more of a solver of learning problems. Students working at their own pace will make the teacher's life "more interesting," while the solution to the teacher development problem is to have them educated by computers!

On a more somber note, factors such as values, motivation, training, and the organization of the school lead Cuban (1986) to predict that computer use in schools will seldom exceed 10 percent in elementary schools and 5 percent in secondary schools. He feels that utilization will be low because we have failed to ask "what schools are for, why teachers teach certain content, how they should teach, and how children learn" (Cuban, 1986, p. 98).

Licklider (1983) has been predicting the uses of computers in education for more than two decades and still retains considerable enthusiasm for the task. He sees "lots of computers" and observes that almost everyone who tries the new technology "really has a ball. It's exciting. It's motivating. It's energizing" (p. 73). This sets the tone for a chapter in which his concern for leisure time is that it be "used well," where home economics students learn to shop for, prepare, and understand the significance of a meal through access to the commodity futures market, and where finding yourself a little further from the real situation is seen as an advantage of using computers to solve problems. The level of enthusiasm, where "technology will motivate the student the rest of the way" (p. 75) is unbroken until he responds to a question about why he talks about technology rather than demonstrating it. The enthusiasm abates as he declares, "It can possibly be done, but at great expense, at great cost, and then usually it turns out not to work at the critical time" (p. 81).

Chambers and Sprecher (1983), in discussing "The Future of CAI and Traditional Education," also follow Bork in seeing the end of education as it now exists, with much of the instruction taking place in the home. They foresee extensive entertainment/learning centers in homes, intelligent CAI modules with live actors portraying relevant scenarios, and traditional schools providing a supervisory service by the year 2000. That is, they don't see traditional schools as disappearing, but rather emphasizing a supervisory, advising, counseling function in what they call a "traditional Oxford type of learning" (p. 187).

Berg and Bramble (1983) make comments about technological advances which are similar to those of the preceeding authors, but they also put stress on the importance of the teacher, a title they see as commanding more respect in the information age. Moursund (1984) also emphasizes the role of the teacher, along with parents and students, as being essential in improving education.

Goodson's view of the future puts more emphasis on the immediate future, the steps which must be taken in 1985-90, what she calls "the window of opportunity" (*TechTrends*, 1985, p. 24). She feels that this five-year period must be used to bring technology and curriculum together, with curriculum in the dominant role. However, she also sees a need for curriculum to change, particularly in terms of its limitations, such as confining the teaching of writing skills to English and writing classes. She also urges secondary schools to prepare for an influx of students who no longer need to learn basic computer skills, but need opportunities to use them and a more extensive investigation into the ways in which technology, including videodiscs, can help in all of the content areas. Most of all, she sees a great part of the task as being related to attitudes, a preparation for and acceptance of direction and change. In this regard she echoes Cronbach's (1963) prophetic observation that it was probably more important to know that the effectiveness of programmed instruction was dependent on the teacher's attitude than to know the average effectiveness of programmed instruction. One hopes that the recognition of this relationship will do more for the effective use of computers than it did for programmed instruction.

Goodson's views are based on her work with a committee which was preparing a report for the U.S. Secretary of Education, but the general tenor of her comments (in this mid-1985 interview) are compatible with most of the ideas put forward in this chapter. Goodson's background includes 12 years of junior high school teaching, which possibly accounts for her pragmatic view of the future of computers in education.

Goodson describes the report of the committee on which she has served as being "upbeat" and "positive," illustrating their belief "in the future of education with technology as a partner" (p. 24). This belief is certainly characteristic of the typical computer educator's view of the future of educational computing. If this is the projected future, what do computer educators see as the necessary research needed in order for us to be able to reach this future?

Goals for Educational Computing Research

Some suggestions for research are for very specific areas of inquiry, such as Norton's (1985) agenda of questions dealing with the differences between print-oriented (books, worksheets, etc.) and computer-oriented methods of problem solving, the development of these skills, their applications, and how one might maximize the potentials inherent in learning to use computers. The last of these is the most general, echoing Postman's (1982) and Harlow's (1984) concern that inherent does not mean inevitable.

White's (1983) approach to clarifying the inherent potentials of computers is to set a goal of developing a psychology of electronic learning. She sees electronic learning as progressing through three stages: television, computer, and electronic environment. She feels that television has broken the school's monopoly on formal learning and our understanding of the effects of computers depends on our application and extension of reinforcement theory, developmental learning theory, and information processing. Her entrance into a psychology of electronic learning would be similar to Norton's, an analysis of print learning versus electronic learning.

Some calls for research emphasize the urgency of acting quickly, not only from Goodson, but also from Bork (1984) and Lepper (1985). Lepper mentions a "research window," presumably much like Goodson's "window of opportunity" for implementation, stating that much of the needed research on motivational and social issues can only be done in the next two to eight years, while students without previous computer experience can still be found. The issues he raises are primarily in the area of intrinsic motivation, the aspects of instructional tasks which make children want to do them, and its implications for the use of computers in instruction. In addition, he raises concerns about social equity, social development, such as family relationships, and the activities which will be displaced by computers.

Salomon and Gardner (1986) also stress the need for early research, basing their arguments on lessons learned from television research. They suggest avoiding questions such as "does it teach better?" in favor of more detailed study of unique features of the medium. Their other three main suggestions have to do with the richness of the computer-student interaction, as they encourage holistic research, emphasize the learner's role in affecting the results, and stress the wide range of outcomes which can be produced. Salomon (1984) had earlier proposed a research agenda in which he urged the study of similar issues, but also stressed the need for long-range study of cumulative computer effects, the importance of the effective transfer of learning to noncomputer contexts, and his concern that schools would assimilate computers without making the changes necessary to make effective use of them.

In the domain of CAI, Chambers and Sprecher (1983) suggest a number of issues relating to the effectiveness of CAI, beginning with the amount and type of human interaction which will make it most effective. They also raise issues relating to types of students, types of subject matter, and the degree of CAI which might be most effective for learning via CAI. Roblyer (1985) is also concerned with the use of computers in instruction and defines four areas of investigation. Her first is similar to Salomon and Gardner's first point, finding the specific aspects of computer learning that are most effective. The second is the area of cost/benefit studies, similar to those done by Levin, Glass, and Meister (1987). The remaining areas of concern are those of evaluation for learning materials before they are published, and increased study of the social impact of computer learning.

Becker's (1987) research plan is most concrete. He called for schools to participate in "National Field Studies of Instructional Uses of School Computers." The project is underway and involves 40 pairs of classrooms in grades five through eight, each pair located in one school, with one classroom using computers (at least one per four students) for mathematics instruction, and the other not using computers. A wide range of achievement test, questionnaire, observation, and other data are being collected in the mathematics study, which is the first year of what is expected to be a three-year project. Other subject matter areas and grade levels are being studied in the remaining years.

Sheingold, Kane, and Endreweit (1983) have the most specific basis for their research agenda, deriving it out of three case studies of one-week duration each in three different school systems. The case studies were to determine the ways in which the system used microcomputers and led to the definition of six areas: access to microcomputers, new roles for teachers and students, integration into classrooms and curricula, the appropriate quantity and quality of software, preparation of teachers for using microcomputers, and the social, cognitive, and learning consequences of using microcomputers.

Teacher as Researcher

Based on this restricted, but varied, sampling of views on research into educational computing, plus the future which computer educators envisage, what might be seen as the dominant theme(s)? If you interpret the agenda and futures as I do, or if the introduction to this section has been written convincingly, then your answer should be the importance of the teacher as researcher. Many factors lead to this conclusion, but the most important ones seem to be the need for research to be done soon, the wide range of issues which need to be considered, and the crucial role of teachers in facilitating (or obstructing) the implementation of computers in the schools.

The need for research on the impact of computers in education to be done very soon is stated specifically by Bork (1984), Lepper (1985), and Salomon and Gardner (1986), but it is implicit not only throughout the proposed research agendas, but also in the projected futures of computers in education as well. In particular, Goodson's (*TechTrends*, 1985) view of the future can be seen as meshing with the proposals that the results of research are needed quickly. Her stress on the attitudinal change, curriculum change, and intensive implementation over a five-year period, 1985-90, imply that research results, in order to have any effect on practice, must be obtained from a process which runs concurrent with implementation. Pea also suggests a merging of research and development, but his focus is not so much on the teacher as on the view that "theory and practice will need to be unified through the invention of research-informed electronic learning systems that work in educational settings" (Pea, 1986, p. 21).

The research cycle

The usual view of educational research is that researchers gather their data from laboratory and/or field (school) settings, analyze their results, and then disseminate the findings and conclusions in various forms, including reports, books, revised curricula, curriculum materials, etc. Obviously, a concurrent process of research and implementation does not allow effective use of the traditional research cycle. In order to decrease the time which elapses between the collection of data and changes in teacher practice, changes must be made. Chapter 2 describes some of the differences that arise from a greater emphasis on "naturalistic inquiry" rather than controlled experiments.

The preceding is not to be interpreted as saying that careful longitudinal studies are not useful. For example, preschool education has been a topic of controversy for at least two decades, with most of the empirical results confined to immediate benefits, such as achievement in grade one. Now a recent longitudinal study includes results from *sixteen years* after the preschool experience and shows differences in unemployment, teen-age pregnancies, arrests, and school dropping out (Shanker, 1984). Such lengthy studies are perhaps more common in medicine, where an evaluation of behavioral factors affecting heart disease took ten years and $115 million to complete.

Schwarz (1985) describes the use of "reconnaissance" in evaluation, directing the evaluation activities toward the decisions which need to be made. He applied this technique to an educational environment in which activities were constantly being changed on the basis of what worked and what didn't. A major focus of the technique was to regard the participants in the study as also being "observers" of all that transpired in the schools. As such, their value was not limited to simply responding to predetermined questions, but they could play a more active role in the research process.

Carmichael et al. (1985) also made use of their teacher participants as classroom observers, but they comment on how difficult it is to continue to be an alert observer in the classroom, whether as teacher or researcher. The teachers in this study found it particularly difficult to keep records of their observations, though they were good sources of such data when interviewed. These teachers had the added difficulty of being asked to introduce computers to their students *with minimal support*, but the question of time being available is important for any teacher. Any suggestions that the teacher function as a researcher must bear the time constraints in mind.

Data collection is often the longest part of the research process, particularly when data are to be collected from many locations and a limited number of researchers must make regular visits for the purpose of observation, testing, interviews, or other forms of data collection. One way to shorten the time required for data collection is to reduce the number of sites from which they are collected, but this also limits the value of the results, since a number of sites are usually chosen to try and represent a variety of different environments. Using the teacher as researcher permits the possibility of increasing the number of researchers to collect the same amount of data from all sites in the same length of time, and with the same level of intensity, as it would normally take to collect data from one site.

Of course, the substitution of the teacher for a researcher is not all that simple. Obvious complications arise in that the teacher may be biased in expectations, is usually untrained in collecting observational data, and is already extremely busy. At the same time, a benefit of the teacher as researcher is that the teacher is already in the classroom and does not create an intrusion, or abnormal environment as the presence of an outside observer often does.

Analysis of the collected data can also be a time consuming experience, particularly if the data are collected in a relatively unstructured way, such as through observation or interviews. For example, a researcher might discover that students in the sixth classroom visited, when asked a specific question, gave very unexpected and interesting answers. Analyzing these responses should involve a comparison with the responses given in the first five classrooms, but if the question was not asked in the first five, either the analysis will be incomplete or additional visits must be made. That is, in a naturalistic form of research (discussed in more detail in Chapter 2) the analysis of data and the collection of data often interact. Therefore, if teachers are collecting data in their own classrooms, the interaction of data analysis and data collection can be accomplished more efficiently.

If teachers are actively involved in the collection and analysis of data, then the dissemination of results is already taking place before the study is even completed. Not all teachers will be functioning as researchers, so of course not all of them will be receiving results as the study progresses, but if part of the role of teacher as researcher is seen as ongoing dissemination, then many teachers can be reached during the study. Teachers involved as researchers in the study can also serve as informed distributors of information when more formal results become available.

Needless to say, the issue of time dominates any consideration of teachers as researchers. The time invested must be seen as satisfying a need, not only for teachers, but also for those who allocate teachers' time: principals, superintendents, school trustees, taxpayers, parents, etc. Recent contract negotiations in Ontario have included 'planning time' as a major issue for elementary school teachers. Time for research will only be made available if it is seen as satisfying needs as important as those addressed by planning time (among others).

Wide range of issues

Having spent considerable time and words on how the teacher as researcher might shorten the time of the research cycle, it should not take quite so long to deal with the remaining factors, the wide range of issues to be investigated and the crucial role of the teacher in implementation. If one research study can consider a limited number of factors, and the number of studies done simultaneously is limited by the number of researchers, the teacher-researcher seems an obvious answer. In addition, the wide range of teacher backgrounds and teaching environments, often seen as hampering research by introducing more variation in results, can be seen as an advantage when a variety of factors needs to be considered. Since the identification of the important questions is still incomplete, a variety of inputs from teachers can only help make the identification more comprehensive.

Teacher's role in implementation

The crucial role of the teacher in facilitating (or obstructing) implementation of computers in the schools brings the relationship between teacher development and the teacher as researcher more sharply into focus. If teacher development is seen as giving teachers all that is known about the use of computers in education, then researchers will not gain much from taking part, since little is currently known. If instead, the emphasis is on how little we know and the process by which we can find out about computers in education, then teachers can take a much more professional role in their own development.

Developing teachers for research

Rather than telling teachers what to expect from computers being used in their classrooms, we could be helping them to see what is really happening, perhaps through an explanation of the principles underlying ethnographic evaluation (Dorr-Bremme, 1985), or other forms of naturalistic inquiry. We should be helping them to see the unexpected, by observing the side effects of computer use. At the same time, teachers should be aware of the personal nature of many side effects, that not every student or every teacher reacts in the same way to a particular application of computers. Instead of waiting to find the effects of computers they were told about in a course actually happening in their classrooms, teachers can be helped to focus on what is really happening to them and their students as they work with computers. As a side effect of teachers becoming adept at looking for side effects, they should also become more sensitive to the effects of other classroom techniques and procedures on them and their students. The teacher as professional can be enhanced through functioning as the teacher/researcher.

In most teacher development programs, a subset of the total group is initially trained so that they may instruct the rest. For example, the French "Informatique pour Tous" plan involves the rapid training of about 110,000 teachers, or about one in eight, who will then instruct the others. A plan to create teacher/researchers might proceed in a similar manner, through a combination of short courses and on the job education. The emphasis in the short course would be on observation techniques, perhaps using video tape case studies of classroom scenes (Ingle, 1984) and examples of the kind of "unexpected" results which might be found. A local collection of anecdotal information would satisfy the latter requirements, but until it is developed, Carmichael et al. (1985) can provide ample material for consideration. In looking at previously collected data, the emphasis should be not only on the unexpected results but also on the diversity between students, between teachers, and between classrooms.

Teachers should also receive guidance in recording their observations, probably in a daily journal, and in presenting them so they can be shared with a group of other researchers. It is particularly important that teachers learn to keep an effective record of their observations without it taking excessive amounts of their already limited time. On-the-job education will deal with such issues as developing a group report and selecting interesting incidents for group validation. Sharing of research findings with other teachers will also be part of this ongoing experience. Eventually, when teacher/researchers are confident enough of their own skills, they can develop research groups within their own school or region.

Initially, research groups probably should be quite homogeneous, elementary teachers or a single subject at the secondary level, so that the range of observed behaviors does not exceed the ability of the members of the group to cope with it. Later, more variation might be introduced into groups so that the migration of results between groups is encouraged. Variety of background other than grade level, such as urban-rural, size of school, ethnic composition, etc., could also be introduced as the local conditions permit.

It is probably most important that the teacher/researcher not be seen as an appendage to the teacher development program, nor that teacher development be seen merely as being an avenue through which one might encourage teacher/ researchers. Both of these processes are a necessary component of the successful use of computers in education, the professional status and job satisfaction of teachers, and the education of students. Unless teacher growth is based on what is actually happening in the classroom it cannot become an important part of their professional lives. And unless the teacher/researchers see this activity as being important to their professional lives, it cannot succeed.

In-service Programs

Although the specifications of computer use in the schools may still be incomplete, several principles for in-service programs seem to emerge from the preceding discussions. One of them is that such a program should be based on plans, probably at the school board level or higher, for the use of computers at the higher grades being built on the experience that students acquire in the earlier grades. This means that teachers will be able to have some idea of what computer skills their students will be bringing with them on entering the class and what they should have when they leave.

It also seems important that the programs be nonthreatening to teachers. One obvious step in this direction is to recognize that teachers, as adult learners, have different needs than do their students (Rawitsch, 1981). Another useful step is to reduce the emphasis on technical details about the computers themselves (hardware), including only what is necessary for their effective use. That is, users need some information about the workings of a program and computer in order to increase their understanding of the tasks they can accomplish. Instead of an emphasis on hardware and programming, teachers should be given instruction on applications of computers, particularly what computers can do for the teacher.

Finally, the beneficial effects of the preceding can all be lost if the instructors are not patient. Many teachers are already under stress related to computers and the increased pressure of (what seems to them to be) a rapid pace may prevent effective learning from taking place and lead to their dropping out. Moreover, the instructors must be particularly sensitive to the possible personal side effects which teachers may suffer from computer use. Without sensitivity, the value of the program of instruction may be lost for some, if not all, teachers.

Appendix

STATISTICAL SIGNIFICANCE

One of the persistent problems related to the analysis of experimental results is the undue emphasis placed on achieving statistical significance. Often, the significance of results is used to judge their importance, so that results significant at the .01 level are *better* than those that are significant at the .05 level. At the same time, it could be argued that in many instances obtaining significant results may tell you very little, perhaps nothing at all of value.

Consider, as an example, a (hypothetical) courseware package which is designed to prepare students for taking the Scholastic Aptitude Test (SAT). This test is given to students in their last year of high school and is used as an admission criterion by some universities. The SAT is designed so that the mean score is 500 and the standard deviation of the scores is 100.

If we were advising students who wished to enter a university requiring a score of 600 on the SAT, how useful would it be to know that a controlled experiment had shown that students using the courseware package had obtained significantly higher scores than those who did not use the package? This would be of little value, even if we knew that the significance level was .001, for it doesn't say anything about the actual score a student is likely to get. If we learned that the controlled study used a sample size of 10,000 students per group, we would not find that any more useful, for a large sample size can permit very small differences to become statistically significant. The increase in sample size is like increasing the power of a microscope, in that it may allow us to measure very small differences accurately. But if we found consistent differences between razor blades with a powerful electron microscope, it would not necessarily follow that users of the blades would notice a difference.

An alternative to reporting statistical significance (alone) is the use of the "effect size," basically the size of the difference one might expect to find. The effect size is usually given in standard deviation units, to permit some comparison over different types of measures, but since the SAT has a fixed standard deviation we will talk about effect size in terms of score units. Let's assume that the average difference, or effect size between students using the courseware and those who don't is 20 points. This would give us much better information on which to base our advice, but is still insufficient. Our next concern would be for the reliability of this effect size.

We usually express information about the reliability (or variability) of an effect size in terms of a "confidence interval." For example, a confidence interval for an effect size of 20 points might be expressed as being a 95 percent chance that the actual difference between the groups is between 10 and 30 points. Once you have determined a confidence interval, a separate statement about statistical significance is not needed, for it is included in the interval definition. If a 95 percent confidence interval does not include zero, or no difference, as part of the interval, the effect size is significant at the .05 (one minus .95) level of significance. Therefore, not only does a confidence interval provide information that is not present in a simple statement of statistical significance, but the original information is also retained.

With the additional information provided by the confidence interval, we are now closer to being able to offer advice. If the interval is from -5 to +45, we would still have an effect size of 20 (the midpoint of the interval), but the result would no longer have statistical significance (the interval includes zero). Note that even without statistical significance, this second interval does provide useful information. We could tell students that although the courseware might provide no benefit at all (they could even score lower), it would not be unlikely for their gain to be as high as 45 points. With the 10 to 30 interval (with the same effect size of 20), our advice would be different since a gain of at least 10 points is very likely, but it is unlikely that the gain would be more than 30. Note that these statements of expected gain are related to group averages, with individual student scores showing greater variation due to other variables (changes in health, for instance).

Although the confidence interval provides a great deal more information than the statement of statistical significance, crucial information must still be obtained in order to give useful advice. The missing information is in terms of a needs assessment, or how large a gain would these students need in order to score the necessary 600 points. In the case of the SAT, this information can be obtained in more than one way. A preliminary form of the SAT (the PSAT) is administered to students in the penultimate year of high school and the score on this test may be used to estimate the score that is likely to be obtained on the SAT a year later. In addition, sample forms of the SAT itself are publicly available and may be used by students to estimate their likely score. Once we have needs assessment data in terms of the estimated SAT score (without training) our advice can be much more specific. Obviously a student whose estimated score is 520 is not likely to reach the goal of 600 after using the courseware if the effect size is 20 points (with a 95 percent confidence interval of 10 to 30).

The knowledge that confidence intervals are more useful for making evaluative decisions than simple statements of statistical significance has been available for decades. Nevertheless, these more useful techniques are still not as widely used as they should be. Those who read the educational research literature should be aware of the advantages of confidence intervals and insist on their being used.

Bibliography

Adams, K. A. (1983). Needs sensing: The yeast for R&D Organizations. *Educational Evaluation and Policy Analysis, 5*(1), 55-60.

Anderson, J. R., Boyle, C. F., & Reiser, B. J. (1985). Intelligent tutoring systems. *Science, 228*, 456-462.

Anderson, R. E., Welch, W. W., & Harris, L. J. (1984). Inequities in opportunities for computer literacy. *The Computing Teacher, 11*(8), 10-12.

Arons, A. B. (1984). Computer-based instructional dialogs in science courses. *Science, 224*, 1051-1056.

Arons, S. (1984, November 7). The myth of value-neutral schooling. *Education Week*, pp. 24; 19.

Attewell, P., & Rule, J. (1984). Computing and organizations: What we know and what we don't know. *Communications of the ACM, 27*(12), 1184-1192.

Balkovich, E., Lerman, S., & Parmelee, R. P. (1985). Computing in higher education: The Athena experience. *Communications of the ACM, 28*, 1214-1224.

Barclay, W. (1956/1975). *The Letter to the Romans.* Burlington, Ontario: Welch Publishing Company.

Becker, H. J. (1985, August). The Second National U.S. School Uses of Microcomputers Survey. Paper presented at the World Conference on Computers in Education, Norfolk, Virginia meeting of the IFIP.

Becker, H. J. (1986). Our national report card: Preliminary results from the new Johns Hopkins survey. *Classroom Computer Learning, 6*(6), 30-33.

Becker, H. J. (1987, April 23). The impact of computer use on children's learning: What research has shown and what it has not. Paper presented at the Washington D.C. meeting of the American Educational Research Association.

Bennett, W. J. (1987). The role of the family in the nurture and protection of the young. *American Psychologist, 42*(3), 246–250.

Bereiter, C. (1985). Toward a solution of the learning paradox. *Review of Educational Research, 55*(2), 201–226.

Berg, P., & Bramble, W. J. (1983). Computers and the future of education. *AEDS Journal, 17*(1&2), 101–108.

Bitter, G. G., & Camuse, R. A. (1984). *Using a Microcomputer in the Classroom.* Reston, VA: Reston Publishing.

Blair, D. C., & Maron, M. E. (1985). An evaluation of retrieval effectiveness for a full-text document-retrieval system. *Communications of the ACM, 28* (3), 289–299.

Bloom, B. S. (1984). The 2 sigma problem. *Educational Researcher, 13*(6), 4–16.

Boden, M. A. (1984). AI and human freedom. In M. Yazdani & A. Narayanan (Eds.), *Artificial Intelligence: Human Effects* (pp. 196–221). Chichester: Ellis Horwood.

Bolter, J. D. (1984). *Turing's Man.* Chapel Hill, NC: The University of North Carolina Press.

Bork, A. (1984). Computer futures for education. *Creative Computing, 10*(11), 178–180.

Bork A. (1985). *Personal Computers for Education.* New York: Harper & Row.

Bourque, J. H., & Ramage, K. (1984). The hidden costs of computer innovation. *Educational Technology, 24*(11), 36–39.

Boyd, G. (1983). Education and miseducation by computer. In J. Megarry, D. R. F. Walker, S. Nisbet, & E. Hoyle (Eds.), *World Yearbook of Education 1982/83* (pp. 50–54). London: Kogan Page.

Bracey, G. W. (1982, Nov.–Dec.). Computers in education: What the research shows. *Electronic Learning,* pp. 51–54.

Brod, C. (1984). *Technostress.* Reading, MA: Addison-Wesley.

Brooks, L. (1978). Nonanalytic concept formation and memory for instances. In E. Rosch & B. Lloyd (Eds.), *Cognition and Categorization* (pp. 169–211). Hillsdale, NJ: Erlbaum.

Brooks, H., & Bowers, R. (1970). The assessment of technology. *Scientific American, 222*(2), 13–21.

Brown, J. S. (1977). Uses of artificial intelligence and advanced computer technology in education. In *Computers and Communications* (pp. 253–270). New York: Academic Press.

Brown, J. S. (1985). Process versus product: A perspective on tools for communal and informal learning environments. *Journal of Educational Computing Research, 1*(2), 179–201.

Brown, J. S., & Burton, R. R. (1978). Diagnostic models for procedural bugs in basic mathematical skills. *Cognitive Science, 2,* 155–192.

Browne, M. W. (1985, October 17). Dinosaur-size robot with laser eyes ready to take first steps. *International Herald Tribune,* p. 8.

Bruner, J. (1985). Models of the learner. *Educational Researcher, 14*(6), 5–8.

Bryson, M., Lindsay, P. H., Joram, E., & Woodruff, E. (1986, April). Augmented Word-Processing: The Influence of Task Characteristics and Mode of Production on Writers' Cognitions. Paper presented at the San Francisco meeting of the American Educational Research Association.

Burke, J. (1978). *Connections.* London: MacMillan.

Burns, M. (1980). Getting kids ready for computer thinking. *The Computer Teacher, 8*(1), 28–32.

Burton, R. R., & Brown, J. S. (1982). An investigation of computer coaching for informal learning activities. In D. Sleeman & J. S. Brown (Eds.), *Intelligent Tutoring Systems* (pp. 79–98). New York: Academic Press.

Bywater, M. (1985, February 24). Myth of techno-change. *The Observer*, p. 37.

Calfee, R. (1985). Computer literacy and book literacy: Parallels and contrasts. *Educational Researcher, 14*(5), 8–13.

Cameron, A. (1985, May). Grandmothers, Teachers, and Little Girls. Paper presented at the Technology and Culture: Computers, Values, Creativity meeting of the University of Ottawa.

Campbell, J. A. (1984). Three uncertainties of AI. In M. Yazdani & A. Narayanan (Eds.), *Artificial Intelligence: Human Effects* (pp. 249–273). Chichester: Ellis Horwood.

Capra, F. (1982). *The Turning Point.* New York: Simon & Schuster.

Carlson, R. O. (1965). *Adoption of Educational Innovations* (Tech. Rep.). Eugene, OR: Center for the Advanced Study of Educational Administration.

Carlyle, R. E. (1985). Can AI save COBOL? *Datamation, 31*(18), 42–43.

Carlyle, R. E. (1987, March 15). Technology—sword or shield? *Datamation, 33*(6), 85–86.

Carmichael, H. W., Burnett, J. D., Higginson, W. C., Moore, B. G., & Pollard, P. J. (1985). *Computers, Children and Classrooms: A Multisite Evaluation of the Creative Use of Microcomputers by Elementary School Children.* Toronto: The Ontario Ministry of Education.

Case, R. (1978). A developmentally based theory and technology of instruction. *Review of Educational Research, 48*, 439–463.

Catania, A. C., & Cutts, D. (1963). Experimental control of superstitious responding in humans. *Journal of the Experimental Analysis of Behavior, 6*(2), 203–208.

Chambers, J. A., & Sprecher, J. W. (1980). Computer assisted instruction: Current trends and critical issues. *Communications of the ACM, 23*, 332–342.

Chambers, J. A., & Sprecher, J. W. (1983). *Computer-Assisted Instruction: Its use in the Classroom.* Englewood Cliffs, NJ: Prentice-Hall.

Chance, P. (1984). The revolutionary gentleman. *Psychology Today, 18*(9), 42–48.

Chancellor, A. (1985, September 15). (untitled). *The Sunday Telegraph*, p. 18.

Chion-Kenney, L. (1984, November 7). Houston families borrow, buy, train on computers for learning. *Education Week*, pp. 10, 18.

Christoff, K. A. (1985). Simon says . . . . *Datamation, 31*(23), 109–110; 112.

Church, V. (1926). *Teachers are People.* Hollywood, CA: David Graham Fischer Corp.

Clark, R. E. (1983). Reconsidering research on learning from media. *Review of Educational Research, 53*(4), 445–459.

Clark, R. E. (1985). Evidence for confounding in computer-based instruction studies: Analyzing the meta-analyses. *Educational Communication and Technology Journal, 33*(4), 249–262.

Collis, B. (1985, November). Sex-related differences in attitude toward computers: Implications for counselors. *The School Counselor*, pp. 120–130.

Collis, B., & Muir, W. (1986). A survey of computer education courses in Canadian faculties of education. *The Canadian Journal of Higher Education, 16*(1), 61–71;

Collis, B., Ollila, L., & Muir, W. (1987, March). Interim report on the Victoria installation of Writing to Read (WTR). *SEE Newsletter,* (4), pp. 5–7.

Computer requirements for teachers. (1984, October 24). *Education Week*, p. 11.

Craig, D. (1984). Suzuki calls for more public awareness on technology. *Computing Canada, 10*(25), 1.

Crawford, D. G., & Crawford, G. C. (1984). On-line and off-line courseware: The weakest link. *Computers and Education, 8*(4), 343–348.

Cronbach, L. J. (1963). Course improvement through evaluation. *Teachers College Record, 64*(8), 672–683.

Cronbach, L. J., Ambron, S. R., Dornbusch, S. N., Hess, R. C., Hornik, R. C., Phillips, D. C., Walker, D. F., & Weiner, S. S. (1980). *Toward Reform in Program Evaluation.* San Francisco: Jossey-Bass.

Csikszentmihalyi, M., & McCormack, J. (1986). The influence of teachers. *Phi Delta Kappan, 67*(6), 415–419.

Cuban, L. (1986). *Teachers and Machines: The Classroom Use of Technology Since 1920.* New York: Teachers College Press.

Cuffaro, H. K. (1984). Microcomputers in education: Why is earlier better? *Teachers College Record, 85*(4), 559–568.

Daiute, C. (1985). *Writing and Computers.* Reading, MA: Addison-Wesley.

Daiute, C. (1986). Physical and cognitive factors in revising: Insights from studies with computers. *Research in the Teaching of English, 20*(2), 141–159.

Darwin, F. (Ed.). (1958). *The Autobiography of Charles Darwin and Selected Letters.* New York: Dover Publications.

Davis, P. J., & Hersh, R. (1986). *Descartes' Dream.* San Diego, CA: Harcourt Brace Jovanovich.

Davy, J. (1984). Mindstorms in the lamplight. *Teachers College Record, 85*(4), 549–558.

de Sola Pool, I. (1983). *Forecasting the Telephone: A Retrospective Technology Assessment.* Norwood, NJ: Ablex.

Della-Piana, G. M. (1982). Film criticism and micro-computer courseware evaluation. In N. Smith (Ed.), *New Directions for Program Evaluation: Field*

Assessments of Innovative Evaluation Methods (pp. 11-28). San Francisco: Jossey-Bass.

Des maîtres mécontents dénoncent. (1986, mars 13). *24 heures*, p. 21.

Dickson, W. P. (1985). Thought-providing software: Juxtaposing symbol systems. *Educational Researcher, 14*(5), 30-38.

Dorn, P. H. (1985). Learning from lemons. *Datamation, 31*(2), 72-74; 76; 78; 80.

Dorr-Bremme, D. W. (1985). Ethnographic evaluation: A theory and method. *Educational Evaluation and Policy Analysis, 7*(1), 65-83.

Dreyfus, H. L. (1972/1979). *What Computers Can't Do* (Revised ed.). New York: Harper Colophon.

Dreyfus, H. L., & Dreyfus, S. E. (1984). Putting computers in their proper place: Analysis versus intuition in the classroom. *Teachers College Record, 85* (4), 578-601.

Dreyfus, H. L., & Dreyfus, S. E. (1986). *Mind over Machine*. New York: The Free Press.

Duda, R. O., & Shortliffe, E. H. (1983). Expert systems research. *Science, 220*, 261-268.

Eaton, J., & Olson, J. (1985, June). 'Doing computers?' The micro in the elementary curriculum. Paper presented at the Montreal meeting of the Canadian Society for the Study of Education.

Eggers, J. R., & Wedman, J. F. (1984). The growing obsolescence of computers in education. *Educational Technology, 24*(7), 27-29.

Ellul, J. (1964). *The Technological Society*. New York: Vintage Books.

Ellul, J. (1980). The power of technique and the ethics of non-power. In K. Woodward (Ed.), *The Myths of Information: Technology and Postindustrial Culture* (pp. 242-247). Madison, WI: Coda Press.

Elmer-DeWitt, P. (1984, December 3). Let us now praise famous hackers. *Time*, p. 76.

Elmer-DeWitt, P. (1986, February 10). The (digitized) eye of the beholder. *Time*.

Emerson, A., & Forbes, C. (1984). Living in a world with thinking machines. *Christianity Today, 28*(2), 14-18.

English, R., & Edwards, G. (1984, February). Programming as a writing activity. *The Computing Teacher, 11*(6), 46-47.

Ershov, A. P. (1981). Programming, the second literacy. In R. Lewis and E. D. Tagg (Eds.), *Computers in Education* (1-7). Amsterdam: IFIP.

Etheridge, J. (1985). French micro lessons. *Datamation, 31*(13), 119-120.

Farine, A., & Hopper, C. (1987, Janvier). *La Micro-Informatique et les Parents* (Tech. Rep.). Montreal: Groupe de recherche en administration des applications de l'ordinateur, Faculte des sciences de l'education, Universite de Montreal.

Flaherty, D. (1985). Computers and the new culture: Where are the role models? *Educational Technology, 25*(6), 34-36.

Florman, S. C. (1981). *Blaming Technology*. New York: St. Martin's Press.

Follman, J. (1984, September). Pedagogue–paragon and pariah–20% of the time: Implications for teacher merit pay. *American Psychologist, 39*(9), 1069-1070

Francis, L., Goldstein, M., & Call-Himwich, E. (1975). *Lesson Review* (PLATO User's memo No. 3). University of Illinois.

Friedrich, O. (1983, January 3). The computer moves in. *Time*, pp. 8-16.

Frude, N. (1983). *The Intimate Machine*. London: Century Publishing.

Fullan, M. (1982). *The Meaning of Educational Change*. Toronto: OISE Press.

Fullan, M., & Connelly, F. M. (1987, January). *Teacher Education in Ontario: Current Practice and Options for the Future*. (Position Paper.) Toronto: Ontario Ministry of Colleges and Universities.

Galanter, E. (1984). Homing in on computers. *Psychology Today, 18*(9), 30-33.

Gilliland, K., & Pollard, M. (1984, August/September). Ethics and computer use. *The Computing Teacher, 12*(1), 19-23.

Gochenouer, J. (1985). *Computing needs of knowledge workers*. Unpublished doctoral dissertation, Florida Institute of Technology.

Goldenberg, E. P. (1979). *Special Technology for Special Children*. Baltimore, MD: University Park Press.

Good, M. D., Whiteside, J. A., Wixon, D. R., & Jones, S. J. (1984). Building a user-defined interface. *Communications of the ACM, 27*(10), 1032-1043.

Goodlad, J. I. (1984). *A Place Called School*. New York: McGraw-Hill.

Gottfredson, G. D. (1984). A theory-ridden approach to program evaluation. *American Psychologist, 39*(10),1101-1112.

Goudzwaard, B. (1984). *Idols of our time*. Downers Grove, IL: Inter-Varsity Press.

Graves, D. H. (1983). *Writing: Teachers and Children at Work*. Exeter, NH: Heinemann Educational Books.

Gray, L. (1983). Teachers' unions and the impact of computer-based technologies. In J. Megarry, D. R. F. Walker, S. Nisbet, & E. Hoyle (Eds.), *World Yearbook of Education 1982/83: Computers and Education* (pp. 29-41). London: Kogan Page.

Green, M. (Ed.). Polanyi, M. (1969). *Knowing and Being: Essays by Michael Polanyi*. London: Routledge & Kegan Paul.

Green, J. O. (1984a). Kids and writing: An interview with Donald Graves. *Classroom Computer Learning, 4*(8), 20-23, 28.

Green, J. O. (1984b, February). B. F. Skinner's technology of teaching. *Classroom Computer Learning, 4*(7), 22-24; 28-29.

Green, J. O. (1985). A conversation with Seymour Papert: Logo under fire. *Classroom Computer Learning, 5*(6), 28-29; 58-59.

Greenbaum, J. (1985). A Swedish Experiment. *Datamation, 31*(1), 127-128.

Grubb, R. E. (1964). *The Effects of Paired Student Interaction in the Computer Tutoring of Statistics* (Tech. Rep.). Yorktown Heights, NY: IBM.

Guba, E. G., & Lincoln, Y. S. (1982). The place of values in needs assessment. *Educational Evaluation & Policy Analysis, 4*(3), 311-320.

Hannah, L. S., & Matus, C. B. (1984, August/September). A question of ethics. *The Computing Teacher, 12*(1), 11-14.

Harlow, S. (1984). The computer: Humanistic considerations. *Computers in the Schools, 1*(1), 43-50.

Hassett, J. (1984). Computers in the classroom. *Psychology Today, 18*(9), 22-28.

Hawkins, C. A. (1979). The performance and the promise of evaluation in computer based learning. *Computers and Education, 3*(3), 273-280.

Hawley, D. E., Fletcher, J. D., & Piele, P. K. (1986, November). *Costs, Effects, and Utility of Microcomputer-Assisted Instruction* (Tech. Rep. No. 1). Eugene, OR: Center for Advanced Technology in Education, University of Oregon.

Hayes, J. R., & Flower, L. S. (1986). Writing research and the writer. *American Psychologist, 41*(10), 1106-1113.

Hazen, M. (1980). An argument in favor of multimethod research and evaluation in CAI and CMI instruction. *AEDS Journal, 13*(4), 275-284.

Hirschheim, R. A. (1986, June). The effect of a priori views on the social implications of computing: The case of office automation. *Computing Surveys, 18*(2), 165-195.

Hofstadter, D. R. (1979). *Godel, Escher, Bach: an Eternal Golden Braid.* New York: Basic Books.

Hofstadter, D. R., & Dennett, D. C. (Eds.). (1981). *The Mind's I.* Toronto: Bantam Books.

House, E. R., & Gjerde, C. (1973). *The Politics of Educational Evaluation.* Berkeley, CA: McCutchan.

Howard, G. S. (1985). The role of values in the science of psychology. *American Psychologist, 40*(3), 255-265.

Hoyle, E. (1983). Computers in education: A solution in search of a problem?. In J. Megarry, D. R. F. Walker, S. Nisbet, & E. Hoyle (Eds.), *World Yearbook of Education 1982/83: Computers and Education* (pp.55-65). London: Kogan Page.

Hunt, R. A. (1985). Computers and families—an overview. In M. B. Sussman (Ed.), *Personal Computers and the Family* (pp. 11-25). New York: The Haworth Press.

Illich, I. (1977). *Toward a History of Needs.* New York: Pantheon Books.

Imhoff, H. (1984). Jenny of the Prairie. (review). *The Computing Teacher, 11* (8), 35.

Ingle, H. T. (1984). Microcomputers in schools: The video case study as an evaluation tool. In J. Johnston (Ed.), *Evaluating the New Information Technologies* (pp. 43-51). San Francisco: Jossey-Bass.

Jacob, E. (1987). Qualitative research traditions: A review. *Review of Educational Research, 57*(1), 1-50.

Johnson, E. M. (1987a, June 1). The Development of Computer Applications in Context: The Case of Social History in Ontario Schools. Paper presented at the Hamilton, Ontario meeting of the Canadian Society for the Study of Education.

Johnson, E. M. (1987b). *Social History in the Information Age: The Role of Computers and Database Management.* Unpublished doctoral dissertation, University of Toronto. Toronto.

Johnson, R. T., Johnson, D. W., & Stanne, M. B. (1986). Comparison of computer-assisted cooperative, competitive, and individualistic learning. *American Educational Research Journal, 23*(3), 382-392.

Jonas, H. (1973). Technology and responsibility: Reflections on the new tasks of ethics. *Social Research, 40*(1), 31-54.

Kernighan, B. W., & Plauger, P. J. (1974). *The Elements of Programming Style.* New York: McGraw-Hill.

Kiesler, S., Siegel, J., & McGuire, T. W. (1984). Social psychological aspects of computer-mediated communication. *American Psychologist, 39*(10), 1123-1134.

King, A. J. C., & Warren, W. K. (1987, June 2). Toward the "Good" School: Secondary School Student and Teacher Perspectives. Paper presented at the Hamilton, Ontario meeting of the Canadian Society for the Study of Education.

Kinnucan, P. (1984, January). Computers that think like experts. *High Technology,* pp. 30-37; 40-42.

Kleiner, A. (1985, (Fall)). The health hazards of computers. *Whole Earth Review,* (98), pp. 80-94.

Knapp, L. R. (1986). *The Word Processor and the Writing Teacher.* Englewood Cliffs, NJ: Prentice-Hall.

Koch, H. W. (1985—Direct mail advertising brochure). Englewood Cliffs, NJ: Executive Reports Corporation.

Komoski, K. (1984). Guest editorial. *The Computing Teacher, 11*(8), 5-6.

Krathwohl, D. R. (1980). The myth of value-free evaluation. *Educational Evaluation and Policy Analysis, 2*(1), 37-45.

Kubey, R. W. (1986). Television use in everyday life: Coping with unstructured time. *Journal of Communication, 36*(3), 108-123.

Kurtz, P. (Ed.) (1973). *Humanist Manifestos I and II.* Buffalo, NY: Prometheus Books.

Larkin, J. H. (1983). A general knowledge structure for learning or teaching science. In A. C. Wilkinson (Ed.), *Classroom Computers and Cognitive Science* (pp. 51-70). New York: Academic Press.

Latamore, G. B. (1984, April). Services link home computers. *High Technology, 4*(4), 18-19.

Lee, I. A. (1987, April). Microcomputer Labs in Elementary Schools: A Case Study in Planned Change. Paper presented at the Toronto meeting of the Educational Computing Organization of Ontario.

Lenat, D. B. (1984). Computer software for intelligent systems. *Scientific American, 233*(3), 204-209; 211-213.

Lepper, M. R. (1985). Microcomputers in education: Motivational and social issues. *American Psychologist, 40*(1), 1-18.

Lepper, M. R., & Malone, T. W. (1986). Intrinsic motivation and instructional effectiveness in computer-based education. In R. E. Snow & M. J. Farr (Eds.), *Aptitude, Learning, and Instruction: III. Conative and Affective Process Analysis.* Hillsdale, NJ: Erlbaum.

Leron, U. (1985). Logo today: Vision and reality. *The Computing Teacher, 12* (6), 26-32.

Levin, H. M., & Rumberger, R. W. (1986). Education and training needs for using computers in small businesses. *Educational Evaluation and Policy Analysis, 8*(4), 423-434.

Levin, J. A., Boruta, M. J., & Vasconcellos, M. T. (1983). Microcomputer-based environments for writing: A writer's assistant. In A. C. Wilkinson (Ed.), *Classroom Computers and Cognitive Science* (pp. 219-232). New York: Academic Press.

Levin, H. M., Glass, G. V., & Meister, G. R. (1984). *Cost-Effectiveness of Four Educational Interventions* (Tech. Rep. No. 84-A11). Palo Alto, CA: Institute for Research on Educational Finance and Governance, Stanford University.

Levin, H. M., Glass, G. V., & Meister, G. R. (1987, February). Cost-Effectiveness of Computer-Assisted Instruction. *Evaluation Review, 11*(1), 50-72.

Lewis, C. S. (1933/1977). *The Pilgrim's Regress.* Glasgow: William Collins Sons.

Lewis, C. S. (1943/1978). *The Abolition of Man.* Glasgow: William Collins Sons.

Lias, E. J. (1982). *Future Mind.* Boston: Little, Brown.

Licklider, J. G. R. (1983). The future of electronic learning. In M. A. White (Ed.), *The Future of Electronic Learning* (pp. 71-85). Hillsdale, NJ: Erlbaum.

Lincoln, Y. S., & Guba, E. G. (1985) *Naturalistic Inquiry.* Beverly Hills, CA: Sage Publications.

Linn, M. C. (1985). The cognitive consequences of programming instruction in classrooms. *Educational Researcher, 14*(5), 14-16; 25-29.

Lipson, J. I., & Fisher, K. M. (1985). Technologies of the future. *Education and Computing, 1*(1), 11-23.

Lockheed, M. E., & Frakt, S. B. (1984). Sex equity: Increasing girls' use of computers. *The Computing Teacher, 11*(8), 16-18.

Loucks-Horsley, S., French, L., Rubin, A., & Starr, K. (1985). *The Role of Teacher Incentives and Rewards in Implementing a Technological Innovation* (Tech. Rep.). The NETWORK, Inc.

Lyon, D. (1985). From 'Pacman' to 'Homelink': Information technology and social ethics. *Faith and Thought, 3*(1), 13-21.

Malone, T. W. (1985). Designing organizational interfaces. In *CHI '85 Proceedings* (66-71). ACM.

Martins, G. R. (1984). The overselling of expert systems. *Datamation, 30*(21), 76; 78; 80.

Matheson, K., & Strickland, L. (1986). The stereotype of the computer scientist. *Canadian Journal of Behavioral Science, 18*(1), 15-24.

Mathinos, D. A., & Woodward, A. (1987, April). The status of instructional computing in the classroom: Removing those rose-colored glasses. Paper presented at the Washington, D.C. meeting of the American Educational Research Association.

McKelvey, B. (1983). *Sex roles and computer use: A study of equity in the classroom.* Unpublished master's thesis, University of Toronto.

McKelvey, B. (1984). *Group writing projects.* Paper presented at the annual meeting of the Association for Educational Communications and Technology in Dallas, Texas, January 22, 1984.

McLaughlin, M. W., Pfeifer, R. S., Swanson-Owens, D., & Yee, S. (1986). Why teachers won't teach. *Phi Delta Kappan, 67*(6), 420-426.

McLean, R. S. (1985). Spelling activities on the ICON. *ECOO Output, 6*(3), 31-34.

MCSR (1983). *Computer Learning and the Public Need* (Tech. Rep.). Minneapolis, MN: Minnesota Center for Social Research.

Megarry, J. (1983). Thinking, learning and educating: The role of the computer. In J. Megarry, D. R. F. Walker, S. Nisbet, & E. Hoyle (Eds.), *World Yearbook of Education 1982/83: Computers and Education* (pp. 15-28). London: Kogan Page.

Menosky, J. A. (1984). Computer literacy and the press. *Teachers College Record, 85*(4), 615-621.

Menzies, H. (1981). *Women and the Chip.* Montreal: The Institute for Research on Public Policy.

Merrill, M. D. (1980). Learner control in computer based learning. *Computers and Education, 4*(2), 77-95.

Merrill, M. D. (1987, Summer). An expert system for instructional design. *IEEE Expert*, pp. 25-37.

Merrill, P. F., Tolman, M. N., Christensen, L., Hammons, K., Vincent, B. R., & Reynolds, P. L. (1986). *Computers in Education.* Englewood Cliffs, NJ: Prentice-Hall.

Michaelsen, R. H., Michie, D., & Boulanger, A. (1985, April). The technology of expert systems. *BYTE*, pp. 303-307; 309-312.

MICROgram. (1983). *The Computing Teacher, 10*(5), 34-45.

Minsky, M. L. (1966). Artificial Intelligence. *Scientific American, 215*(3), 246-260.

Minsky, M. L. (1979). Computer science and the representation of knowledge. In M. L. Dertouzos & J. Moses (Eds.), *The Computer Age: A Twenty-year view* (pp. 392-421). Cambridge, MA: The MIT Press.

Mitchell, E. (1985). The dynamics of family interaction around home video games. In M. B. Sussman (Ed.), *Personal Computers and the Family* (pp. 121-135). New York: The Haworth Press.

Moravec, H. P. (1984, September 11). *Robots that rove.*

Morgan, M. (1984). Reward-induced decrements and increments in intrinsic motivation. *Review of Educational Research, 54*(1), 5-30.

Morris, J. M. (1985). Hacker meets star wars. *Datamation, 31*(8), 161-162.

Moursund, D. (1984). To improve education. *Creative Computing, 10*(11), 183-186.

Mueller, E. T., & Dyer, M. G. (1985, May). *Daydreaming in Humans and Computers* (Tech. Rep. No. UCLA-AI-85-16). Los Angeles, CA: Artificial Intelligence Laboratory, UCLA.

Mumford, L. (1970). *The Myth of the Machine: The Pentagon of Power.* New York: Harcourt, Brace, & World.

Murphy, J. (1985, December 9). A convert to the write stuff. *Time*, pp. 98-99.

Murphy, R. T., & Appel, L. R. (1977). *Evaluation of the PLATO IV Computer based Education system in the Community College* (Tech. Rep.). Princeton, NJ: Educational Testing Service.

Neatby, H. (1953). *So Little for the Mind.* Toronto: Clarke, Irwin & Company.

Nelson, R. R., & Cheney, P. H. (1987, May 15). Training today's user. *Datamation, 33*(9), 121-122.

(1984). *New Webster's Computer Dictionary.* New York: Delair Publishing.

Noble, D. (1984). Computer literacy and ideology. *Teachers College Record, 85* (4), 602-613.

Noble, D. F. (1984a). Is progress what it seems to be? *Datamation, 30*(19), 140; 142; 146; 148; 152; 154.

Noble, D. F. (1984b). *Forces of Production: A Social History of Industrial Automation.* New York: Alfred A. Knopf.

Norton, P. (1985). Problem-solving activities in a computer environment: A different angle of vision. *Educational Technology, 25*(10), 36-41.

O'Dell, J. W., & Dickson, J. (1984, July). ELIZA as a "therapeutic" tool. *Journal of Clinical Psychology, 40*(4), 942-945.

O'Donovan, O. (1984). *Begotten or Made?* Oxford: Oxford University Press.

O'Shea, T., & Self, J. (1983). *Learning and Teaching with Computers: Artificial Intelligence in Education.* Englewood Cliffs, NJ: Prentice-Hall.

Olson, J. K. (1985). Information Technology and Teacher Routines: Learning from the Microcomputer. Paper presented at the bi-annual Conference, Tillburg University, Netherlands meeting of the ISATT.

Olson, J. K. (1986, April). Computers in Canadian Elementary Schools: Curriculum Questions from Classroom Practice. Paper presented at the San Francisco meeting of the American Educational Research Association.

Olson, J., & Eaton, S. (1986). *Case Studies of Microcomputers in the Classroom.* Toronto: Queen's Printer for Ontario.

Osborne, K. (1983). In defence of history. In J. Parsons, G. Milburn, & M. Van Manen (Eds.), *A Canadian Social Studies* (pp. 55-69). Edmonton, Alberta: University of Alberta.

Pacey, A. (1983). *The Culture of Technology*. Cambridge, MA: The MIT Press.

Page, E. B. (1966). The imminence of grading essays by computer. *Phi Delta Kappan, 47*(5), 238-243.

Papert, S. (1980a). Teaching children thinking. In R. P. Taylor (Ed.), *The Computer in the School: Tutor, Tool, Tutee* (pp. 161-176). New York: Teachers College Press.

Papert, S. (1980b). *Mindstorms: Children, Computers and Powerful Ideas*. New York: Basic Books.

Papert, S. (1987). Computer criticism vs. technocentric thinking. *Educational Researcher, 16*(1), 22-30.

Parnas, D. L. (1985). Software aspects of strategic defense systems. *Communications of the ACM, 28*(12), 1326-1335.

Pask, G. (1982). *Microman: Computers and the Evolution of Consciousness*. New York: Macmillan.

Pea, R. D. (1985). Integrating human and computer intelligence. In E. L. Klein (Ed.), *Children and Computers* (pp. 75-96). San Francisco: Jossey-Bass.

Pea, R. D. (1986, March). *Beyond Amplification: Using the Computer to Reorganize Mental Functioning* (Tech, Rep. No. 38). New York: Bank Street College Center for Children and Technology.

Pea, R. D., & Kurland, D. M. (1984). On the cognitive effects of learning computer programming. *New Ideas in Psychology, 2*(2), 137-168.

Pepper, J. (1981). Following students' suggestions for rewriting a computer programming textbook. *American Educational Research Journal, 18*(3), 259-269.

Perkins, D. N. (1985). The fingertip effect: How information-processing technology shapes thinking. *Educational Researcher, 14*(7), 11-17.

Pogrow, S. (1987, March). The HOTS program: The role of computers in developing thinking skills. *TechTrends, 32*(3), 10-13.

Postman, N. (1982). *The Disappearance of Childhood*. New York: Delacorte Press.

Pratt, D. (1983). Curriculum for the 21st century. *Education Canada, 23*(4), 41-47.

Ragsdale, R. G. (1978). Evaluating curricula for the teaching of programming. In R. G. Montanelli, Jr., & A. M. Wildberger (Eds.), *Topics in Instructional Computing. Evaluation of the Use of Computers in Instruction* (pp. 11-21). ACM (SIGCUE.)

Ragsdale, R. G. (1980). Empirically based myths: Astrology, biorhythms, and ATIs. *Canadian Journal of Education, 5*(1), 40-51.

Ragsdale, R. G. (1982). *Computers in the Schools: A Guide for Planning*. Toronto: OISE Press.

Ragsdale, R. G., & McKelvey, B. (1985). A possible future for the teaching of programming in Canada. In M. Griffiths & E. D. Tagg (Eds.), *The Role of Programming in Teaching Informatics*. (pp. 43-49). Amsterdam: Elsevier Science Publishers.

Rawitsch, D. G. (1981). Teaching educators about computing: A different ball game. *The Computing Teacher, 9*(4), 27-32.

Redish, K. A., & Smyth, W. F. (1986). Program style analysis: A by-product of program compilation. *Communications of the ACM, 29*(2), 126-133.

Roads, C. (1985). Research in music and artificial intelligence. *Computing Surveys, 17*(2), 163-190.

Roberts, M. J. (1974, Summer). On the nature and condition of social science. *Daedalus*, pp. 47-64.

Roblyer, M. D. (1981). Instructional design versus authoring of courseware: Some crucial differences. *AEDS Journal, 14*(4), 173-181.

Roblyer, M. D. (1982). Developing courseware must be easier than some things. *Educational Technology, 22*(1), 33-35.

Roblyer, M. D. (1985). The greening of educational computing: A proposal for a more research-based approach to computers in instruction. *Educational Technology, 25*(1), 40-44.

Rogers, P. C. (1984). AI as a dehumanising force. In M. Yazdani & A. Narayanan (Eds.), *Artificial Intelligence: Human Effects* (pp. 222-234). Chichester: Ellis Horwood.

Rose, G. A. (1986). *Understanding the Interaction Between Teachers and Computers.* Unpublished doctoral dissertation, University of Toronto.

Roszak, T. (1986). *The Cult of Information.* New York: Pantheon Books.

Rust, V. D., & Dalin, P. (1985). Computer education Norwegian style: A comprehensive approach. *Educational Technology, 25*(6), 17-20.

Salisbury, D. F. (1984). How to decide when and where to use microcomputers for instruction. *Educational Technology, 24*(3), 22-24.

Salomon, G. (1984). Computers in education: Setting a research agenda. *Educational Technology, 24*(10), 7-11.

Salomon, G. (1986). *Information Technologies: What you see is not (always) what you get* (Tech. Rep.). Tel Aviv: Tel Aviv University School of Education.

Salomon, G., & Gardner, H. (1986). The computer as educator: Lessons from television research. *Educational Researcher, 15*(1), 13-19.

Salomon, G., & Perkins, D. N. (1986). *Transfer of Cognitive Skills from Programming: When and How?* (Tech. Rep.). Tel Aviv: Tel Aviv University School of Education.

Sanders, J. S., & Stone, A. (1986). *The Neuter Computer: Computers for Girls and Boys.* New York: Neal-Schuman.

Sardello, R. J. (1984). The technological threat to education. *Teachers College Record, 85*(4), 631-639.

Scarr, S. (1985). Constructing psychology: Making facts and fables for our time. *American Psychologist, 40*(5), 499-512.

Schaeffer, F. A. (1968). *The God Who is There.* London: Hodder & Stoughton.

Schaeffer, F. A. (1972). *Back to Freedom and Dignity.* Downers Grove, IL: InterVarsity Press.

Schaeffer, F. A. (1976). *How should we then live?* Old Tappan, NJ: Fleming H. Revell Company.

Schank, R. G. (1984). *The Cognitive Computer.* Reading, MA: Addison-Wesley.

Scheffler, I. (1986). Computers at school? *Teachers College Record, 87*(4), 513-528.

Schlossberg, H. (1983). *Idols for Destruction.* Nashville, TN: Thomas Nelson Publishers.

Schneider, B. R. Jr. (1984). Programs as essays. *Datamation, 30*(7), 162; 164; 166; 168.

Schooltech News (1984, November). Educate parents in micro teaching, schools told. *Schooltech News, 2*(3).

Schwartz, B. (1984). *Psychology of Learning and Behavior.* New York: W. W. Norton & Company.

Schwartz, H. J. (1985). *Interactive Writing.* New York: Holt, Rinehart and Winston.

Schwarz, P. A. (1985, August). Evaluation of the Pakistan primary education project: A methodological case study. In B. Searle (Ed.), *Education and Training. Evaluation in World Bank Education Projects: Lessons from Three Case Studies* (pp. 73-105). Washington, DC: The World Bank.

Science Council of Canada. (1983). *A Workshop on Artificial Intelligence* (Tech. Rep.). Ottawa: Science Council of Canada.

Scriven, M. (1974). Prose and cons about goal-free evaluation. In W. J. Popham (Ed.), *Evaluation in Education* (pp. 34-67). Berkeley, CA: McCutchan.

Scriven, M. (1981a). Product evaluation. In N. L. Smith (Ed.), *New Techniques for Evaluation* (pp. 121-166). Beverly Hills, CA: Sage Publications.

Scriven, M. (1981b). *Evaluation Thesaurus.* Point Reyes, CA: Edgepress.

Scriven, M. & Roth, J. (1978). Needs assessment: Concept and practice. *New Directions for Program Evaluation, 1,* 1-11.

Seidman, W. H. (1983). Goal ambiguity and organizational decoupling: The failure of "rational systems" program implementation. *Educational Evaluation and Policy Analysis, 5*(4), 399-413.

Self, J. (1985). *Microcomputers in Education: A Critical Appraisal of Educational Software.* Brighton: Harvester Press.

Shallis, M. (1984). *The Silicon Idol.* Oxford: Oxford University Press.

Shanker, A. (1984, October 24). Some just can't believe good news. *Education Week,* p. 9.

Sheil, B. A. (1981). The psychological study of programming. *Computing Surveys, 13*(1), 101-120.

Sheingold, K., Kane, J. H., & Endreweit, M. E. (1983). Microcomputer use in schools: Developing a research agenda. *Harvard Educational Review, 53*(4), 412-432.

Shneiderman, B. (1980). *Software Psychology.* Cambridge, MA: Winthrop.

Sigel, E. (1985). Alas poor Visicorp. *Datamation, 31*(2), 93-94; 96.

Sinclair, C. (1984). Predictions on our computerized future. *Creative Computing, 10*(11), 256-258.

Skinner, B. F. (1984, September). The shame of American education. *American Psychologist, 39*(9), 947-954.

Sleeman, D., & Brown, J. S. (1982). Introduction: Intelligent tutoring systems. In D. Sleeman & J. S. Brown (Eds.), *Intelligent Tutoring Systems* (pp. 1-11). New York: Academic Press.

Sloan, D. (1984). On raising critical questions about the computer in education. *Teachers College Record, 85*(4), 539-547.

Smith, W. C. (1975). Methodology and the study of religion: Some misgivings. In R. D. Baird (Ed.), *Methodological Issues in Religious Studies* (pp. 1-30). Chico, CA: New Horizons Press.

Smith, F. (1983). The promise and threat of microcomputers for language learners. In J. Handscombe, R. A. Oren, & B. P. Taylor (Eds.), *On TESOL 83: The Question of Control* (pp. 1-18). Washington: TESOL.

Solomon, C. (1986). *Computer Environments for Children.* Cambridge, MA: MIT Press.

Spradley, J. P. (1980). *Participant Observation.* New York: Holt, Rinehart and Winston.

Stonier, T. (1984). Thinking about thinking machines. *Creative Computing, 10* (11), 252-254.

Stott, C. (1985, September 22). When TV morals guide the child. . . . *The Sunday Telegraph,* p. 12.

Strehlo, K. (1986, February). The video game syndrome. *PC World*, pp. 65-66, 72; 74; 76; 78.

Sturdivant, P. (1984). Access to technology: The equity paradox. *The Computing Teacher, 11*(8), 65-67.

Sullivan, E. V. (1983). Computers, culture, and educational futures: A critical appraisal. *Interchange, 14*(3), 17-26.

Sullivan, E. V. (1985). Computers, culture, and educational futures—A meditation on Mindstorms. *Interchange, 16*(3), 1-18.

Suppes, P. J. (1966). The use of computers in education. *Scientific American, 215*(3), 207-220.

Suzuki, D. (1985, February 23). Man can't resist lure of technology. *The Toronto Star.*

Swinton, S. S., Amarel, M., & Morgan, J. A. (1978). *The PLATO Elementary Demonstration Educational Outcome Evaluation* (Tech Rep.). Urbana, IL: The University of Illinois. [ED 1860201].

Taffee, S. J. (1984, August/September). Computers, kids and values. *The Computing Teacher, 12*(1), 18.

Taylor, G. R. (1982). *The Great Evolution Mystery.* London: Secker & Warburg.

Taylor, R. P. (1980). *The Computer in the School: Tutor, Tool, Tutee.* New York: Teachers College Press.

Taylor, R. P. (1982). *Programming Primer: A Graphic Introduction to Computer Programming with BASIC and Pascal.* Don Mills: Addison-Wesley.

TechTrends interview: Bobby Goodson. (1985). *TechTrends, 30*(7), 23–27.

The Conditions of Teaching. (1984). Advice to the Minister of Education, Quebec: Conseil Superieur de l'Education.

Thiessen, E. J. (1985). Review of A. Adams & E. Jones, *Teaching Humanities in the Microelectronic Age. Canadian Journal of Education, 10*(3), 317–320.

Thompson, G. B. (1979). *Memo from Mercury: Information Technology is Different* (Occasional paper No. 10). Montreal: Institute for Research on Public Policy.

(1984). *Un ordinateur a la maison: Pourquoi? Pour quoi?* Paris: Thomson Micro-Informatique Grand Public.

Tillich, P. (1963). *The Eternal Now.* New York: Charles Scribner's Sons.

Tinnell, C. S. (1985). An ethnographic look at personal computers in the family setting. In M. B. Sussman (Ed.), *Personal Computers and the Family* (pp. 59–69). New York: The Haworth Press.

Trumbull, D. J. (1986, March). Games children play: A cautionary tale. *Educational Leadership*, pp. 18–21.

Turkle, S. (1984). *The Second Self: Computers and the Human Spirit.* New York: Simon and Schuster.

Turner, J. A. (1984). Computer mediated work: The interplay between technology and structured jobs. *Communications of the ACM, 27*(12), 1210–1217.

Van Dyke, C. (1987, May). Taking "computer literacy" literally. *Communications of the ACM, 30*(5), 366–374.

Vanderburg, W. H. (Ed.). Ellul, J. (1981). *Perspectives on Our Age.* Toronto: Canadian Broadcasting Corporation.

Vitalari, N. P., Venkatesh, A., & Gronhaug, K. (1985). Computing in the home: Shifts in the time allocation patterns of households. *Communications of the ACM, 28*(5), 512–522.

Walker, D. F. (1983, October). Reflections on the educational potential and limitations of microcomputers. *Phi Delta Kappan, 65*(2), 103–107.

Weick, K. E. (1984). Small wins: Redefining the scale of social problems. *American Psychologist, 39*(1), 40–49.

Weinberg, G. M. (1971). *The Psychology of Computer Programming.* New York: Van Nostrand Reinhold.

Weizenbaum, J. (1966). ELIZA—a computer program for the study of natural language communication between man and machine. *Communications of the ACM, 9*(1), 36–45.

Weizenbaum, J. (1976/1984). *Computer Power and Human Reason.* San Francisco: W. H. Freeman and Co.

Weizenbaum, J. (1984, June). Another view from MIT. *Byte, 9*(6), 225.

Whitby, B. (1984). AI: Some immediate dangers. In M. Yazdani & A. Narayanan (Eds.), *Artificial Intelligence: Human Effects* (pp. 235-245). Chichester: Ellis Horwood.

White, M. A. (1983). Toward a psychology of electronic learning. In M. A. White (Ed.), *The Future of Electronic Learning* (pp. 51-62). Hillsdale, NJ: Erlbaum.

Wilkinson, A. C., & Patterson, J. (1983). Issues at the interface of theory and practice. In A. C. Wilkinson (Ed.), *Classroom Computers and Cognitive Science* (pp. 3-13). New York: Academic Press.

Williams, D. D. (Ed.). (1986). *Naturalistic Evaluation*. San Francisco: Jossey-Bass.

Wilton, J. A., & Rubincam, I. (1985). Featured speakers' symposium. *ECOO Output, 6*(3), 8-17.

Winner, L. (1986). *The Whale and the Reactor*. Chicago: University of Chicago Press.

Winograd, T., & Flores, F. (1986). *Understanding Computers and Cognition*. Norwood, NJ: Ablex.

Wong, R. E., Uhrmacher, P. B., & Siegfreid, D. P. (1984). Computers and equity: A pilot program. *The Computing Teacher, 11*(8), 52-55.

Woodward, K. L. (1985, June 24). Islam versus the West. *Newsweek*, pp. 28-30.

Worsthorne, P. (1985, September 22). Hot air and high technology. *The Sunday Telegraph*, p. 18.

Yazdani, M., & Narayanan, A. (Eds.). (1984). *Artificial Intelligence: Human Effects*. Chichester: Ellis Horwood.

Yourdon, E. (1979). *Structured Walkthroughs*. Englewood Cliffs, NJ: Prentice-Hall.

Zajonc, A. G. (1984). Computer Pedagogy? Questions concerning the new educational technology. *Teachers College Record, 85*(4), 569-577.

Index

About the Author

RONALD G. RAGSDALE has been active in the field of computers and education for over 25 years. Since 1966 he has been at the Ontario Institute for Studies in Education and is an Associate Professor in the Department of Measurement, Evaluation, and Computer Applications. His primary interest is evaluating the impact of computers on the educational process. He has authored two other books, entitled *Computers in the Schools: A Guide for Planning* (1982) and *Evaluation of Microcomputer Courseware* (1983).